EMBODIMENT AND REPRESENTATIONS OF BEAUTY

ADVANCES IN GENDER RESEARCH

Series Editors: Vasilikie Demos and
Marcia Texler Segal

Recent Volumes:

Volume 14:	Interactions and Intersections of Gendered Bodies at Work, at Home, and at Play – Edited by Marcia Texler Segal, 2010
Volume 15:	Analyzing Gender, Intersectionality, and Multiple Inequalities: Global, Transnational, and Local Contexts – Edited by Esther Ngan-Ling Chow, Marcia Texler Segal and Lin Tan, 2011
Volume 16:	Social Production and Reproduction at the Interface of Public and Private Spheres – Edited by Marcia Texler Segal, Esther Ngan-Ling Chow and Vasilikie Demos, 2012
Volume 17:	Notions of Family: Intersectional Perspectives – Edited by Marla H. Kohlman, Dana B. Krieg and Bette J. Dickerson, 2013
Volume 18A:	Gendered Perspectives on Conflict and Violence: Part A – Edited by Marcia Texler Segal and Vasilikie Demos, 2013
Volume 18B:	Gendered Perspectives on Conflict and Violence: Part B – Edited by Marcia Texler Segal and Vasilikie Demos, 2014
Volume 19:	Gender Transformation in the Academy – Edited by Marcia Texler Segal and Vasilikie Demos, 2014
Volume 20:	At the Center: Feminism, Social Science and Knowledge – Edited by Vasilikie Demos and Marcia Texler Segal, 2015
Volume 21:	Gender and Race Matter: Global Perspectives on Being a Woman – Edited by Shaminder Takhar, 2016
Volume 22:	Gender and Food: From Production to Consumption and After – Edited by Marcia Texler Segal and Vasilikie Demos, 2016
Volume 23:	Discourses of Gender and Sexual Inequality: The Legacy of Sanra L. Bem – Edited by Marcia Texler Segal and Vasilikie Demos, 2016
Volume 24:	Gender Panic, Gender Policy – Edited By Vasilikie Demos and Marcia Texler Segal, 2017
Volume 25:	Marginalized Mothers, Mothering from the Margins – Edited by Tiffany L. Taylor and Katrina R. Bloch, 2018
Volume 26:	Gender and the Media: Women's Places – Edited by Marcia Texler Segal and Vasilikie Demos, 2019
Volume 27:	Gender and Practice: Insights from the Field – Edited by Vasilikie Demos, Marcia Texler Segal and Kristy Kelly, 2019
Volume 28:	Gender and Practice: Knowledge, Policy, Organizations – Edited by Vasilikie Demos, Marcia Texler Segal and Kristy Kelly, 2020
Volume 29:	Advances in Women's Empowerment: Critical Insight from Asia, Africa and Latin America – Edited by Araceli Ortega Diaz and Marta Barbara Ochman, 2020
Volume 30:	Gender and Generations: Continuity and Change – Edited by Vasilikie Demos and Marcia Texler Segal, 2021
Volume 31:	Producing Inclusive Feminist Knowledge: Positionalities and Discourses in the Global South – Edited by Akosua Adomako Ampofo and Josephine Beoku-Betts , 2021
Volume 32:	Advances in Trans Studies: Moving Toward Gender Expansion and Trans Hope – Edited by Austin H. Johnson, Baker A. Rogers and Tiffany Taylor, 2022
Volume 33:	Gender Visibility and Erasure – Edited by Marcia Texler Segal and Vasilikie Demos, 2022
Volume 34:	People, Spaces and Places in Gendered Environments – Edited by Vasilikie Demos and Marcia Texler Segal, 2024

EDITORIAL ADVISORY BOARD

Miriam Adelman
Universidade do Paraná, Brazil

Franca Bimbi
University of Padua, Italy

Max Greenberg
Boston University, USA

Marla Kohlman
Kenyon College, USA

Preethi Krishnan
O. P. Jindal Global University, India

Chika Shinohara
*Momoyama Gakuin University,
(St Andrew's University), Japan*

Shaminder Takhar
London South Bank University, UK

Tiffany Taylor
Kent State University, USA

ADVANCES IN GENDER RESEARCH   VOLUME 35

EMBODIMENT AND REPRESENTATIONS OF BEAUTY

EDITED BY

ESTHER HERNÁNDEZ-MEDINA
Pomona College, USA

and

SHARINA MAÍLLO-POZO
University of Georgia, USA

United Kingdom – North America – Japan
India – Malaysia – China

Emerald Publishing Limited
Emerald Publishing, Floor 5, Northspring, 21-23 Wellington Street, Leeds LS1 4DL.

First edition 2024

Editorial matter and selection © 2024 Esther Hernández-Medina and Sharina Maíllo-Pozo.
Individual chapters © 2024 The authors.
Published under exclusive licence by Emerald Publishing Limited.

Reprints and permissions service
Contact: www.copyright.com

No part of this book may be reproduced, stored in a retrieval system, transmitted in
any form or by any means electronic, mechanical, photocopying, recording or otherwise
without either the prior written permission of the publisher or a licence permitting
restricted copying issued in the UK by The Copyright Licensing Agency and in the USA
by The Copyright Clearance Center. Any opinions expressed in the chapters are those
of the authors. Whilst Emerald makes every effort to ensure the quality and accuracy of
its content, Emerald makes no representation implied or otherwise, as to the chapters'
suitability and application and disclaims any warranties, express or implied, to their use.

British Library Cataloguing in Publication Data
A catalogue record for this book is available from the British Library

ISBN: 978-1-83797-994-3 (Print)
ISBN: 978-1-83797-993-6 (Online)
ISBN: 978-1-83797-995-0 (Epub)

ISSN: 1529-2126 (Series)

Printed and bound by CPI Group (UK) Ltd, Croydon, CR0 4YY

CONTENTS

About the Editors   ix

About the Contributors   xi

Series Editors' Preface   xiii

The Power of Beauty: Intersectional Feminist Approaches to its Embodiment and Representation
Esther Hernández-Medina and Sharina Maíllo-Pozo   1

Chapter 1   Mamá Fit Goes to El Salvador: Fitness in a Transnational Society
Noelle K. Brigden   13

Chapter 2   Shifting Perceptions of Women's Weight
Courtney Dress   33

Chapter 3   Doing Beauty, Doing Health: Embodied Emotion Work in Women Cancer Patients' Narratives of Hair Loss
Marley Olson   55

Chapter 4   "How Do They Really See Me?": The Sexual Politics of Multiracial Desirability
Julia Chin   73

Chapter 5   Body Image and Sexual Pleasure in Women and Genderqueer Individual's Sexual Experiences
Spencier R. Ciaralli   91

Chapter 6   I Don't Wear Black: Professional Muslim Workers and Personal Dress Code
Salam Aboulhassan   117

Chapter 7   Millennial Agency and Liberation within Black American Beauty Standards
Jaleesa Reed   137

Chapter 8 Ballet Is [White] Woman: Anti-Black Standards of Beauty Within Ballet
Sekani L. Robinson   *159*

Chapter 9 Consuming Beauty, Constructing Blackness: A Constructivist Grounded Theory Analysis of Racialized Gendered Embodiment Practices Through Shampoo Product Descriptions
Shameika D. Daye   *177*

Chapter 10 *Mulata* in Repose
Jennifer Báez   *197*

ABOUT THE EDITORS

Esther Hernández-Medina is Assistant Professor of Latin American Studies and Gender & Women's Studies at Pomona College. She is a feminist academic, public policy expert, and activist from the Dominican Republic. Her research and teaching revolve around the question of how historically marginalized groups such as women, racial, ethnic, and sexual minorities are able to change public policy in their favor. She has studied the Dominican feminist movement and citizen participation in urban policies in Mexico City, São Paulo, and the Dominican Republic. She was a Humanities Studio Faculty Fellow (2021–22, and 2023–24) at Pomona College, and Open Education Faculty Fellow (2019) at the Claremont Colleges Center for Teaching and Learning and the Claremont Colleges Library. Her most recent publication is the book chapter "The Right to A Complete Life: The Struggles of the Dominican Feminist Movement" in *Women's Rights in Movement: Dynamics of Feminist Change in Latin America and the Caribbean* (Springer, editors Inés M. Pousadela and Simone Bohn). She is also co-founder of the feminist group Tertulia Feminista Magaly Pineda in the Dominican Republic.

Sharina Maíllo-Pozo is Assistant Professor of Latinx studies in the Department of Romance Languages at the University of Georgia. She specializes in Latinx and Caribbean literature and culture, with special attention to the cultural production of the Dominican Republic and its diaspora in the United States. Some of her research papers and reviews have appeared in various edited volumes, mid-high tier academic journals. She was a Dominican Studies Fellow (2016–2017), Lilly Teaching Fellow (2019–2021), Willson Center for the Humanities Fellow (2020–2021), and UGA Teaching Academy Fellow (2022–2023). In 2021, she was the recipient of the Sandy Beaver Excellence in Teaching Award at the University of Georgia. She is working on two book manuscripts: *Beyond Borderlands. Popular Music in Contemporary Dominican/Dominicanyork Literature* and *Tracing the Legacy of Camila Henríquez Ureña Through Translation and Beyond* (co-authored with Dr Anne Roschelle).

ABOUT THE CONTRIBUTORS

Salam Aboulhassan is a PhD candidate in the Department of Sociology, Wayne State University, Detroit, MI, USA. Her current research focuses on the experiences of Muslims within US workplaces and was awarded the National Science Foundation Doctoral Dissertation Improvement grant.

Jennifer Báez is Assistant Professor of Art History in the School of Art, Art History, and Design at the University of Washington. She specializes in the visual, material, and religious culture of Latin America and the African diaspora under the global Spanish empire. She received her PhD in Art History from Florida State University, where she taught courses in museum studies and the history of African art.

Noelle K. Brigden, PhD, is an Associate Professor in the Department of Political Science at Marquette University. Her research and teaching interests include gender, human security, international relations, borders, transnationalism, violence, the politics of the body, trauma, fieldwork ethics, and political ethnography. Her book, *The Migrant Passage: Clandestine Journeys from Central America* (Cornell University Press, 2018), won the Yale Ferguson Award.

Julia Chin earned a BA in Sociology with distinction from UC Santa Barbara in 2021. She now works at Over Zero, an NGO which focuses on identity-based and political violence prevention. She is a contributor to the University of Georgia Press edited volume, *Books Through Bars* (2024).

Spencier R. Ciaralli, PhD, is Assistant Professor in the Department of Sociology, Augustana University, USA. They work in the areas of sexual behavior, gender, and sexuality, as well as medical sociology. Their publications appear in journals such as *Women's Reproductive Health* and *Consumption Markets & Culture*.

Shameika D. Daye, MPA, is Doctoral candidate in the Department of Sociology, University of Central Florida, Orlando, Florida, USA. Working at the intersection of race, gender, and embodiment of Black women, she explores how Black women navigate the politics of identity, authenticity, and beauty through the lens of consumerism and the workplace.

Courtney Dress is a Doctoral candidate in the Department of Sociology and Criminology at Kent State University, USA. She studies inequalities, focusing on issues of race and gender, as well as sexuality/asexuality. Her dissertation examines racial, gender, and intersectional disparities in Computer Science education.

Marley Olson, PhD, is an Instructor of Sociology at Walla Walla Community College, Washington, USA. She earned her PhD in Sociology at the University of Colorado Boulder specializing in gender, medicine, health, and disability. Her research examines nonvisible disabilities and contested illnesses, with a focus on gender disparities.

Jaleesa Reed, PhD, is Assistant Professor in the Department of Human Centered Design at Cornell University, USA. Her research focuses on the intersections of beauty culture, identity, and place informed by human geography, feminist studies, and merchandising in the fashion and beauty industries.

Sekani L. Robinson is an Assistant Professor at California State Polytechnic University, Pomona in the Sociology Department. She earned her PhD in Sociology at the University of California, Santa Barbara. Her research focuses on race, gender, culture, embodiment, sport, and class.

SERIES EDITORS' PREFACE

We welcome this extensive focus on embodiment and representation to our Advances in Gender Research series. The guest editors and contributors from the United States, El Salvador, and the Dominican Republic take intersectional and interdisciplinary approaches to the body and its representation. The research settings are varied from the ballet and the gym to the college campus and media. The authors demonstrate that beauty varies not only with gender, race, ethnicity, class, body configuration, and location but also with one's perception of self and others. The impacts of stereotypes and European norms are evident in everything from the clothing choices of Muslim office workers to the self-images of mixed-race women and non-binary individuals in the dating scene, as is the importance of self-care in the face of such symbolic violence. Hair is a focus not only for women losing theirs during cancer treatment but also for Black women shopping for haircare products and ballerinas. A focus on weight and body type occurs across chapters and countries as well. We hope readers will come away from the volume with new definitions of beauty and a new understanding of embodiment.

Vasilikie Demos, University of Minnesota, Morris, USA
Marcia Texler Segal, Indiana University Southeast, USA

THE POWER OF BEAUTY: INTERSECTIONAL FEMINIST APPROACHES TO ITS EMBODIMENT AND REPRESENTATION

Esther Hernández-Medina[a] and Sharina Maíllo-Pozo[b]

[a]*Latin American Studies and Gender and Women's Studies, Pomona College, USA*
[b]*Department of Romance Languages, The University of Georgia, USA*

ABSTRACT

Contributions to this volume showcase the current state of gender research as it relates to the embodiment and representation of beauty. In particular, the authors highlight a more open-ended concept of beauty that goes beyond esthetics. The authors call our attention to the fact that beauty definitions and standards in any given society closely reflect the distribution of power in it. For this purpose, the authors in this volume share findings of research and conducted in multiple sites in the United States (i.e., Southern California, the Midwest, the Northwest, New York City, Salt Lake City, Houston, Boston, and Washington, DC), El Salvador, and the Dominican Republic. Contributors also use a variety of qualitative and quantitative methodologies to expand notions of beauty and its embodiment across diverse areas and experiences. The authors ask and invite us to ask ourselves how race, class, disability, gender identity or sexual orientation, and other dimensions of inequality inform our definitions of what beauty is and is not. They exhort us to interrogate who defines who and what is beautiful and why. Finally, rather than being problem-oriented, the premise of each study is to effect collective change in the ways we construe, see, represent, and embody beauty.

Keywords: Beauty standards; race; gender; disability; gender identity; body size

Contributions to this volume highlight a more open-ended concept of beauty that goes beyond esthetics. They call our attention to the fact that beauty definitions and standards in any given society closely reflect the distribution of power in it. The authors ask and invite us to ask ourselves how race, class, disability, gender identity or sexual orientation, and other dimensions of inequality inform our definitions of what beauty is and is not. They encourage us to interrogate who defines who and what is beautiful and why. In a time of global political lethargy where public dialog is mostly centered on collective frustration, painful events, and overall disillusionment, the chapters of this volume foreground alternative discussions on beauty that remind us of what and who we are as people and bring us back to our humanity. Borrowing from West's (1993) reflections on race in America, each chapter of *Embodiment and Representations of Beauty* guides us through the process of learning "a new language of empathy and compassion" (p. 8) across different geographical spaces. The research sites include multiple sites in the United States (i.e., Southern California, the Midwest, the Northwest, New York City, Salt Lake City, Houston, Boston, and Washington, DC), El Salvador, and the Dominican Republic. The authors also use a variety of qualitative and quantitative methodologies to expand notions of beauty and its embodiment across diverse areas and experiences.

The chapters in this volume use what C. Wright Mills called the sociological imagination. Wright Mills proposed this concept to help the public at large (not only sociologists) make sense of the uncertain world around them. He defined it as "a quality of mind that will help them to use information and develop reason in order to achieve lucid summations of what is going on in the world and what may be happening within themselves" (Wright Mills, 2016 [2000, 1959], p. 3). The sociological imagination allows us to understand any phenomenon (a date, a microchip, or a religious ceremony) by looking at the general patterns of the society they are part of (for instance, gender roles, the predominance of Western technology, or people's need for shared meaning and symbols).

ON BEAUTY

One of the most illuminating aspects of the studies in this volume is the centering on an inclusive cultural history of beauty that transcends and disrupts US- and Eurocentric beauty standards, especially as they relate to race, ethnicity, gender and sexuality, body image, illness, and new technologies. Through an interdisciplinary approach, the pieces in this volume evince multiple approaches to the understanding of beauty representations and embodiment in popular culture, fitness culture, print and social media, beauty markets, professional environments, and everyday life.

In this vein, the pieces in *Embodiment and Representations of Beauty* posit that beauty "is not a frivolous concept nor practice" (Havlin & Báez, 2018, p. 13). Following the footsteps of and in dialog with the 2018 issue of *WSQ: Women's Studies Quarterly* co-edited by Natalie Havlin and Jillian Báez, the 10 chapters comprising this volume reclaim beauty "by unraveling hegemonic normativities and imagining new liberations through art [and real life experiences]" and provoke new considerations of beauty as a critical entry point to understanding not only the material and ideological structures of violence and inequity produced through the matrix of hetero-cis patriarchy and racial capitalism but also the radical potential of mobilizing beauty to imagine and create new liberatory practices. (p. 22)

Beauty and Power

The authors challenge and expand our understandings of beauty in a manner similar to the way in which Baldwin (1993 [1963]) and Camp (2015) challenged distorted understandings of it based on race and class. In fact, many of the chapters reminded us of Baldwin's own expansion of the idea of beauty, understanding it not only as a dimension present in all bodies but also as a moral quality of dignity and resilience against impossible odds (Baldwin, 1993 [1963]). He found beauty even in indignity. He found it, for instance, in how working-class Black people swallowed their pride to be able to navigate the white world of their time in order to be able to build their own.[1]

The connection between power and beauty is especially visible in dehumanizing social institutions like slavery. Despite Europeans having been both fascinated and repulsed by Africans at the beginning of the fateful contact between the continents, Camp (2015) calls our attention to the fact that: "It was within the context of modern slavery in the Americas that African and black bodies came to be seen as singularly and uniformly ugly" (p. 681). As Aníbal Quijano (2000) famously argued, the very idea of race as "the codification of the differences between conquerors and conquered" (p. 533) was a new invention that European empires created specifically in the process of colonizing the Americas. Classifying entire groups of people based on phenotypic features was necessary to coerce free labor from them in the context of the "new global model of labor control" (Quijano, 2000, p. 535) the European powers created.

Moreover, María Elena Cepeda (2018) contends that "the machinations of racial capital – a bodily resource attached to gradients of skin color and phenotype grounded in existing racial hierarchies – proves particularly potent in former European colonies and nations that experience a significant U.S. presence" (p. 125). Along these lines, Alok Vaid-Menon emphasizes that "[b]eauty can be a violent system: one which sanctions whose lives matter and whose do not" (Berne et al., 2018, p. 244) based on how useful they are to capitalism as Malcolm Shanks also reminds us (Berne et al., 2018). Hernández (2018) makes a similar critique while examining the commodification of the deaths of poor Mexican women in Ciudad Juárez by US-based makeup companies and asks: "How can one woman become beautiful through the death of another?"

Beauty and the Body

Bodies continue to be the central location for defining beauty precisely because of the centrality of sight as a source of knowledge and the obsession with categorization the Western world inherits from the Enlightenment and continues to reproduce today (Camp, 2015). This is the case particularly in relation to race as it was "through hierarchical visual representations of human bodily difference that the social category of race came into existence" (Camp, 2015, p. 680). Such European hierarchies were also highly gendered yet with the purpose of ungendering the female Black body as "voluptuous and unwomanly" in order to justify its exploitation as slave labor using the construct of "the thick black woman" (Gentles-Peart, 2018, p. 200). Moreover, they have survived through "controlling images" of Black women like the mammy or the Jezebel as Patricia Hills Collins famously argued and Gentles-Peart (2018) found in her research about English-speaking Caribbean women in New York City. In this volume, the chapter by Sekani L. Robinson showcases similar results as controlling images like the Jezebel, the highly sexualized Black woman, are still used to marginalize Black female dancers in ballet culture.

More broadly, scholars and activists alike have shown how marginalized communities that do not conform to dominant social expectations about race, gender, ability, sexual orientation, gender identity, and other identity markers have "been positioned to be in conflict with our bodies" in the words of Patricia Berne, co-founder of the disability justice Sins Invalid collective (Berne et al., 2018, p. 241). For instance, the chapter by Courtney Dress in this volume shows how pervasive and acceptable anti-fat biases still are, particularly when directed toward women. In a similar manner, Noelle Bridgen demonstrates how the new standard for feminine beauty related to a fit body in El Salvador reinforces traditional gender roles and creates a market for thinning products. Conversely, Berne et al. (2018) advocate for a more holistic understanding that resonates with Baldwin's idea of beauty as dignity: "a beauty based in our integrity, our lineages, our aesthetics, in self-possession of our sexualities and being desirable to ourselves; a beauty that radiates from our hearts, not from symmetrical bone structure" (p. 241); an invitation the authors in this volume clearly accepted.

In the 18th and 19th centuries, an increased focus on the body became even more crucial as potential explanations about human behavior moved from emphasizing environmental factors to internal ones. As Camp (2015) highlights in her seminal article about the history of the relationship between blackness and beauty:

> This modern rethinking of race in ever more biological and physiological terms deepened the importance of looks. For if race arose from and was reflected in human physiognomy, physical appearance did more than embellish biologically distinct "varieties" of mankind: *beauty and ugliness defined one way of thinking about the world's people and human inequality*. [p. 682; emphasis added]

Moreover, the "body is also both a medium *of* culture and a metaphor *for* culture" (Anastasia, 2010, p. 17) as it reflects and recreates the social norms of its time. In this sense, the body "can also be viewed as a locus of social control" (Anastasia, 2010, p. 17) following the works by Pierre Bourdieu and Michel Foucault. A social control that is reinforced through the daily practices of those involved since their participation in "beauty practices has played a crucial role in their embodied experience of femininity" (Vanderberg, 2018, p. 170) and those practices vary greatly over time. Nonetheless, as Vanderberg (2018) also reminds us, not paying attention to individuals' agency and participation in manipulating their bodies while enacting beauty practices can end up overlooking "the capacity of individuals and groups to resist, challenge, and expand beauty norms, as well as the potential for women to engage in beauty practices as part of an expression of selfhood and individual identity" (p. 173). The centrality of the body in the constant negotiation of these norms is evident in all the chapters herein, for instance, in those by Jaleesa Reed on millennials' perspectives about Black standards of beauty, Sekani L. Robinson's chapter on the anti-Black standards of beauty prevalent in ballet, Julia Chin's analysis of the desirability of multiracial people, and Shameika D. Daye's take on the important role of Black hair products.

Beauty and Rebellion

The chapters in this volume show that, even when we understand beauty in the narrow sense of physical representation, it still holds possibilities for agency and rebellion. Similar to White's (2018) exploration of makeup online tutorials' potential to empower women echoing Lorde's definition of self-care as "an act of political warfare,"[2] Salam Aboulhassan analyzes the ways in which Muslim women strategically use clothing to navigate the tensions between the very different yet equally gendered understandings of beauty and honor in their two cultures. The study also reveals how Muslim women and men negotiate the biases and unspoken rules concerning how they, as racialized subjects, should look in the workplace. Along the same lines, Marley Olson examines how white breast cancer survivors redefine their relationships with their own physicality and self-presentation in an attempt to retain some degree of control in their profoundly disrupted lives. And similar to Gentles-Peart's (2018) analysis of the voluptuous Black female body as a disruptor of beauty standards based on whiteness, Shameika D. Daye's chapter shows how Black hair products still mirror Eurocentric beauty standards yet allow Black women to embody their own definitions of beauty.

Indeed, women and gender non-conforming individuals can use beauty to challenge societal norms and other people's attempt to control their destinies and their bodies. For instance, Anastasia (2010) found that the women she interviewed wore tattoos as a way to increase their own self-confidence and sense of beauty. However, they also did it to challenge collective expectations related to beauty and femininity and what is considered appropriate for women to do with their bodies. In their own words, they didn't want to be "placed into a box" and wanted to be free to be "themselves" instead. In fact, the main result from Anastasia's (2010) study was that her participants held an "entirely different definition of beauty than society's ideal" (p. 30). We found a similar theme in several of the chapters in this volume. Nonetheless, Spencier R. Ciaralli's chapter in this volume also highlights that breaking away from narrow and patriarchal standards of beauty is a complicated venture. Even the women and genderqueer people in Ciaralli's study show ambivalence in attempting to do so when it comes to the connection between their body image and their sexual pleasure.

A similar level of complexity can be found in the relationship between beauty and race including a dimension that is less often studied: the perspectives of multiracial individuals in the United States, Latin America, and the Caribbean as shown in Julia Chin's and Jennifer Báez's contributions. Julia Chin's study argues that there is a gap in the studies of multiracial individuals and desirability. Rather than focusing on the perception of external groups, Chin examines how mixed-raced women and non-binary people perceive their own desirability. Through an intersectional approach to mixed-race studies that consider race, sexuality, and gender, Chin shows the impact of these interactions on the sexual politics of dating for multiracial people. Jennifer Báez's intersectional approach to the historical misrepresentation of *mulatas* (half Black, half white women) shifts the conversation toward the ways mixed-race women do not question their desirability, rather they embrace their beauty, sensuality, and race. Through the analysis of Josefina Báez's *CarmenFotonovelArte* and performance pieces by Joiri Minaya, Báez argues that the *mulata* in the works of both Afro-Latina artists disrupts traditional constructions and misperceptions of beauty as they relate to mixed-race women, thus offering new pathways toward the liberation of Afro-Latinas.

CHAPTER DESCRIPTIONS

In "*Mamá Fit* Goes to El Salvador: Fitness in a Transnational Society," Noelle K. Bridgen traces the racialized and gendered practices of fitness in El Salvador in a diasporic context by analyzing print and social media. Bridgen takes the *Mamá Fit* memes, other social media phenomena, and popular print media to trace the racialized and gendered practices in new fitness cultures in El Salvador. Bridgen argues that the word *fit* in English illustrates a crucial cultural change in conventional understandings of the body in a Spanish-speaking society. By charting the emergence of this new beauty and health norm in a transnational domain, Noelle examines the relationship between shifting patterns of gendered corporeal discipline and changes in El Salvador's location within the global political economy. She argues that fitness discourse in El Salvador has become a subtle but powerful conduit for coloniality during a renegotiation of the meaning of gender to fit a neoliberal reality. Grounded in feminist textual analysis, this chapter shows the role of mainstream media in constructing standard sexual politics as it pertains to the public presentation of female bodies and embodied beauty. Bridgen's piece demonstrates this politics of national rebranding through fit culture.

Courtney Dress' chapter "Shifting Perceptions of Women's Weight" presents the results of a quantitative online study on the ways in which people's ideas about women's weight are starting to change in the context of the US Midwest. Based on a sample of 320 mostly female, white and college educated respondents, the author found that anti-fat biases continue to be acceptable to the general public. Even though both thin and fat women were perceived less favorably than average weight women, fat women were perceived less favorably than both average and thin women. Interestingly, in a trend that seems to be consistent with the gendered dimensions of beauty examined in this volume, men were harsher than women in their evaluations of only fat women. As the author highlights in the chapter, her findings add to the emerging evidence that women's weight standards are in transition although not necessarily in favor of overweight women. The study also underscores the need for more extensive research on attitudes of people across the entire weight spectrum.

In "Doing Beauty, Doing Health: Embodied Emotion Work in Women Cancer Patients' Narratives of Hair Loss," Marley Olson addresses the role of hair loss in women's illness narratives of cancer using in-depth interviews with 16 white women in the US Northwest. Interviewees varied in age, marital status, diagnoses, and treatments yet all the women in the study went to great lengths to emotionally manage the effects of their appearance. By examining hair loss, a relatively less studied impact of cancer on women, Olson is able to analyze the features and depth of the emotion work these women engage in. As the author highlights in the chapter and confirmed in her findings, hair loss provokes an explicit and direct confrontation with the gender system and the complex dynamics underlying the accomplishment of proper femininity, including emotions and health. In particular, using Hochschild's concept of gendered emotion work, Olson found that women are taught to be emotion managers and prioritize others' wellness, yet they also must do emotion work on themselves when faced with a cancer diagnosis.

Julia Chin's "'How Do They Really See Me?': The Sexual Politics of Multiracial Desirability" focuses on the experiences of mixed-race women and non-binary people. Chin examines how multiraciality, sexuality, and gender affect self-perceptions of desirability among women and people who identify as non-binary of three multiracial combinations (Black/white, Asian/white, and Latinx/white) at a Southern California public university. The study demonstrates that for mixed-race women, situating into just one racial identity becomes a point of contention with romantic partners and themselves. Moreover, it shows the impact of racial expectations of others and the constant fetishization of mixed-race women and non-binary individuals on their confidence levels, self-esteem, and sense of belonging and authenticity. The findings of this study contribute to research on desirability and critical mixed-race studies. They also open dialogs about the possibility of mixed-race women finding joy through accepting aspects of their mixed-race identities or being open to dialog about their race with their partners in a positive light.

Spencier R. Ciaralli's chapter "Body Image and Sexual Pleasure in Women and Genderqueer Individual's Sexual Experiences" analyzes the relationship between body image, sexual behavior, and pleasure among women and genderqueer or non-binary individuals who are all assigned-female-at-birth with 26 out of 30 participants identifying as LGBTQIA+. The author used a life history method, which highlighted participants' voices and used stories to draw out the social processes being discussed. Ciaralli also employed grounded theory methods in order to identify themes and concepts emerging directly from the data. The first finding points to the presence of genital panic among participants as they experienced anxiety regarding their bodies that impacted their fulfillment in sexual experiences. A related theme was the connection between genital panic and embodied racism, and the aspiration of thinness. Through a very detailed analysis of the data, and in particular of five life stories selected as a panoramic view of the rest, Ciaralli found that participants are both resisting notions of ideal feminine beauty, while reckoning with its tight hold on their actions. Even though they are aware of the patriarchal nature of impossible beauty standards, they often found themselves attempting to embody those standards.

In "I Don't Wear Black: Professional Muslim Workers and Personal Dress Code," Salam Aboulhassan analyzes qualitative data to examine the experiences of Muslim women and men in diverse workplaces in the United States. Grounded in theories of orientalism and social identity, the study interrogates hegemonic representations of organizational power using the context of dress. It considers the interconnections between beauty, work esthetics, hegemonic structures, and systems of marginalization. Furthermore, Aboulhassan shows how Muslim women and men, as well as other racial/ethnic minorities, are marginalized in the workplace while also highlighting the negotiation strategies they use to fit in US work environments. The findings of the study showed gender discrepancies between Muslim men and women in US work settings. In the case of men, they could employ masculine practices to navigate anti-Muslim discourse and foster a sense of belonging at work. At the same time, women tend to face cultural backlash for appropriating Western styles considered immodest within immigrant-centered workplaces. Yet, the study also revealed that while working outside their community, women who wore hijabs emphasized their femininity through softer colors, makeup, or "unpinning" their veil to offset the visceral reaction to their hijab. In sum, this chapter demonstrates how the intersections of gender, religion, and workplace location affect how Muslim men and women dress in their workplaces.

Jaleesa Reed's "Millennial Agency and Liberation within Black American Beauty Standards" examines millennial Black women's relationship with beauty standards in the United States. Through a quantitative analysis, Reed looks at how millennial Black women define Black, the United States, and millennial beauty standards. The findings reveal that participants described these three standards of beauty distinctly. Whereas US beauty was associated with mainstream media representation and Eurocentric features, millennial beauty standards were aligned with tolerance and political consciousness. Conversely, Black American beauty standards were described as an alternative to US beauty conventions and more accepting of the wide range of Black hair textures and skin hues present in the African diaspora. The study demonstrates that millennials value the representation of different gender, racial, and sexual identities in beauty while continuing to engage in beauty practices that require significant time and financial investment. In this sense, the findings showed that beauty can also be construed as a form of capital and a commodity that, at times, can express the interviewees' creativity or a means to achieve professional success. Despite some of these contradictions, one thing is clear: millennials favor a Black American standard of beauty within their community.

Sekani L. Robinson's chapter "Ballet Is [White] Woman: Anti-Black Standards of Beauty Within Ballet" examines the problematic relationship between race, gender, and beauty within the ballet industry. The author highlights the challenges that Black women experience and the anti-Blackness that takes place within the discipline due to enduring Eurocentric beauty standards. Robinson employs Patricia Hill Collins' concept of controlling images to analyze the ways in which those associated with Black women limit the roles and opportunities available to them even today. By delving into the emphasis on hair texture, flesh-tone tights, pointe shoes, and the racist history of the United States and ballet, the chapter demonstrates how ballet continues to discriminate against and marginalize Black women. Nonetheless, based on the results from more than 50 interviews with currently active and retired Black women and men within ballet, the author argues that Black women challenge the narrow model of woman the industry still has in mind: a thin, young, white, middle-class heterosexual woman.

In "Consuming Beauty, Constructing Blackness: A Constructivist Grounded Theory Analysis of Racialized Gendered Embodiment Practices through Shampoo Product Descriptions," Shameika D. Daye closely examines the advertised descriptions of more than 124 shampoos marketed for Black hair textures to understand the messages such products communicate both about beauty and about Blackness. Taking this impressive array of descriptions from the websites of two of the largest distributors in the United States (Target and Walmart) as the starting point, the author used grounded theory methodology to understand phenomena where there is limited available knowledge, such as the embodiment of Black beauty through analyzing hair care products. Daye coded the emerging themes in the analysis by focusing on the ways each description appealed to each of the five senses. Based on the findings from the study, Daye argues that by constructing visual interpretations of racial signifiers through text, marketing strategies encourage otherness, creating a racialized space for Blackness consumption. Moreover, combining the five senses in the descriptions of shampoo products marketed for Black hair textures allowed the author to show how beauty embodiment practices reinforce racialized and gendered practices to subjugate the Black body.

In "*Mulata* in Repose," Jennifer Báez examines various pieces by performance artists who intervene, complicate, and dismantle scripts of othered life. Through a close-reading and critical analysis of the intergenerational pieces of two New York City-based Afro-Dominican artists who arrived in the United States on different migration waves, Joiri Minaya (1983) and Josefina Báez (1960), this study proposes that Afro-Latina women enact an esthetics of "not doing sh*t" as a way to reclaim their agency. The author subverts the idea of repose as passive and attributes a dynamic quality to it, revealing the hidden labor behind historic images of *mulatas* as relaxed, inviting, and welcoming to their consumption. Ultimately, Báez demonstrates that these women artists articulate, problematize, and dismantle oppressive and reductive representation systems through the trope of repose.

CONCLUSION

Drawing from qualitative and quantitative data, the chapters in this volume offer new alternatives to how beauty is conceptualized through a wide range of themes. Beauty is presented and understood as an avenue to create alternative knowledge as well as a conduit to engage in critical conversations on race, ethnicity, gender and sexuality, illness, and fitness. The studies compiled here also exhort us to think critically about the role of hair industries, workplaces, visual arts, and classical dance – to name a few examples – on how beauty is socially construed and conceptualized. In spite of some challenges put forth by the authors, one thing is clear: there is a feminist research ethos in each chapter. Rather than being problem-oriented, the premise of each study is to effect collective change in the ways we construe, see, represent, and embody beauty. Borrowing from Elaine Scarry, "[t]hrough its beauty, the world continually recommits us to a rigorous standard of perceptual care: if we do not search it out, it comes and finds us" (Pérez Rosario, 2018, p. 282). Every essay is a significant contribution to advances in gender research and the volume as a whole indicates that current research in gender and sexuality studies remains committed to social justice and equity. In so doing, each of them also invites us to think of beauty as an emancipatory path to liberation.

NOTES

1. "They did not like saying 'Yes, sir' and 'No, Ma'am,' but the country was in no hurry to educate Negroes, these black men and women knew that the job had to be done, and they put their pride in their pockets in order to do it .... But we must avoid the European error; we must not suppose that, because the situation, the ways, the perceptions of black people so radically differed from those of whites, they were racially superior. I am proud of these people not because of their color but because of their intelligence and their spiritual force and their beauty. The country should be proud of them, too, but, alas, not many people in this country even know of their existence. And the reason for this ignorance is that a knowledge of the role these people played – and play – in American life would reveal more about America to Americans than Americans wish to know" (Baldwin, 1993 [1963], pp. 100–101).

2. "Rather than extending postfeminist claims that cosmetics are inherently empowering, feminist vloggers show how makeup can be part of a feminist language and that feminism can be part of a beauty language. For instance, narratives about foundation allow feminist vloggers to consider what is hidden and parodic product names offer ways to consider intolerance and objectification" (White 2018, p. 149).

REFERENCES

Anastasia, D. J. M. (2010). Living marked: Tattooed women and perceptions of beauty and femininity. *Interactions and Intersections of Gendered Bodies at Work, at Home, and at Play Advances in Gender Research, 14*, 11–33.

Baldwin, J. (1993 [1963]). *The fire next time*. Vintage International.

Berne, P., Lewis, J. T., Milbern, S., Shanks, M., Vaid-Menon, A., & Wong, A. (2018). "Beauty always recognizes itself": A roundtable on sins invalid. *WSQ: Women's Studies Quarterly, 46*(1 & 2), 241–251. https://www.jstor.org/stable/26421177

Camp, S. M. H. (2015). Black is beautiful: An American history. *The Journal of Southern History, 81*(3), 675–690.

Cepeda, M. E. (2018). Putting a good face on the nation. *WSQ: Women's Studies Quarterly, 46*(1 & 2), 121–138. https://www.jstor.org/stable/26421166

Gentles-Peart, K. (2018). Controlling beauty ideals: Caribbean women, thick bodies, and white supremacist discourse. *WSQ: Women's Studies Quarterly, 46*(1 & 2), 199–214. https://www.jstor.org/stable/26421171

Havlin, N., & Báez, J. (2018). Introduction: Revisiting beauty. *WSQ: Women's Studies Quarterly, 46*(1 & 2), 13–24. https://www.jstor.org/stable/26421158

Hernández, B. (2018). Dying to be beautiful: (Re)Membering the women of Juárez, the commodification of death, and the nonuniversal standards of beauty. *WSQ: Women's Studies Quarterly, 46*(1 & 2), 70–87. https://www.jstor.org/stable/26421162

Pérez Rosario, V. (2018). On beauty and protest. *WSQ: Women's Studies Quarterly*, *46*(1 & 2), 279–285. https://www.jstor.org/stable/26421190

Quijano, A. (2000). Coloniality of power, eurocentrism, and Latin America. *Nepantla: Views from South*, *1*(3), 533–580. https://www.muse.jhu.edu/article/23906

Vanderberg, A. (2018). Toward a phenomenological analysis of historicized beauty practices. *WSQ: Women's Studies Quarterly*, *46*(1 & 2), 167–180. https://www.jstor.org/stable/26421169

West, C. (1993). *Race matters*. Beacon Press.

White, M. (2018). Beauty as an "act of political warfare": Feminist makeup tutorials and Masquerades on YouTube. *WSQ: Women's Studies Quarterly*, *46*(1 & 2), 139–156. https://www.jstor.org/stable/26421167

Wright Mills, C. (2016 [2000, 1959]). The sociological imagination. The promise. In K. McGann (Ed.), *SAGE readings for introductory sociology* (pp. 1–8). SAGE.

CHAPTER 1

MAMÁ FIT GOES TO EL SALVADOR: FITNESS IN A TRANSNATIONAL SOCIETY

Noelle K. Brigden

Department of Political Science, Marquette University, USA

ABSTRACT

Taking the Mamá Fit *memes and other social media eruptions as a starting point and delving deeper into popular print media, this chapter traces the racialized and gendered practices that constitute fitness in El Salvador in a diasporic context. Importantly, the word* fit *is now often expressed in English, captured in the names of commercial gyms and diet advertisements; the use of this word signals an important cultural change in conventional understandings of the body in a Spanish-speaking society. By charting the emergence of this new health/beauty norm in a transnational domain, this chapter explores the relationship between shifting patterns of gendered body discipline and changes in El Salvador's location within the global political economy. This chapter argues that fitness discourse has become a subtle, but powerful, conduit for coloniality during a renegotiation of the meaning of gender to fit a neoliberal reality. The argument ends by pointing in the direction of future research to explore how this discourse is experienced in embodied practice with potentially contradictory impacts in Salvadoran society.*

Keywords: Physical culture; body image; fat phobia; coloniality; symbolic violence; neoliberal feminism

The one-piece, backless spandex jumper clung to her body, accentuating curves with a tight seam down the backside of the shorts and ties at her hips. While clearly proud of the muscles that she had built in the gym, she, nevertheless, maintained an image of feminine beauty: voluptuous, flat bellied, and tanned. She kept her fingernails groomed and her highlighted-blond hair long. She waited dutifully for her young son to emerge from school. Filmed from the back without consent by a woman hoping to shame her for the revealing attire, Bolivian lawyer and model Vanessa Medina became a global social media sensation when she responded online by proclaiming herself *Mamá Fit*.[1] Memes with her image ignited spin-offs with jokes, people around the world debated the appropriateness of her wardrobe, and avid gym-goers passionately defended her lifestyle and praised the discipline required to obtain her physique. In El Salvador, one of many Spanish-speaking countries where this image resonated, *Mamá Fit* heralds a new standard for feminine beauty that reinforces traditional gender roles while incorporating fitness ideals.

Taking the *Mamá Fit* memes and other social media eruptions as a starting point and delving deeper into popular print media, I trace the racialized and gendered practices that constitute fitness in El Salvador. Importantly, the word *fit* is often expressed in English, captured in the names of commercial gyms and diet advertisements[2]; the use of this word in English signals an important cultural change in conventional understandings of the body in a Spanish-speaking society. By charting the emergence of this new beauty and health norm in a transnational domain, I explore the relationship between shifting patterns of gendered corporeal discipline and changes in El Salvador's location within the global political economy.

Salvadoran *fitness* is intimately connected to that international context. El Salvador's recent economic repositioning and service sector growth have not disrupted older patterns of inequality, international economic dependence, and patriarchy but instead hastened social changes compatible with their contemporary retrenchment. Within these older patterns, coloniality is an ongoing conquest by gendered subjectivities rooted in racism, patriarchal exercise of power, and global inequality (Lugones, 2008; Martin Alcoff, 2020). Modernization and ideals linked to "modernity" institutionalize and internalize an atomized individualism that perpetuates inequities and obscures the racist origins of the global system (Quijano, 2000). As Mignolo (2000, p. ix) explains, "there is no modernity without coloniality." Thus, across Latin America, the contemporary neoliberal reality, in which state–society relations become unmoored and re-ordered according to capitalist rationalities, both emerges from past colonialism and reinforces coloniality in the present (Mignolo, 2000; Quijano, 2000). Under these conditions, fitness internalizes racist and gendered imagery, generating pressure for personally and ecologically destructive capitalist consumption. As people begin to read images of lean, muscular bodies as an embodiment of discipline and modernity, fitness classifies differences between worthy and unworthy humans. This process is one example of what Quijano (2000) calls "the coloniality of power."

This chapter maps how newspapers and social media communicate fitness in El Salvador. Following feminist textual analyses, such as Cabas-Mijares and

Jenkins (2023, p. 2), I show how mainstream media "construct a normative sexual politics around the public presentation of female bodies." However, I look specifically at how fitness discourse, known colloquially in English as fitspo, structures normative politics. Fitspo is a contraction of two words: fitness and inspiration. This discourse forms a vital transmission medium for fitness culture, and it circulates with accelerating intensity on contemporary social media platforms, often selling consumer products or services while providing motivating imagery, words, or advice to achieve physical transformation goals. As Silva (2022, p. 3) explains, in his analysis of Brazilian wellness and beauty trends, fitness culture is "a set of racial, ethnic, gendered sexual, and ableist discourses and signifiers of normativity at the level of corporality-images of the body, what it should look like, and how it should function." In the US context, Carlan (2021, p. 1) draws attention to how discursive constructions of diet and fitness, and often even the body positive rhetoric meant to thwart such constructions, subtly constitute a "racial language of fatphobia." As a hierarchical and stigmatizing system that values some bodies over others, fitness often reinforces other symbolic and material inequities based on race, class, and gender. Fitness thereby becomes a form of symbolic violence, defined by Bourdieu and Wacquant (2002) as harm experienced with the complicity of the sufferer. In this vein, I argue that fitspo has become a subtle, but powerful, conduit for coloniality during a renegotiation of the meaning of gender to fit a neoliberal reality.

EL SALVADOR: A SITE OF TRANSNATIONAL BODY POLITICS

In a context of international migration and a communications technology boom, a transnational imaginary of fitness emerged in El Salvador and across the Americas.[3] In El Salvador, multinational corporations leverage a body panic over obesity to sell diet fads, gym memberships, drugs, cosmetic surgery, workout supplements, and fitness equipment. The growth of this transnational consumer market dovetails with neoliberal economic restructuring in the aftermath of the civil war (1980–1992). Salvadoran policymakers began to court "remitting subjects," understanding good citizens to embody neoliberal values and send money home (Hernández & Coutin, 2006; Pedersen, 2013). With these migrant dollars as the mainstay national economy, Salvadoran elites shifted their financial interests away from traditional agriculture and toward banking, services, tourism, and import industries, increasingly dependent on the stimulation of consumption rather than the control of production (Warnecke-Berger, 2020). Today, contemporary El Salvador has more *Instagram* fitness influencers and bitcoin enthusiasts than sugar barons.[4]

In the Salvadoran post-conflict setting, still reeling from the geopolitical legacies of Cold War proxy struggles in Central America, this fitness imaginary constitutes a form of symbolic violence. Despite the increased pressure to conform to specific corporeal standards of beauty and health, socio-economic realities limit fitness opportunity for many Salvadorans.[5] The impossibility of achieving these standards manifests the multiple forms of political and economic violence experienced by Salvadorans as everyday life (Bourgois, 2001; Walsh & Menjívar, 2016). Since the end of its civil war (1980–1992), El Salvador has gained renewed international notoriety for violence as the "murder capital of the world" and home to, allegedly, the "most dangerous gang in the world."[6] Several generations of refugees fled the region, first from a spiral of political repression and then from an escalation of policing and gang activity: a so-called war on gangs.

Salvadoran society sits at a geographical crossroads in the Americas, located (at least in the US foreign policy imagination) on a strategically important land bridge connecting north and south. As a result of repeated US political interventions, El Salvador also inhabits a transnational diasporic position within a global economy dominated for roughly a century by the United States. Indeed, as a result of decades of violence and economic dislocation with roots in Cold War politics and US Foreign policy (Brigden & Hallett, 2020; Chomsky, 2021), approximately 25% of Salvadoran citizens live in the United States, often referred to as *Departamento 15*, and migrant remittances constitute approximately 15% of the annual gross domestic product (Menjívar & Gomez Cervantes, 2018; Velásquez et al., 2021).[7] This broader geopolitical context contributes to the messages people receive about the worth of their bodies.

El Salvador's resulting, entrenched diasporic cultural setting corresponds to Anzaldúa's (2015, p. 127) description of the *nepantla* (Borderlands). She defines Borderlands, not only as a specific territorial site at the US–Mexico divide but more broadly as liminal spaces of colonial contact. These spaces not only provoke anxiety and ambiguity but also conversely generate improvisation, cultural hybridity, and resistance to oppression. Central America and the Caribbean are, in this sense, the extended Borderlands of US Empire. In this chapter, following inspiration from decolonial scholarship, I show how transnational fitness worlds have become a conduit for symbolic violence to and through El Salvador. However, at the close of this argument, I gesture in the direction of Anzaldúa's (2015) analysis to pose an additional question about the potential for resistance to this violence for future research.

METHODS

For this chapter, data collection and analysis center primarily on popular print media. I began with a review of the *La Prensa Gráfica* newspaper and then examined social media and articles found online. While I focus on content that would be widely available to and circulating among domestic Salvadoran audiences (whether in print or online), I emphasize the transnational domain that constitutes a global gym culture (Andreasson & Johansson, 2014).

To situate contemporary notions of *fit*, I identified key shifts in economic and political structures in the narrative of the Salvadoran body politic. Since the 1992 peace accords that ended the civil war, these shifts include: the post-2001 period of failed peace, marked by dollarization and earthquake, as the world hurled headlong into a US-led War on Terror; and the post-2019 rise of populist authoritarianism with the presidential election of Nayib Bukele as a third-party candidate, the consolidation of his power during and after the Covid-19 crisis, and the adoption of Bitcoin as national currency. I trace changes in gendered images and discourses of fitness around these flexion points.

I analyze *La Prensa Gráfica* newspaper since 2001 and social media circulations on *Facebook* post-2014. Founded in 1915, *La Prensa Gráfica* is one of the two most circulated national papers alongside *El Diario de Hoy*. Beyond its broad circulation and national coverage with large readership, I chose *La Prensa Gráfica* as a starting place because of its long-term transnational engagement. In 2001, the paper launched a regular *Departamento 15* section, referring to Salvadorans in the diaspora as an integral part of the nation. In 2004, the paper entered an information-sharing agreement with the multinational communications giant, *Univision*, merging its coverage with global media. To explore its content and knowing that new years' resolutions generate increased discussion of body transformations, I read issues from cover to cover for the first two weeks each January from 2001 to 2014. I paid particular attention to sections on health, beauty, lifestyle, and sport, and I cataloged advertisements for a variety of body-changing treatments, products, and equipment. By 2014, the internet had become an important source of beauty and wellness information for most Salvadorans, with newspaper coverage easily accessible online. For my exploration of this contemporary period, I switched my strategy to keyword searches of online media materials, as well as my own *Facebook* feed from Salvadoran friends over the years. During the Covid-19 crisis in 2020, Salvadoran use of social media, including but not limited to *Twitter*, YouTube, *Facebook*, and *Instagram*, skyrocketed (Marroquin & Carballo, 2021). My iterative attempts at coding and interpretation of this text have been informed by and situated within immersive and embodied knowledge accumulated over years of participant observation in fitness spaces in both the United States and El Salvador.[8]

FIT HISTORY: CONTEXTUALIZING CONTEMPORARY SOCIAL MEDIA CIRCULATIONS IN AN URBAN LANDSCAPE

The incorporation of the English words *fitness* and *fit* into daily discourse signals a change in the relationship between body, gender, and self in El Salvador since my first visit to the country in 2008. This social transformation can only be fully understood in reference to a broader national, historical trajectory and shifts in the global political economy. Indeed, by examining notions of fitness, we learn a great deal about these broader socio-economic and political trends. To restate this chapter's argument: in El Salvador, fitspo (online fitness images, ostensibly circulated as exercise and diet motivation) constitutes a form of symbolic violence that reinforces a coloniality of bodies while renegotiating the meaning of gender to fit a neoliberal reality.

The growth of the gym industry and contemporary understandings of *fitness* in El Salvador emerged in tandem with the development of private shopping malls.

Previously, department stores (e.g., *Siman*) organized commercialism. However, malls built with multiple (often multinational franchise-style) stores and complete with food courts and other spaces for leisure became the preferred place for family recreation. Their popularity soared as security anxieties over street gangs escalated in the late 1990s and early 2000s, both reflecting and contributing to the privatization of public space and fragmentation of the experience of citizenship within the urban environment (see Caldeira, 2001 on Brazil). *Metrocentro*, among the first of these developments in Central America, opened in 1971. In the three decades that followed, the spatial model diffused and transformed the urban landscape of San Salvador. A shopping mall called *Galerias*, located in upscale commercial district of Colonia Escalon, opened in 1994. *Multiplaza*, an impressive upgrade from *Metrocentro* that advertised itself with the slogan, "the future is built here! It's an entire city" with chapel, corporate offices, hotel, apartments, and every shopping need, opened in 2004. A luxury race among malls across the city has been a constant since that time, most recently with the extravagant *Plaza Millennium* (connected by an enclosed overhead walkway to *Galerias*), which advertises in its promotional materials that the development is "more than a lifestyle, it is a new philosophy of urban life."

In 2010, *BeFit* Fitness Centers became El Salvador's first major (Central American-based) multinational chain modeled after US commercial gyms to expand into shopping malls. The air-conditioned, highly regulated, and clean facilities boast "modern exercise machines" and claim to "promote a healthy lifestyle" with staff on hand to track progress and assist beginners (Ortiz, 2014, p. 1). Their self-proclaimed modernity was a major selling point. As they entered shopping malls with their stylized brand, *BeFit* and its imitators began to attract new clientele, including women and novice exercisers. The population of gym-goers diversified and expanded. These consumers had previously shunned the more affordable, ubiquitous, working-class local-chain *Coach Gym* for its grittiness and masculine intimidation factor. Even prior to the *Coach Gym* chain, a handful of gyms with relatively affordable rates, such *as Gimnasio Olímpico* and *Gimnasio Libertad* downtown, had catered primarily to the devout (overwhelmingly male) lifter but never "modernized" (according to former members). In contrast, the upscale and expensive *World Gym* or *Balley's*, both US name brands with co-ed appeal, made early entry into the Salvadoran landscape and are still located in a wealthy part of town near the US embassy and the campus-neighborhood outside the Jesuit University, respectively.

Unlike these gyms, *BeFit* lowered membership fees to make "modern" and "hygienic" facilities accessible to greater numbers of people from the middle classes. However, to become a member, gym-goers need a credit card or bank account to set up monthly autopay under a longer-term contract: no day-by-day passes allowed, and no cash accepted. As a result, the primary barrier to luxurious, user-friendly exercise spaces shifted away from the cash cost and toward whether the would-be gym goer could engage with the formal economy. People caught in the informal economy with unpredictable salaries hesitate to sign contracts, and without access to the institutional infrastructure for autopay, they could not become members. Other gyms soon followed this membership model, including *LevelUp* gyms.

The entry of *BeFit* into the gym landscape of San Salvador, thus, sat at the nexus of important, interconnected changes that co-occurred in both the notion of *fitness* and the political economy. A perfect storm of migrant remittances, transnational commercial messaging from the United States, and ongoing urbanization fueled middle-class consumerism. This new socio-economic reality unmoored traditional class distinctions differentiating *humilde* rural *campesino* from upper-class urban dweller; the creep of consumerist culture, urbanization, and transnationalism renders such distinctions ambiguous, as people across class sectors adopt new dress, food, and recreation. In that transition moment, *fitness* as a lifestyle, including modes of self-presentation, consumption, and daily practices worn on the body, became a class aspiration and a way of signaling worth. Finally, *BeFit* changed the language of exercise and wellness. The word *fit* in the gym name soon became a hegemonic signifier for goals and lifestyle practices that conflate health, beauty, athleticism, and the capacity to participate in consumerism. More recently, *SmartFit*, a mega-chain from Brazil conquered the Latin American market, expanded aggressively into El Salvador, and, uncoincidentally, also has a franchise in the new *Plaza Millennium*. The future is here, and fitness has become (as the *Plaza Millennium* slogan suggests) "more than a lifestyle; it is a new a philosophy of urban life."

Prior to this mall-gym expansion, fitness (as we now know it) did not exist in El Salvador. However, the pivotal events of the year 2001 set forces set into motion that would profoundly transform the Salvadoran body politic and, ultimately, define the future of fitness for the country. That year, two key disasters struck the poor, causing widespread economic displacement: a destructive earthquake and a destabilizing dollarization. Dollarization, the moment when El Salvador officially shed its national currency in favor of US currency, caused a sudden, painful inflation for the working classes. The political elite justified this monetary policy as the most efficient approach to the country's overwhelming economic dependence on migrant remittances from the United States. In 1999, El Salvador received $1,373.8 million in remittances from the US-based diaspora, and by 2005, $2,830 million (Granados, 2006, citing data from the Central Bank of El Salvador). However, the embrace of dollarization by policymakers also institutionalized the neoliberal economic paradigm, including attempts to limit government spending on social systems and to privatize the health sector. Despite continued spending on military and police, public safety also fell into the hands of private actors, such as hired mall security guards. Thus, by 2001, the early euphoria and optimism of the immediate post-conflict period had receded (Moodie, 2011). Deportations from the United States soared, and newspaper headlines decried gang extortion and escalating murder rates. The world would soon be engulfed in a US-led War on Terror with deep reverberations for El Salvador's own War on Gangs, which ramped up *Mano Dura* (Iron Fist) policing in 2004 and labeled street gangs "terrorists" in 2010 (Wolf, 2017; Zilberg, 2011). Since that time, security priorities have overshadowed civil liberties with deleterious consequences for Salvadoran democracy, culminating in the election of the (very popular) authoritarian, President Nayib Bukele, in 2019.

Throughout the early 2000s, *La Prensa Gráfica* expressed these concerns. The newspaper documents El Salvador's ongoing shift from an agricultural economy to a remittance-dependent consumer economy. Stories of regional free trade agreements, the multinational expansion of the Salvadoran financial sector, privatization of public sectors, updates on remittances, US immigration politics, and the birth of new shopping mall development projects fill the economy and national sections, alongside increasingly alarming stories of gang violence. Throughout this newspaper coverage, multinational food chains regularly advertise cheap burgers and pizzas, often sharing a page with promotions from beauty and weight loss centers hawking mysterious creams and treatments, adorned with images of thin, scantily clad, white women. A market for thinning products surges. Promotions of cellulite creams, diet pills, and other treatments claim to help women *perder peso* (lose weight) and *ponerte en forma* (get in shape) or *estar en forma* (be in shape). While McDonalds expanded its reach into Salvadoran market, growing 30% in 2007, a 2008 gated-housing development advertises its own gym, which provided "everything you need to stay in shape." New dedicated spaces for fitness and the gated fragmentation of the city, driven by crime anxieties, went hand in hand with a rural reorganization of agriculture and the urban entry of a multinational food industry.

However, in articles and advertisements of this period and in the 2010s, the English word *fitness* is not yet used. Ideas of a specific exercise lifestyle, replete with its own philosophy of life and values, and associated with imagery of toned or even muscular forms, had not yet taken hold. Nevertheless, key elements of this concept emerge, including the gendered and racialized conflation of health and beauty norms, and the idea that physical presentation that conforms to those norms unlocks broader class ambitions for individuals. Both health and beauty sections of the paper advise women on weight loss, and the key phrase repeated in these sections is to *ponerte en forma* (get in shape). No mention is made of *fitness* or *la vida fit*, but women are encouraged to seek a *new body* in English. Uncoincidentally, small gyms throughout San Salvador use the English word *body* in their names today: *Good Body Gym, Body Impact, BodyTek, Bodynolimitgym, Perfect Body Gym*, among others. In both ads and articles, the desired female body is described as *eseblto* (svelte) and in English *slim*. Photographs that illustrate this ideal are almost universally thin, white women, and often, blond. For example, a health article providing advice on how to manipulate diet to lose weight acknowledges that

> In our society, a beauty ideal that rhymes with slenderness governs. A svelte body has become a calling card that can open many doors: that of professional achievement, emotional satisfaction, and social affirmation. But when one is *gordita* (a little fat), dissatisfaction arrives.

In the accompanying image, a thin white woman, long-legged and laughing happily, bends over a refrigerator overflowing with fruits. Importantly, *gordita* had traditionally been a term of endearment in many Spanish-speaking societies (Yates-Doerr, 2015, p. 86), including El Salvador, but now took the blame for dissatisfaction in many areas of life, ranging from relationships to career.

In the two decades after 2001, the newspaper increasingly conveys concerns over the growth of obesity as a health risk, often uncritically conflating good health and thinness. An article implores women to "begin the year with health" but illustrates health with an emaciated, air-brushed, pale-skinned waist, wrapped in measuring tape. Throughout the beauty section of this period, articles that lump "health" and "a better figure" or "shape" and "weight loss" into the same sentence proliferate. The health sections also routinely borrow from *Univision* and *Reuters*, transnationally transmitting fears about a global obesity pandemic. While obesity has grown in El Salvador as US-based franchises spread and disrupted traditional food cultures, the body panic, discrimination, and fat phobias that accompany this shift in body mass index (BMI) numbers have their roots in a global hysteria transmitted via traditional and social media (see Boero, 2013; Brewis & Wutich, 2019; Dworkin & Wachs, 2009).

In the early 2000s, articles decrying the risks of obesity for cardiovascular health or cancer were the only newspaper content to mention the need for male weight loss or provide images of men seeking body transformations; there is no beauty section for men. Conversely, athletic male bodies populate the sports section, and few women adorn its pages. Notable exceptions include international tennis stars and elite Salvadoran athletes in international competitions, such as the Pan-American games. Unlike the male soccer stars and other male athletes that dominate the pages, a notable portion of the already scarce attention paid to these female athletes centers on their beauty and body. Occasionally, the female athletes in the sports section appear in street clothes, bathing suits, and evening wear, rather than in the context of their athletic pursuit.

Perhaps unsurprisingly then, the newspaper advises women to prioritize beauty over athletics. One article from the lifestyle section, titled "A feminine privilege that you should take care of yourself," explains that

> the breasts are, par excellence, an attribute of beauty in all women, but at the same time, an organ destined for lactation with few rewinding mechanisms to put the brakes on factors that affect their beauty and youth. In fact, only five percent of women 35 years old maintain the look of a perfect chest.

As a solution to this crisis of imperfect breasts among middle-aged women, the article proposes cold showers, massages, and sports like swimming and controlled repetitions of weights but warns that women "should ignore, however, practices such as the *jogging*, aerobics, equitation, and in general, any physical activity that provokes sudden agitation." The image of a youthful, thin, white woman lifting a tiny silver barbell in a bicep curl while sucking in her smoothly air-brushed stomach accompanies this advice. The camera angle looks downward toward her cleavage, bursting from a baby blue push-up bra. According to the newspaper in 2010, women have *nada de excusas* (no excuses) for not exercising. Women experiencing "that classic feeling of guilt and remorse for all they have eaten on vacation" need not worry because they too could lose weight in their daily activities. A slender-illustrated figure demonstrates that it is easy to burn 100 calories by simply ironing, carrying grocery bags, washing the car, cooking, pushing a baby stroller, jogging, gardening, dancing, walking, climbing steps, and sweeping. The message: slender bodies and traditional women's work are perfectly compatible.

Of course, women who work outside the home also have no excuses. Several articles demonstrate how to do gentle exercises at your office desk, thereby rendering capitalist work discipline compatible with fitness.

In 2005, the word *fitness* surfaces only in relation to the women's competitive bodybuilding category, which is so named. At the time, the sport represented a marginalized subculture in El Salvador, viewed as a novelty for men and an oddity for women. The article calls attention to the "tremendous show" that the sport offers potential spectators with its title: "when the bodybuilder inflated their muscles until one fears they will explode." The article does not imply that these bodies represent ideals for which everyday people should strive; body builders were a spectacle, not role models.

The English word *fitness* first entered *La Prensa Gráfica* newspaper as a mainstream goal for exercise enthusiasts in an article imported from *Reuters* in 2011 about how to achieve New Years' resolutions. For that article, an image of white women in a step cardio class accompanied advice from *Hollywood* trainers about how to get into shape so that the machine you received for Christmas does not go to waste. Indeed, around that time, the discussion of "getting into shape" turned toward weights and machines available for home purchase or for use in commercial gyms. Retailers began to market home exercise equipment in the newspaper, alongside fashionable workout clothing. In 2010, the major department store which sells such apparatus, *Siman*, offered a *Vida Sana* (Healthy Lifestyle) fair with a variety of sponsors, ranging from multinational *Herbalife* to *Yes* yogurt. In media, fitness became a comprehensive lifestyle, signaling not only health and beauty but also the financial capacity to consume in the new Salvadoran economy. By 2017, the newspaper more frequently provides advice columns on how to have a *fit body* or achieve fitness goals like popular *Instagram* influencers, beauty pageant winners, the "abuela de *fitness* mas *sexy* del mundo" (the sexiest grandmother in the world), and JLo.

In recent years, US celebrity men (not only women) increasingly appear in media representations of fitness. One newspaper article from 2022, originally a story from *La Nacion* Argentina but re-circulated in *La Prensa Gráfica* online, discusses a muscle-building diet and routine from Dwayne "the Rock" Johnson. His hyper-muscular physique represents a changing beauty norm for men in a country where soccer stars have long been the male body ideal (Landaverde & Valladares Lemus, 2006). A 2023 article, re-circulated from *El Tiempo* Colombia, gives *tips* to get started in the *fitness* world and displays a muscular, white, co-ed group of athletes, glowing with sweat and performing high-intensity exercise.

Indeed, a slightly more *marcado* or *tonificado* ideal (less exaggerated than the Rock with emphasis on lean muscle in gender-appropriate places) emerges for women in the newspaper. This new feminine image of *fitness* (now often explicitly named such) coincides with the rise of *CrossFit* boxes in wealthy neighborhoods of the city, where practitioners perform high-intensity exercise with heavy weights in co-ed groups. In a 2017 newspaper article espousing the benefits of *CrossFit*,[9] a celebrity Costa Rican trainer notes that both men and women can participate, albeit usually for different goals: "Generally, women look to tone the body, create resistance and improve physical condition, while some men work for muscle strengthening." A year later, the newspaper announced that Maria Jose (Majo) Alger, host of a popular daytime talk show, could boast of a *six pack* thanks to a beauty regimen that included being a *CrossFit girl* and cryogenic freezing. After retiring from television, Alger went on to found her own *CrossFit*-style gym.[10]

The new body ideal coincides with the entry of bodybuilding into the mainstream with a *bikini fitness* category, in which a physique looks more akin to a beauty pageant eschews the stereotypes of extreme muscularity associated with the sport. The new ideal also coincides with the rising global influence of female bodybuilders proudly displaying their *Brazilian Butt* workouts on transnational social media (Silva, 2022). In El Salvador, the newspaper and national sports federation herald these new bikini fitness champions as examples of "perseverance," "discipline," and "achievement," no longer muscled oddities but instead role models with hyper-feminine physiques and muscles that accentuate curves rather than give an impression of pure strength.

FIT POLITICS: ERUPTIONS OF FEMINIST CONTESTATIONS AND EMERGENT POST-COVID-19 CITIZENSHIP

In the wake of traditional media representations of fitness, online fitspo has become an important site to negotiate what it means to be a good woman and a good citizen. In this discourse, the body and its imagery perform both neoliberal gender identity and modern citizenship. The *Mamá Fit* memes and comments provide just one example of how *fitness* became more than simply a "toned" or "muscular" body ideal. *Facebook* pages where such memes and messages circulate in Spanish language include, but are not limited to, *Vida Fitness, Gym Mi Estilo de Vida, Adictos Gym, Memo Fit, Motivacion Gym, Bestias del Gym, PonteFit21, Yo Amo el Gym,* and *Forever Fitness.* Those pages often re-post the same reappropriated images with advertisements for a variety of supplements and drugs. Those listed here also appear most frequently in my own *Facebook* feed from Salvadoran friends. As of the time of writing, none of the anonymous managers of these pages, who appear to be based outside El Salvador, have responded to requests to be interviewed about their selection of content or their geographic location. The result is a transnational discourse with ambiguous origins. Such memes also re-circulate on the pages of various Salvadoran gyms, as well as through personal accounts. As this circulation accelerated, fitness became an aspirational lifestyle and philosophy of life.

Online fitspo, uncoincidentally, is compatible with the neoliberal project undertaken by the Bukele regime, which also relies heavily on social media propaganda to buttress popular support. Neoliberalism is "a fluid process of ordering disordering and re-ordering state-society relations, attended by a legitimizing individualizing ideology" (Brigden & Vogt, 2015, p. 4). Over time, this process becomes an everyday logic generating self-governance with internalized notions of discipline (Brigden & Vogt, 2015, p. 2, citing Ong, 2006). In El Salvador, neoliberalism predates the rise of Bukele's *Nuevas Ideas* (new ideas) political party.

However, Bukele's rule intensified its manifestations, such as the privatization of public goods, the normalization of extreme forms of economic inequality, the militarization of domestic policing, and the abrogation of institutionalized democracy and civil liberties that had been promised by the 1992 Peace Accords.

One of *Nuevas Ideas*' new ideas is engagement with the fit body of its citizens, and this gendered national fitness agenda takes shape within a neoliberal feminist framework. Neoliberal feminism is a logic grounded in assumptions of atomized individual rationality that valorizes women who can productively manage work–family balance, as well as her own self-care (Rottenberg, 2018). In the Global North, lean-in-style strategies for coping with gendered inequalities, rather than collective mobilization to dismantle the intersections of patriarchy and capitalism, characterize feminist action moved by this logic (Rottenberg, 2013). Similarly, in El Salvador, the gendered citizen subjects generated in neoliberal feminist discourse tend to accept and internalize modes of patriarchal rule and capitalist inequities, focusing instead on the perfection of their own minds and bodies.

Within this context, bodybuilding no longer represents an oddity for some women in Salvadoran society. The President's brother now leads the National Sports Institution of El Salvador (INDES), the government agency that provides the interface between federal funding and sports federations for a variety of athletic disciplines that mobilize elite national athletic teams. The social media public relations for INDES and its federated athletes extend the regime's propaganda campaigns, and Salvadoran success in international bodybuilding competitions figures prominently in that promotional material. Imagery about this extreme physical maintenance, particularly to the muscle-building regimens of elite bodybuilding sport, also establishes a new feminine expectation for recreational athletes. This expectation circulated previously, but it now dovetails with other messages from the regime.

Even before Bukele entered the presidency, a 2018 *La Prensa Gráfica* article heralds this shift, announcing the arrival of *A Supermama Fisicoculturista* in a Mother's Day special sports section. The article focused on Susan de Hernández, a woman who took care to stay in shape during her second pregnancy and competed in a *bodyfitness* category only six months after giving birth. The article identifies her as "mother, wife, athlete and trainer. All *fitness*." After 2017, articles like this one become more commonplace and claim that women really can have it all, including a *fit* body. The neoliberal template for feminism found a home in El Salvador.

A 2021 article from the online periodical *Diario El Salvador* clearly illustrates the links between broader neoliberal shifts in the economy, the feminist ideological accessory to those shifts, fitspo, and the new political moment. That article, titled "A woman can be mother, wife, professional and fight every day to achieve her goals," profiles Lorena Fuentes, a *Nuevas Ideas* congresswoman from Santa Ana. The first image accompanying the text shows a smiling Lorena Fuentes in stylish *lycra* pants and sports bra, performing a bicep curl. The caption explains that she had previously been a professional bodybuilder. In the article, Ms Fuentes explains how uncomfortable she felt looking in the mirror after becoming a mother and gaining weight and how this discomfort with her image motivated her. After her last baby at age 25 via c-section, she began to go to the gym, tracked her nourishment, and saw that her body changed rapidly: "However, I was left with the trauma of putting on a bathing suit to go to the beach." She recognized it as a "mental block." So, she decided to compete in bodybuilding to break that block. When asked about how her life as an athlete has helped her in her new life as a politician, she responds, "In all periods life, the first is discipline. One begins with motivation, but often this motivation disappears and it's there that the role of discipline enters, the knowledge that a "should-do" must be completed, independent of how one feels." Ultimately, Ms Fuentes concludes that "… women have the internal strength to move the world, and through that, seek to promote a true equality in El Salvador, demonstrating that every woman can strengthen herself until she achieves her goals and develops all her capacities." In answer to the question about how women can balance personal and professional lives, she says that she restricts work on Sundays to dedicate time to her family, but

> It's all in knowing how to organize and having clear goals and objectives that one wants to achieve, and of course, strengthening oneself every day to achieve it. Today, technology helps a lot in this aspect. I am in the Legislative Assembly, but I am always attentive of my children, I make videocalls in moments that I have free, and that way I do not lose my link with them and I do not neglect my legislative labors …. I want to leave a clear message for all women: the family domain should not clash with the professional. Both things can be balanced/maintained.

Such media representations of wealthy women contrast sharply with the continued daily experience of many working-class Salvadoran women, who receive criticism from family members and male partners for spending time at the gym rather than attending to their endless household duties (Argueta & Brigden, 2023, p. 161). Nevertheless, the *Mamá Fit* controversy erupted during this shift toward neoliberal feminism, an ideology that encourages women to embody self-discipline to achieve an ideal of success in both public (masculine) and private (feminine) domains. As noted by feminist scholars (e.g., Rottenberg, 2018), such cultural norm changes tend to occur as women develop the double burden of capitalist labor entry with continued responsibilities for reproductive labor. In El Salvador, the demands of being a good woman just intensified.

After Covid-19, the Bukele regime employed fitness as a paradigm within which to message both foreign and domestic audiences about Salvadoran national identity and citizenship responsibilities. While the mechanisms that underpin the correlation between BMI and Covid-19 mortality remain unclear, the global call for active lifestyles has become urgent in the pandemic context (Pause et al., 2021). For example, the Salvadoran government recently released a public relations campaign calling upon its citizens to commit to healthy habits, ranging from regular exercise to better nutrition.[11] The advertisement (subtitled in English) encourages Salvadorans to accept responsibility for their own self-care and health, as a matter of national pride. Based on my own interactions with Salvadorans, it seems unlikely that many people in El Salvador have seen this advertisement. Instead, the primary audience appears to be the Salvadoran diaspora. Thus, the public relations campaign simultaneously explains the duty to be fit, while projecting a message of auspicious fitness consumption that signals how El Salvador has acquired the "modernity" to which so many Latin American countries aspire. In this way, the advertisement speaks to the Salvadoran diaspora, within a pattern of economic dependence and the ongoing socio-political courtship of remittance-sending emigrants (Coutin, 2007; Hernández & Coutin, 2006).

Globally, these campaigns do harm by presenting unachievable lifestyle goals and increasing fat shaming (Brewis & Wutich, 2019; Pause et al., 2021). Rather than depicting more accessible wellness scenes for most low-income urban women, the recent Salvadoran message included lean men and women, jogging, and practicing yoga in fashionable athletic wear and comfortable spaces, interspersed with images of avocado toast and yogurt with berries and granola. However, more problematic than such aspirational imagery are the accusations hurled at obese people in social media and, even sometimes, within doctors' offices. Deeply held fat biases easily fuse with wellness messages and tend to conflate beauty with health (Boero, 2013; Bordo, 2003; Dworkin & Wachs, 2009). An individualistic health discourse centered on self-care as preemptive medicine often strays into ableism; fat people come to bear the blame for their health vulnerabilities, which doctors and others frequently attribute to their perceived lack of discipline and failure to comply with fitness recommendations. Indeed, ample research and personal testimony demonstrates the connections between fat shaming, trauma/re-traumatization, and the medicalization of obesity in both public discourse and private medical practices (Brewis & Wutich, 2019; Gay, 2017; Morgan, 2020; Palmisano et al., 2016).

Pressure to conform to increasingly demanding (and for most women, impossible) beauty standards has intensified with transnational social and economic integration. Commercialized messages and popular imagery disseminated on social media conflate health and esthetics, generating widespread anxiety about the failure to conform to body ideals. In 2006, even before the explosion of social media and smartphone technologies, 67% of 285 high-school students surveyed in San Marcos, a municipality in Greater San Salvador, reported feeling, on at least one occasion, that their body did not look good (Landaverde & Valladares Lemus, 2006). In that survey, youth generally reported feeling satisfied with their body image, but most of the respondents also aspired to achieve esthetic ideals projected by prominent singers, athletes, and actors, and they often judged themselves by the appearances of others.

Most of the students had sought advice on how to transform their appearance in popular media. In their analysis of this survey, Landaverde and Valladares Lemus attribute the mixed responses to increasing pressure to conform to media images of thin or lean bodies conveyed in television, magazines, and internet. The desperation to conform to body ideals intensifies with widespread and frequent access to social media, including *Facebook* and *Instagram*, as well as more traditional conduits of such imagery such as television and advertising. The use of social media has exploded during the Covid-19 crisis (Marroquin & Carballo, 2020), and fitness imagery circulates widely.

Today, San Salvador hosts a variety of private medical facilities and multinational corporations that profit from such insecurities, including commercial gym chains, *Nutrilife*, and other diet companies or nutrition outlets, plastic surgeons and anti-aging clinics, and others (Brigden & Markowitz, 2022). Furthermore, the Salvadoran government, in cooperation with and at the urging of international organizations, launched a major campaign to address the rise in overweight and obese infants and children (Ministerio de Salud, El Salvador (MINSAL), 2017, pp. 11–13). In step with international organizations' campaigns, doctors in the local public clinics that treat the Salvadoran poor widely recommend weight loss as a primary individual health strategy and rely on globally standardized BMI metrics to evaluate their patients (see Yates-Doerr, 2015 on the local lived reality of global obesity campaigns in Guatemala). This public health emphasis on body weight has unintended consequences, including an increase in body shaming against women, particularly without an awareness of how such body metrics as BMI come burdened with implicit racism, classism, and sexism (Brewis & Wutich, 2019; Campos et al., 2006; Dworkin & Wachs, 2009; Farrell, 2011; Strings, 2019). Such body shaming has intensified globally since public health officials have uncritically linked obesity and poor Covid-19 outcomes (Pause et al., 2021).

FUTURE MOVES FOR PHYSICAL CULTURE STUDIES IN EL SALVADOR

In El Salvador, fitness discourse expresses and reproduces other forms of bodily control. As *fitness* evolves into a consumer lifestyle, and ultimately into a life philosophy that values outward expressions of discipline and capitalist achievement, it encourages neoliberal feminism focused on individual success rather than challenging structural inequities. This ideological framework complements broader economic changes and the upsurge in popular authoritarianism. In the transnational process that unfolds in online fitness spaces, traditional notions of beauty widened to encompass more *marcado* (muscular cut) female physiques, but alongside intense body shaming of gender nonconforming and fat people. The white-washed imagery and illusion of meritocracy that accompanies this media obscures racial injustices and reproduces white supremacist tropes. Not surprisingly then, the comment sections responding to *Mamá Fit* and other fitness memes explicitly make connections between the body and morality, debating the relative merits of humility and understated feminine dress against the visual display of discipline that scantily clad *fit* bodies exude. The stakes are high for such discussions, shaping what a good woman and good citizen should be and how to recognize them. The answer provided by transnational notions of fitness to these questions about who qualifies as a good woman or good citizen is a form of symbolic violence that reproduces coloniality while renegotiating gender in El Salvador.

In this way, the recent intrusion of the English language word *fitness* into the Salvadoran vernacular represents a major shift in how people understand their relationship to their body and their behavioral responsibilities. As I argued in this chapter, fitness has become an imperialist lexicon, loaded with racist, classist, sexist, and ableist ideals. However, rather than conclude this chapter with an unwavering condemnation of Salvadoran fitness discourse as oppressive, I would like to briefly complicate these findings, posing a question for future research.

CONCLUSION

Turning again to the work of decolonial scholarship, an alternative reading of the frequent use of Spanglish in Salvadoran society emerges. For example, Anzaldúa (2012, pp. 77–81) recognizes that Spanglish renegotiates social spaces of colonial contact, generating a "wild tongue" that characterizes the speech of people who inhabit a *nepantla* (Borderlands). For Anzaldúa, this speech represents a form of resistance, creativity, and adaptation to life in liminality, not simply a cultural corruption. Furthermore, for Anzaldúa (2015, p. 1), language must be understood as an embodied experience, practiced physically and materially as "gestures of the body." Similarly, Rosa (2019) proposes a raciolinguistic perspective that understands language as embodied practice, and through that perspective, he cautions against the stigmatization of communication modes developed by marginalized populations. The Spanglish of El Salvador, while unique from such eruptions in US urban environments or the Mexico–US territory studied by these authors, represents a similar rearticulation of race, class, and gender within a context of global coloniality and US hegemony.

If we follow Anzaldúa's and Rosa's lead and explore the embodied dimensions of language, we must also consider the routines and experiences that *fitness* signifies. We cannot assume away the agency of people who adopt such Spanglish practices. Indeed, at the level of the gym floor where people physically practice fitness, contradictions and struggle come into view, not simply symbolic violence. For example, in El Salvador, like the United States and elsewhere around the globe, the "care of the body" is deeply political, and our mundane systems of corporeal management, including fitness practices ranging from muscle building to nutrition, intersect with larger processes of control and contestation (Federici, 2020, p. 55). Thus, fitness can also be a form of self-care, and as Lorde (1988, p. 125) famously argued, "caring for myself is not self-indulgence, it is self-preservation and that is an act of political warfare." Indeed, *fitness* disciplines bodies according to classist, racist, sexist, and ableist norms that reinforce coloniality, but Salvadoran people may also improvise upon these practices as a form of daily empowerment.

Gym-goers might coopt this neocolonial discourse for their own purpose. This chapter's feminist textual analysis of fitness discourse, inspired by the *Mamá Fit* social media phenomenon, provides the context necessary to understand exactly how subversive such daily improvisations would be. Future research should turn to the complexities of everyday, embodied experiences of fitness in El Salvador, asking: Under what conditions does the daily physical practice of fitness generate social meanings that defy the symbolic violence of its discourse?

NOTES

1. See https://www.clarin.com/internacional/caso-mama-hot-lleva-hijo-escuela-llego-diarios-ingleses_0_PnLUP8zWeZ.html#:~:text=Vanesa%20Medina%2C%20una%20abogada%2C%20modelo,Cruz%20de%20la%20Sierra%2C%20Bolivia.

2. I have done all translations from Spanish that appear in this chapter. Sometimes, the original text appears in Spanish. I then translated the original phrases into English. If the phrase is short, I left the Spanish in italics and put my English translation in parenthesis

next to it. For longer prose, I translate the Spanish to English and use quotations or indentation to indicate a long quote, just as I do for untranslated English quotations. However, I must also manage Spanglish. If words were already in English in the original, often surrounded by Spanish text, I left those English words italicized within the translation. Brand names are italicized. The appearance of words in Spanglish is an indication of transnational meaning-making processes, but it also challenges consistency of translation and presentation; the word *fit* in an English sentence and the word *fit* in a Spanish sentence do not necessarily mean the same thing, which is partly what I hope to disentangle with this research.

3. The imaginary of fitness is borderless, dynamic, and emergent across an increasing number of national contexts and, ultimately, global (not just regional) in reach (Andreasson & Johansson, 2014).

4. A landowning elite, that is, sugar and coffee barons, traditionally dominated Salvadoran politics, and they formed an alliance with the military to maintain the status-quo, resulting in the brutal political repression and, ultimately, civil war (1980–1992) (Stanley, 1996; Wood, 2003).

5. For a description of the experience of these pressures by Salvadoran women in the context of a trauma-informed lifting program, see Brigden (2023).

6. See for an example of sensationalist media accounts, the National Geographic documentary by that name: https://www.nationalgeographic.com/tv/movies-and-specials/worlds-most-dangerous-gang-power-of-fear.

7. That is, the 15th department in a country divided officially into 14 territorial departments.

8. For reflexive discussion, see Argueta and Brigden (2023) and Brigden (2022). Ethnography provides important contextual knowledge to interpret media but is not the focus here.

9. *CrossFit* is a trademarked brand developed by Greg Glassman in California in 2001 which gained traction in El Salvador a decade later. This style of workout combines weight training with functional movements and high-intensity impact training in a group class setting. On *CrossFit* as US imperial necropolitics, see Hejtmanek (2023).

10. Alger's gym has received accolades for pioneering accessibility in sports for people with disabilities, a unique innovation among commercial athletic spaces in San Salvador.

11. See President Bukele's *Twitter* at https://twitter.com/nayibbukele/status/1478201251737317385.

REFERENCES

Andreasson, J., & Johanssen, T. (2014). *The global gym: Gender, health and pedagogies*. Palgrave Macmillan.

Anzaldúa, G. E. (2012). *Borderlands/La Frontera: The New Mestiza*. Aunt Lute Books.

Anzaldúa, G. E. (2015). *Light in the dark/Luz en lo Oscuro: Writing identity, spirituality, reality*. Duke University Press.

Argueta, E. A., & Brigden, N. K. (2023). Transformative writing and naming: Gimnasio Elba y Celina. In N. K. Brigden, K. R. Hejtmanek, & M. Forbis (Eds.), *Gender and power in strength sports: Strong as feminist* (pp. 215–218). Routledge Press.

Boero, N. (2013). *Killer fat: Media, medicine and morals in the American obesity epidemic*. Rutgers University Press.

Bordo, S. (2003). *Unbearable weight: Feminism, western culture, and the body* (10th anniversary ed.). University of California Press.

Bourdieu, P., & Wacquant, L. J. D. (2002). *An invitation to reflexive sociology*. University of Chicago Press.

Bourgois, P. (2001). The power of violence in war and peace: Post-cold war lessons from El Salvador. *Ethnography*, *2*(1), 5–34.

Brewis, A., & Wutich, A. (2019). *Lazy, crazy, and disgusting: Stigma and the undoing of global health*. Johns Hopkins University Press.

Brigden, N. (2022). Trauma-informed research methods: Understanding and healing embodied violence. In A. Petillo & H. Hlavka (Eds.), *Researching gender-based violence* (pp. 144–158). NYU Press.

Brigden, N. (2023). Understanding body resistance in El Salvador: Qualitative discussion of a pilot program for embodied empowerment. *Violence Against Women, 29*(12–13), 2393–2417.

Brigden, N., & Markowitz, A. (2022). *Stairs to nowhere: Disciplining and excluding bodies using mobility infrastructures* [Unpublished paper] Presented at confronting urban violence: Global interdisciplinary investigations UK–Brazil workshops, Queen Mary University of London.

Brigden, N. K., & Hallett, M. C. (2020). Time and power in a violent moment: Re-imagining fieldwork as transformation. *Geopolitics*. https://doi.org/10.1080/14650045.2020.1717068

Brigden, N. K., & Vogt, W. A. (2015). Homeland heroes: Migrants and soldiers in the Neoliberal era. *Antipode, 47*(2), 303–322.

Cabas-Mijares, A., & Jenkins, J. (2023). Beauty and the breasts: Constructions of feminist sexual politics in vanity fair's 2017 Emma Watson photoshoot. *Feminist Media Studies, 23*(8), 3976–3993.

Caldeira, T. P. R. (2001). *City of walls: Crime, segregation, and citizenship in Sao Paulo*. University of California Press.

Campos, P., Saguy, A. C., Ernsberger, P., & Oliver, E. (2006). The epidemiology of overweight and obesity: Public health crisis or moral panic? *International Journal of Epidemiology, 35*, 55–60.

Carlan, H. (2021). The racial language of fat phobia. *Anthropology News*. Retrieved May 9, 2024, from https://www.anthropology-news.org/articles/the-racial-language-of-fatphobia/

Chomsky, A. (2021). *Central America's forgotten history: Revolution, violence, and the roots of migration*. Penguin Random House.

Coutin, S. B. (2007). *Nation of emigrants: Shifting boundaries of citizenship in El Salvador and the United States*. Cornell University Press.

Dworkin, S. L., & Wachs, F. L. (2009). *Body panic: Gender, health and the selling of fitness*. New York University Press.

Farrell, A. E. (2011). *Fat shame: Stigma and the fat body in American culture*. New York University Press.

Federici, S. (2020). *Beyond the periphery of the skin: Rethinking, remaking, and reclaiming the body in contemporary capitalism*. Kairos.

Gay, R. (2017). *Hunger: A memoir of (my) body*. Harper.

Granados, K. (2006, January 13). Envíos rompen record y cierra 2005 con 2,830 millones. *La Prensa Gráfica. Nación*.

Hannele, H. (2001). Exercising exclusions: Space, visibility, and monitoring the fat female body. *Fat Studies, 8*(2), 173–186.

Hejtmanek, K. R. (2023). On death and fitness: Hero workouts, US militarism, and the necrosociality of CrossFit. In N. K. Brigden, K. R. Hejtmanek, & M. Forbis (Eds.), *Gender and power in strength sports: Strong as feminist* (pp. 122–142). Routledge Press.

Hernández, E., & Coutin, S. B. (2006). Remitting subjects: Migrants, money and states. *Economy and Society, 35*(2), 185–208.

Landaverde, D. E., & Valladares Lemus, J. (2006). *Relación entre los estados de ánimo depresivos y los trastornos de alimentación en los adolescentes caso específico: imagen corporal* [Tesis Licenciatura de Psicología, Universidad Tecnológica de El Salvador. Facultad de Jurisprudencia y Ciencias Sociales, San Salvador]. Retrieved August 31, 2021, from http://biblioteca.utec.edu.sv/siab/virtual/tesis/941000448.pdf Last

Lorde, A. (1988). *A burst of light: Essays*. Fireband Books.

Lugones, M. (2008). Coloniality of gender. *Worlds & Knowledges Otherwise, 2*(Spring), 1–17.

Marroquin, A., & Carballo, W. (2020). *2020 D.C. Asi dio vulta el consume mediatico en El Salvador durante la Covid-19*. Escuela de Comunicacion Monica Herrera.

Martin Alcoff, L. (2020). Decolonizing feminist theory: Latina contributions to the debate. In A. J. Pitts, M. Ortega, & J. Medina (Eds.), *Theories of the flesh: Latinx and Latin American feminisms, transformation, and resistance* (pp. 11–28). Oxford University Press.

Menjívar, C., & Gomez Cervantes, A. (2018). *El Salvador: Civil war, natural disasters and gang violence drive migration*. Migration Information Source. https://www.migrationpolicy.org/article/el-salvador-civil-war-natural-disasters-and-gang-violence-drive-migration

Mignolo, W. D. (2000). *Local histories/global designs: Coloniality, subaltern knowledges, and border thinking*. Princeton University Press.

Ministerio de Salud, El Salvador (MINSAL). (2017). CARGA DE MORTALIDAD DE ENFERMEDADES NO TRANSMISIBLES EN LA POBLACIÓN IGUAL O MAYOR DE 20 AÑOS DE EL SALVADOR. Retrieved April 13, 2022, from http://ins.salud.gob.sv/wp-content/uploads/2018/07/Carga-de-mortalidad-de-enfermedades-no-transmisibles.pdf

Moodie, E. (2011). *In the aftermath of peace: Crime, uncertainty, and the transition to democracy*. University of Pennsylvania Press.

Morgan, E. (2020). Obesity can't be tackled until we address the trauma that causes it. *The Guardian*. Retrieved May 10, 2024, from https://www.theguardian.com/commentisfree/2020/jul/30/obesity-trauma-fat-covid-19-shame-weight-gain

Ong, A. (2006). *Neoliberalism as exception: Mutations in citizenship and the making of nations*. Duke University Press.

Ortiz, R. (2014). $5 millones ha invertido Be Fit en 3 gimnasios. *El Diario de Hoy*. Retrieved May 9, 2024, from https://historico.elsalvador.com/historico/131612/5-millones-ha-invertido-be-fit-en-3-gimnasios.html

Palmisano, G. L., Innamorati, M., Vanderlinden, J. (2016). Life adverse experiences in relation with obesity and binge eating disorder: A systematic review. *Journal of Behavioral Addiction*, 5(1), 11–31.

Pause, C., Parker, G., & Gray, L. (2021). Resisting the problematisation of fatness in Covid-19: In pursuit of health justice. *International Journal of Disaster Risk Reduction*, 54, 102021.

Pedersen, D. (2013). *American value: Migrants, money, and meaning in El Salvador and the United States*. University of Chicago Press.

Quijano, A. (2000). Coloniality of power and eurocentrism in Latin America. *International Sociology*, 15(2), 215–232.

Quintanilla, L. (2008, January12). *Mc Donald's crecio 30% en El Salvador en 2007*. La Prensa Gráfica. Economía.

Rosa, J. (2019). *Looking like a language, sounding like a race: Raciolinguistic ideologies and learning of latinidad*. Oxford University Press.

Rottenberg, C. A. (2018). *The rise of neoliberal feminism*. Heretical thought. Oxford Academic. https://doi.org/10.1093/oso/9780190901226.001.0001

Silva, D. F. (2022). *Embodying modernity: Race, gender, and fitness culture in Brazil*. University of Pittsburgh Press.

Stanley, W. (1996). *The protection racket state: Elite politics, military extortion, and civil war in El Salvador*. Temple University Press.

Strings, S. (2019). *Fearing the black body: The racial origins of fat phobia*. New York University Press.

Velásquez, A., Resstack, R., & Dempster, H. (2021). *The relationship between migration and development in El Salvador*. Center for Global Development. Retrieved February 28, 2023 from https://www.cgdev.org/blog/relationship-between-migration-and-development-el-salvador last

Walsh, S. D., & Menjívar, C. (2016). Impunity and multisided violence in the lives of Latin American women: El Salvador in comparative perspective. *Current Sociology*. https://doi.org/10.1177/0011392116640074.

Warnecke-Berger, H. (2020). Remittances, rescaling of social conflicts, and the stasis of elite rule in El Salvador. *Latin American Perspectives*, 47(3), 202–220.

Wolf, S. (2017). *Mano Dura: The politics of gang control in El Salvador*. University of Texas Press.

Wood, E. J. (2003). *Insurgent collective action and civil war in El Salvador*. Cambridge University Press.

Yates-Doerr, E. (2015). *The weight of obesity: Hunger and global health in postwar Guatemala*. University of California Press.

Zilberg, E. (2011). *Spaces of detention: The making of a transnational gang crisis between Los Angeles and San Salvador*. Duke University Press.

CHAPTER 2

SHIFTING PERCEPTIONS OF WOMEN'S WEIGHT

Courtney Dress

Department of Sociology & Criminology, Kent State University, USA

ABSTRACT

Body weight has a long history of functioning as a symbol of one's beauty, social status, morality, discipline, and health. It has also been a standard inflicted much more intensely on women than men. While US culture has long idealized thinness for women, even at risky extremes, there is growing evidence that weight standards are broadening. Larger bodies are becoming more visible and accepted, while desire for and approval of a thin ideal has diminished. However, the continued widespread prevalence of anti-fat attitudes and stigma leaves uncertainty about just how much weight standards are changing. This study used an online survey (n = 320) to directly compare evaluations of thin, fat, and average size women through measures of negative stereotypes, prejudicial attitudes, and perceptions about quality of life. Results indicated that, as hypothesized, thin women were perceived less favorably than average weight women. However, fat women were perceived less favorably than both average and thin women. Men were harsher than women in their evaluations of only fat women. Additionally, participants being underweight or overweight did not produce an ingroup bias in their evaluations of underweight and overweight targets, respectively. That is, participants did not rate their own group more favorably, with the exception of overweight participants having lower prejudice toward overweight targets. These findings add to the emerging evidence that women's weight standards are in transition, marked by an increasingly negative perception of thin women, though not necessarily growing positivity toward *fat women. This evidence further points toward the need for more extensive research on attitudes of people across the entire weight spectrum.*

Keywords: Anti-fat attitudes; anti-thin attitudes; weight stigma; thin ideal; body acceptance; weight standards

In her book *The Ministry of Thin*, journalist Emma Woolf (2014) writes that all of us, but women in particular, are signed up at birth to follow the "thin commandments" (originally from Costin, 1997, p. 13). These include putting thinness before health and feeling guilty about eating. In encouraging women to liberate themselves from the all-consuming drive for thinness, Woolf reproduces a common narrative in which being thin is, yes, culturally valued and praised but also comes with hardships. Moreover, she argues, these hardships would be considered discriminatory to inflict on fat women, like commenting on their weight or eating habits. The notion that thin and fat women share the ordeal of their weight being a focal point and burden is brought up frequently in discussions of feminine beauty standards. For years, people have been using social media and blogs to ask why it is acceptable to shame skinny women but not fat women (e.g., Iter, 2020; Wan, 2021; Woolf, 2013). Such sentiments imply, or sometimes even flat-out state, that the weight-based (mis)treatment of fat and thin women is equivalent.

Society's reception of fat and thin women is, of course, not equivalent. Contrary to the claims of online bloggers, weight bias researchers conclude from the ubiquity and pervasiveness that anti-fat biases remain quite acceptable to the general public and quite detrimental (e.g., Andreyeva et al., 2008; Puhl, 2008). Among the most crucial features of anti-fat bias that has yet to be observed toward thinner people is the manifestation as institutional discrimination in settings like education, employment, medicine, and law as a result of cultural beliefs held about weight (Fikkan & Rothblum, 2012; Puhl et al., 2008; Puhl & Heuer, 2009; Spahlholz et al., 2016). Though empirical research on thin stigma is rare, existing evidence can only speak to its occurrence at the interpersonal level, like name-calling and stereotyping, assumptions of eating disorders, and being deemed esthetically undesirable (Beggan & DeAngelis, 2015; Tantleff-Dunn et al., 2009). This leads some to feel that claims of skinny shaming are only brought up to derail, dismiss, or co-opt conversations about fat shaming, or attempt to commiserate over experiences that are not actually comparable (Broadbent, 2021; Gordon, 2020; Mehdi & Frazier, 2021).

The recognition that both fat *and thin* women's experiences often revolve around their size brings to attention the intricacies of weight as a beauty standard for women. If thinness is the ideal form for women to achieve, then fat women are stigmatized for failing to meet that standard. But why do thin women also report stigmatizing reactions to their weight? To answer this question, we must gain a deeper understanding of the nature of perceptions of both thin and fat women. This research begins filling that gap by employing repeated-measures assessments of stereotypes, prejudiced attitudes, and perceptions about the quality of life of thin, average weight, and fat women.

HISTORICAL CONTEXTUALIZATION OF BODIES AND BEAUTY

Old adages say that beauty is in the eye of the beholder, or only skin deep, but the importance and influence of our physical appearance on life outcomes disprove these notions (Cottom, 2019; Rhode, 2010). Weight as an aspect of beauty and social status has historically existed at the intersections of gender, race, class, science, and religion, resulting in degrees of both consistency and change throughout different times and places, and for different subcultural groups.

The Long History of Fat Stigma

Perceptions and attitudes about body size are a cultural product and, thus, must be contextualized by period and location. Many scholars have understood cultural perceptions of weight as resulting directly from the prevalence and attainability of thinness or fatness vis-á-vis socioeconomic conditions. In societies suffering frequent food shortages, heavier weight would reflect wealth, health, prosperity, and fertility. More developed societies, in contrast, would have the food security and lifestyle to allow more of the population to be fatter, making thinness more indicative of higher status or class (Anderson et al., 1992; Ritenbaugh, 1982; Sobal, 2001). This model is a bit too simplistic for at least two reasons.

First, cross-cultural research in the 21st century depicts a less clear-cut relationship between socioeconomic status (SES) and weight attitudes. Some research does find that lower-SES populations show a preference for heavier bodies, while higher-SES populations tend to favor a thin ideal for women (Swami et al., 2010), especially to the extent that they have been influenced by modernization and exposure to Western media (Swami, 2015). But other studies find evidence of a global spreading of the thin ideal and anti-fat bias (Brewis, 2017; Puhl et al., 2015; Rubino et al., 2020), including to lower-SES countries (Brewis et al., 2011, 2018). This attitude shift has been described as happening "... so quickly that even those of us conducting field research around body norms almost missed it" (Brewis, 2017, p. 3). Still, other evidence finds that some nations show no relationship between weight stigma and education or income (Bernard, Fankhänel, et al., 2019). Part of this development is likely that the influence of SES on weight itself has drastically changed in many societies due to global trends in economics, urbanization, technology, and food. Globally, people are getting fatter in both developed and developing countries (Ng et al., 2014). In the world's poorest nations, SES and weight still demonstrate a positive relationship (higher income relates to higher weight, and vice versa). But in wealthier nations, it is lower-SES people who are more likely to be fat, contradicting any associations of fatness with status, power, wealth, and so on (Brewis, 2017; Hruschka, 2017).

The more relevant reason that an SES explanation is insufficient for understanding weight attitudes is that the social meanings and consequences of weight standards have seemingly always been about much more than merely resource availability. Individual and shared understandings of the body are complex sociocultural phenomena (Tiggemann, 2011) with certain patterns and trends repeating throughout history. For millennia, weight has been a convenient attribute based on which to declare some groups inferior, primarily in health, beauty, and moral character (Albala, 2005; Forth, 2019; Vigarello & Delogu, 2013). Additionally, though there are body standards, including weight stigma, aimed at men (e.g., Himmelstein et al., 2018), strict body ideals have been the burden of women as an element of their objectification and subjugation (Chrisler, 2012). Men's body ideals are often more about function and ability, for example, strong muscles suggestive of masculinity, while women's are about appearance, for example, beauty, thinness, and sex appeal (McKinley, 2011; Murnen, 2011).

The linking of slenderness with health, beauty, and goodness is documented as far back as Ancient Greece and Rome when citizens thought themselves physically *and morally* superior to others like Persians and Italians who, in their view, overindulged in food and drink leading to their larger bellies (Carden-Coyne & Forth, 2005; Forth, 2019). Most historical accounts of cultural weight standards, however, focus on the Western world, beginning around Europe's Middle Ages. Despite being centuries after ancient civilization, similar foundational beliefs about size and character were retained, and many people openly admired ancient ideas about austerity (Forth, 2019). This period saw endorsement of contradictory expectations of self-indulgence and self-control: those of more civilized taste should enjoy modern material comforts, but they should also show constraint (Dacome, 2005). Figuring out the right balance of consumption and restriction was puzzling but important, as anything beyond moderate fat continued to be associated with poor character, stupidity, laziness, and so on. In his conclusion that, "modernity did not invent stereotypes about fat people, but it surely sharpened them," Forth (2019, p. 179) credits Enlightenment-era Europe with the creation of modern stereotypes about fatness.

Many centuries of historical trends in attitudinal, medicinal, and philosophical approaches to weight have far too much nuance and complexity to adequately be covered here. What can be taken away from this extremely brief overview is that millennia of Western human history demonstrate similar themes of anti-fatness. Across contexts, fatness has been associated with unfavorable attributes, whether it be stupidity, laziness, sinfulness, immorality, poor physical health, corruption, or ugliness. Moving now into the United States in the 19th century, this thread of fat stigma would strengthen through a series of sociocultural developments.

The United States: Late 1800s to Early 2000s

The period of the late-1800s to mid-1900s is generally portrayed as a major transformative period for US weight norms, ideals, and attitudes. At the start of this period, the United States essentially mirrored Europe's understanding of fat (Stearns, 2005). Then, 19th-century industrialization brought major cultural changes that enabled the middle class to rapidly expand and begin enjoying lifestyles only previously known by the wealthy, including more time for eating and recreation, and less physically strenuous jobs. As seen before elsewhere in the world, fatness among this population was blamed on their stupidity and overindulgence in their new way of life (Farrell, 2011; Fraser, 2009; Saguy, 2013), as well as their sinfulness in lacking the core values of the Anglo-Protestant work ethic like hard work, delayed gratification, and bodily control (Oliver, 2006; Strings, 2019; Yager, 2010). White women and girls were encouraged, especially by books and magazines, to be thin, so they could be healthy, beautiful, tempered Christian women (Strings, 2019). Fat was understood to be unattractive on the outside because it resulted from ugliness and sinfulness within.

Throughout the 20th century, weight came under the purview of the medical profession as concern over supposedly weight-related health detriments grew within a broader cultural trend of medicalization (Pool, 2001; Sobal, 1995; Yager, 2010). This culminated with the Centers for Disease Control and Prevention (CDC) declaring the *obesity epidemic* after rates of US adults with obesity doubled from 15% to 30% between 1976 and 2000 (Engel, 2018; Ogden & Carroll, 2010; Oliver, 2006). Medical professionals were now joined by other powerful authorities like the media and government officials to tactfully use the language of crisis to sound an alarm that the United States was dangerously fat as a nation (LeBesco, 2004; Oliver, 2006; Saguy & Almeling, 2008). With this addition of medical framing and crisis rhetoric pushed by powerful leaders, the view of fatness and fat people grew even more negative. In addition to being deemed unattractive and the result of poor morals and discipline, fat was now also understood to be a dangerous threat to personal and population health.

As the population of the United States got fatter, the bodies admired as symbols and icons of beauty got thinner. Supermodels and *Playboy* centerfolds saw decreasing weight and curviness from the 1960s to the 1990s, including most falling into the underweight body mass index (BMI) category (Owen & Laurel-Seller, 2000; Sypeck et al., 2004). The trend of waif models dominating runways and magazine covers became so extreme that it garnered backlash for promoting a thin ideal that was both unrealistic and dangerous for women attempting to embody it (Rodgers et al., 2017; Sajbel, 1994). These concerns are well-founded as abundant evidence shows that exposure to and internalization of the thin ideal leads women to have issues with body dissatisfaction, self-esteem, anxiety and depression, and eating disorder symptoms (Culbert et al., 2015; Hawkins et al., 2004; Nouri et al., 2011; Thompson & Stice, 2001). It was even proposed that higher rates of depression in women than men could result from women becoming depressed due to their failures to achieve the thin ideal (McCarthy, 1990). The 1990s and early 2000s then were the era of simultaneous glorification of very slender feminine figures, but also very vocal criticism about this beauty standard and the damage created by promoting it to women and girls.

THE NEWEST SHIFT IN BODY STANDARDS

The frustration of women being held to a standard that is difficult to achieve, especially without jeopardizing physical and mental health, may have prompted a resistance and rejection of these cultural ideals, leading to a diminishing idealization of thinness. Though research on this topic is growing, much is still not understood. One weakness in the existing literature is that studies comparing attitudes/behavior toward various weight groups often rely on a fat versus nonfat dichotomy (e.g., Bernard, Riedel-Heller, et al., 2019; Schvey et al., 2013), overlooking any potential differences between average weight and thinner targets.

Studies that have utilized three weight categories (thin, average, overweight) have found differences between perceptions of thin and average targets. For example, Davies et al. (2020a, 2020b) found that average weight women were rated more positively on weight-based attributes than both underweight and overweight women. Another study (Malloy et al., 2012) using Big Five personality traits (extroversion, agreeableness, conscientiousness, emotional stability, and intelligence) similarly found that the thinnest and heaviest targets, both men and women, were rated more negatively than more average-weight ones. Qualitative research has also found that being underweight invites negative attention, leaving thin women feeling dissatisfied with their bodies and the comments they receive. This includes being compared to a "concentration camp victim" and being told "it hurts to look at" them (Beggan & DeAngelis, 2015, pp. 378–379).

Several explanations have been put forth for why thinness may elicit these unfavorable perceptions despite its status as the cultural ideal. Some invoke evolution, suggesting that both thinner and fatter bodies may trigger our animalistic drive to avoid disease or general unhealthiness (Malloy et al., 2012). Similarly, Davies et al. (2020a, 2020b) postulated that stigmatization of thinness may reflect stigmatization of eating disorders. Another explanation, coming out of deviance literature, is that achieving thinness represents an *over*conformity to cultural ideals which is met with negative perceptions of the achiever, just like underconformity or nonconformity is (Beggan & DeAngelis, 2015; Heckert & Heckert, 2002, 2004). This may explain a related phenomenon in which physical attractiveness, though generally advantageous, can also be stigmatizing and leave women "always potentially deviant" no matter how much or how little they achieve it (Tseëlon, 1992, p. 299). More broadly, Posner (1976) proposed the *just right principle*, in which excellence, like deficiency, comes with stigma and subsequent feelings like guilt, alienation, and discomfort at being complimented, all of which Beggan and DeAngelis's (2015) thin women reported. Stereotypes of thin women may point toward self-obsession, conceitedness, superficiality, and the like (Dreisbach, 2012), echoing findings that attractive women are thought to be egoistic, snobby, materialistic, vain, and even immoral (Dermer & Thiel, 1975; Han & Laurent, 2022). Perhaps thin women's weight is not *just right*, but rather *too* right in a way taken to indicate vanity and narcissism.

Our standards for physique may also be in another cultural shifting period trending toward open disregard for the thin ideal and growing desire for the acceptance of all bodies (Betz & Ramsey, 2017). Though social media often contributes to body image issues (Fardouly & Vartanian, 2016), it has been a major setting for educating about and fighting weight stigma, for example, in online communities for fat/body acceptance (Marcus, 2016; Striley & Hutchens, 2020). Social media also enables users to encourage broader definitions of beauty through visibility of diverse and "flawed" bodies (Cohen et al., 2019; Lazuka et al., 2020), exposure to which helps decrease anti-fat attitudes (Smirles & Lin, 2018) and increase viewers' positivity about their own bodies (Devine et al., 2022; Ogden et al., 2020). As for thinness, evidence shows that women are shifting toward striving for more fit/athletic bodies (Benton & Karazsia, 2015; Bozsik et al., 2018; Kelley et al., 2010), or a slim-thick figure with a small waist but large hips and bottom (Gruber et al., 2022; McComb & Mills, 2022). Magazines have become more critical of underweight celebrity women than average or overweight ones (McDonnell & Lin, 2016), and sex symbols like *Playboy* models are now more average weight than underweight (Roberts & Muta, 2017). Thinness-related body dissatisfaction has declined in women over the last few decades (Karazsia et al., 2017), and the mere growing presence and visibility of larger bodies may be helping to shift standards away from thin to more average size bodies (Aniulis et al., 2021).

Still, increasing diversity in body representation in some settings does not mean widespread anti-fat, pro-thin cultural attitudes are budging. Body acceptance and positivity for larger bodies on social media are often met with swift disagreement and hostility (e.g., Bograd et al., 2022; Jeon et al., 2018). Some worry that keeping the focus on physical appearance still entails body objectification and dissatisfaction. The more antagonistic critics posit that not all bodies deserve to be accepted and that anything less than derogation of fatness "promotes" or "glorifies" obesity (Cohen et al., 2021). Furthermore, the increasing diversity of bodies on social media is not yet replicated in other mediums like television, where fat characters remain predominantly depicted in negative and stigmatizing ways (Ata & Thompson, 2010; Kyrölä, 2014). And even though women may be concerning themselves more with muscularity than weight, much "fitspiration" content remains thin-promoting at its core, encouraging dieting, excessive exercise, appearance-motivation, and sexualization/objectification of women's bodies (Alberga et al., 2018; Boepple et al., 2016; Simpson & Mazzeo, 2017).

Furthermore, hegemonic ideas about body type are not consistent across subgroups within a culture. Scholars of race and the body have shed light on the centuries-old role of anti-Blackness in anti-fatness, a side of history often omitted from other accounts. The European slave trade, colonization, and the endeavor to scientifically (and hierarchically) classify racial groups prompted the adoption of body size as a trait with which to distinguish races. European race theorists concluded that Black Africans were larger due to their bountiful lands but were also stupid, primitive, and insatiable in their appetite for food and sex (Harrison, 2021; Strings, 2019). Thus, part of the pressure for White women to be pure, delicate, and thin was so they would be distinct from Black women's supposed hypersexuality, gluttony, and unattractive fatness (Strings, 2019).

Today, ideas about weight are still highly raced and gendered, with prevalence and perception of different body types varying meaningfully across racial and ethnic groups. Among US adults, Black women are most likely to have obesity at 58%[1] (compared to 42% of US adults overall; Stierman et al., 2021). This higher prevalence of fatness in Black women is often incorrectly assumed to be a result of their lower adherence to dominant (White) standards of thinness and beauty. Black women, the belief goes, are less devoted to the thin ideal and are subsequently more likely to be contentedly fat and less likely to endorse fat stigma aimed at themselves or others (Daufin, 2020; McClure, 2017; West, 1996). It is not this simple, however. Some Black (and Latina) women and girls are less invested in thinness, recognizing it as the ideal of White women, and opting instead for curvier figures, more like the slim-thick figure previously mentioned. But others feel competing pressures and uncertainty about whether to emulate Black or Eurocentric ideals (Awad et al., 2015; Cheney, 2011; Gruber et al., 2022; Overstreet et al., 2010). These women's self-perceptions stem from influential but conflicting messages from media, peers, family, and men about what their bodies should be (Capodilupo, 2015; Capodilupo & Kim, 2014). Black people both endorse and endure fat stigma, and both experiences are misunderstood (Daufin, 2020; Hart et al., 2016; McClure, 2017; Purkiss, 2017).

Overall, it seems that the parameters of exactly what constitutes *too* thin or *too* fat have become unclear and inconsistent, leading women of all body types to suffer size-related stigma and its consequences, but much remains under-investigated. This study aims to explore perceptions of thinner, fatter, and more average weight women, to begin understanding if and how weight perceptions are experiencing a transformation.

METHODS

To analyze judgments of women across the weight spectrum, I utilize repeated measures to directly compare participants' evaluations of thin women, average weight women, and overweight/obese women in an anonymous online survey. The final sample was 320 participants. Just over half (51.9%) came from an email listserv at a large Midwestern University. Additional participants (45.9%) were obtained through Amazon Mechanical Turk, creating more diversity in the sample, though participation did require lifelong residence in the United States to limit cultural differences in weight attitudes. Respondents were mostly women (75.2%), White (82.5%), and had at least some college education (87.7%). Participant age was ranged from 18 to 76 years old, with a mean of 30.9 years. Nearly half the sample was classified as having a BMI in the "overweight" or "obese" range (48.1%), about 42% had a BMI in the "normal weight" range, and about 5% had a BMI in the "underweight" range. Another 5% did not report their height/weight, so their BMI was unknown.

Independent Variables

The primary independent variable was target weight category. In random order, participants were instructed to indicate their attitudes (the dependent variable measures) toward each of the three target weight categories: *underweight/thin women, average weight[2] women,* and *overweight/obese women*. Two additional independent variables were utilized to further understand trends in perceptions. First was participant gender, which was dummy coded as *woman* (0) or *man* (1). Second, participant BMI category was calculated using participants' self-reported height (inches) and weight (pounds) and the BMI formula used by the CDC: 703 × weight (lbs)/[height (in)]^2. A BMI < 18.5 is classified as "underweight," 18.5–24.9 as "normal weight," 25–29.9 as "overweight," and >30 as "obese." Because fewer than 4% of the sample were classified as "obese," I collapsed those with BMIs over 25 into one "overweight/obese" group.

Dependent Variables

The first scale measuring evaluations of the target weight categories examined endorsement of negative weight-based stereotypes using 17 semantic differential items scored 1–5, with higher scores indicating more negative stereotyping. For example, *intelligent–unintelligent, humble–vain, industrious–lazy*. Most items came from the Fat Phobia Scale (Bacon et al., 2001). Though developed for evaluating anti-fat attitudes, this scale has been used in other studies evaluating underweight targets (Davies et al., 2020a, 2020b; Tantleff-Dunn et al., 2009). I also incorporated items from Dreisbach (2012) to have both thin and fat stereotypes represented.

The second scale measured prejudiced attitudes toward each target group using 10 Likert-scale items, rated 1 *strongly disagree* to 7 *strongly agree*, with higher scores indicating higher prejudice. These items came from the Revised Anti-fat Attitudes Scale (Wrench & Knapp, 2008; revised from Morrison & O'Connor, 1999) and were adapted to refer to only women and to each target weight category. Example items include, "I dislike women who are [overweight/obese]" and "If I were an employer looking to hire, I might avoid hiring an [overweight/obese] woman."

The final scale used to evaluate the three target categories assessed perceived quality of life (PQOL) based on a scale used in the World Health Organization Quality of Life BREF Field Trial Version (Harper & Power, 1998). The original measure is used to assess one's own quality of life. Here, instructions were reworded so that participants rated their perceptions of the quality of life for underweight/thin, average weight, and overweight/obese women. The 16 components included physical pain, energy for everyday life, satisfaction with self, and enjoyment of life, rated 1 *very low* to 5 *very high*; thus, higher scores indicated higher PQOL.

Hypotheses and Further Questions

- *H1.* On the measure of negative stereotypes, overweight/obese women will be rated most negatively, average weight women will be rated least negatively, and underweight/thin women will fall in between.
- *H2.* On the measure of prejudiced attitudes, overweight/obese women will receive the most prejudice, average weight women will receive the least, and underweight/thin women will fall in between.
- *H3.* On the measure of PQOL, overweight/obese women will be perceived to have the lowest quality of life, average weight women will be perceived to have the highest, and underweight/thin women will fall in between.
- *Q1.* How does participant gender affect perceptions of each target group (underweight/thin women, average weight women, and overweight/obese women)?
- *Q2.* Do participants show any ingroup bias for their own weight group? That is, do participant ratings on the three dependent variables relate to participant BMI category?

RESULTS

Hypothesis Testing

I hypothesized that for each of the three dependent variables (negative stereotypes, prejudiced attitudes, and PQOL), participants would evaluate each target weight group significantly differently, with average weight targets being assessed most positively, overweight/obese targets most negatively, and underweight/thin targets falling in the middle. Due to the repeated measurement of the dependent variables, multilevel regression models were used for analysis.

Beginning with *H1*, results supported the predicted effect of target weight group on negative stereotyping. The target being underweight ($\beta = 4.14$, $p < 0.001$) led to a four-point increase in negative stereotypes, and the target being overweight/obese ($\beta = 7.52$, $p < 0.001$) led to a seven-point increase, relative to evaluating average weight target women. These results were replicated when assessing prejudiced attitudes (*H2*). Compared to average weight targets, underweight targets ($\beta = 5.74$, $p < 0.001$) incurred a five-point increase, and overweight targets ($\beta = 8.45$, $p < 0.001$), an eight-point increase in prejudiced attitudes toward them. Thus, *H 2* was also supported. Results for *H3*, examining PQOL, showed the same pattern. Average weight targets were believed to have the highest quality of life, while underweight targets ($\beta = -4.69$, $p < 0.001$) averaged almost five points lower, and overweight/obese targets, nearly 13 points lower ($\beta = -12.80$, $p < 0.001$). Altogether, as hypothesized, average weight targets were viewed the most favorably, underweight targets were viewed less favorably than average weight targets, but overweight/obese target women were perceived most negatively of all. See Table 2.1 for means and Table 2.2 for regression results.

Further Questions

Additional research questions allowed for a deeper investigation into the influence of specific statuses on ratings of different weight targets. *Q1* sought to understand the effect of participant gender on negative stereotyping, prejudiced attitudes, and PQOL of the three target weight categories. Again, multilevel regression models were used to account for the dependent variables being repeated measures. Table 2.2 displays the results. First, I examined the effect of participant gender on negative stereotype scores for each target weight category. Participant gender had no significant main effect ($\beta = 0.50$, $p = 0.60$), but the interaction between participant gender and target weight category was significant ($\beta = 2.77, p < 0.05$), such that when rating overweight/obese targets, but not average weight or underweight targets, men in the sample were significantly higher than women in their endorsement of negative stereotypes. Next, I examined this effect of participant gender on prejudiced attitude scores, and the results mirrored those of negative stereotypes. Gender had no significant main effect ($\beta = 0.52$, $p = 0.67$), but significantly interacted with target weight category ($\beta = 7.41$, $p < 0.001$) such that men, again, demonstrated higher prejudice than women toward only overweight/obese targets, not average weight or underweight targets. Finally, in examining gender differences in PQOL, participant gender had neither a significant main effect nor significant interaction with target weight category. Thus, in indicating

Shifting Perceptions of Women's Weight

Table 2.1. Stereotype, Prejudice, and PQOL Mean Scores by Target Weight Category, Participant Gender, and Participant BMI Category.

Dependent Variable	Target Category	Overall Mean	Participant Gender		Participant BMI Category		
			Men	Women	Overweight/Obese Participants	Normal Participants	Underweight Participants
Negative stereotypes	Overweight/obese women	53.63	56.14	52.87	52.87	54.71	54.19
	Underweight/thin women	50.27	51.59	49.79	49.88	50.80	48.42
	Average weight women	46.09	46.42	45.92	45.54	46.46	45.94
Prejudiced attitudes	Overweight/obese women	29.92	36.02	28.08	28.53	31.07	32.48
	Underweight/thin women	27.18	28.87	27.06	27.72	26.85	25.13
	Average weight women	21.48	22.04	21.51	21.69	20.82	22.23
Perceived quality of life	Overweight/obese women	42.19	41.89	42.26	42.78	41.43	42.15
	Underweight/thin women	50.30	49.82	50.49	51.37	49.17	50.41
	Average weight women	54.95	55.12	55.05	56.15	53.95	54.67

Table 2.2. Multilevel Regression Results.

Dependent Variable	Independent Variable	H1–H3			Research Q1			Research Q2		
		Coeff.	SE	p	Coeff.	SE	p	Coeff.	SE	p
Stereotypes	Target = overweight/obese	7.52	0.49	0.000	6.95	0.57	0.000	8.25	0.67	0.000
	Target = underweight	4.14	0.49	0.000	3.87	0.57	0.000	4.34	0.51	0.000
	Participant gender = man				0.50	0.94	0.597			
	Participant BMI = overweight/obese							−0.92	0.67	0.166
	Participant BMI = underweight							−0.52	1.45	0.719
	Participant gender * target weight category									
	Man * overweight/obese target				2.77	1.14	0.015			
	Man * underweight/thin target				1.30	1.14	0.256			
	Participant BMI * target weight category									
	Overweight/obese * overweight/obese							−0.91	0.87	0.295
	Underweight * underweight							−1.86	1.98	0.349
	(cons)	46.08	0.40	0.000	45.92	0.47	0.000	46.46	0.54	0.000

(Continued)

Table 2.2. *(Continued)*

Dependent Variable	Independent Variable	H1–H3 Coeff.	SE	p	Research Q1 Coeff.	SE	p	Research Q2 Coeff.	SE	p
Prejudice	Target = overweight/obese	8.45	0.55	0.000	6.57	0.61	0.000	10.25	0.74	0.000
	Target = underweight	5.74	0.55	0.000	5.55	0.61	0.000	6.03	0.57	0.000
	Participant gender = man				0.53	1.23	0.670			
	Participant BMI = overweight/obese							0.87	1.00	0.384
	Participant BMI = underweight							1.41	2.16	0.514
	Participant gender * target weight category									
	Man * overweight/obese target				7.41	1.22	0.000			
	Man * underweight/thin target				1.28	1.22	0.294			
	Participant BMI * target weight category									
	Overweight/obese * overweight/obese							−3.41	0.97	0.000
	Underweight * underweight							−3.13	2.11	0.137
	(cons)	21.45	0.54	0.000	21.51	0.61	0.000	20.82	0.78	0.000
PQOL	Target = overweight/obese	−12.80	0.58	0.000	−12.79	0.68	0.000	−12.52	0.80	0.000
	Target = underweight	−4.69	0.58	0.000	−4.56	0.68	0.000	−4.78	0.62	0.000
	Participant gender = man				0.07	1.11	0.951			
	Participant BMI = overweight/obese							2.20	0.78	0.005
	Participant BMI = underweight							0.72	1.70	0.670
	Participant gender * target weight category									
	Man * overweight/obese target				−0.44	1.38	0.750			
	Man * underweight/thin target				−0.74	1.37	0.592			
	Participant BMI * target weight category									
	Overweight/obese * overweight/obese							−0.85	1.05	0.423
	Underweight * underweight							0.52	2.27	0.819
	(cons)	55.00	0.40	0.000	55.04	0.22	0.000	53.95	0.64	0.000

the quality of life of that overweight, average weight, and underweight women are believed to have, scores did not differ by participant gender. Overall then, the effect of participant gender was that, compared to women, men were harsher in endorsing negative stereotypes and prejudicial attitudes toward overweight/obese women targets, while they were no more negative in their perceptions of average weight or underweight targets.

Q2 asked whether participants showed any ingroup bias, that is, whether participants evaluated targets more favorably when they belonged to the same weight group. For negative stereotyping, analysis revealed no significant interactions between participant BMI and target weight category, indicating no ingroup bias. In other words, participant and target both being underweight ($\beta = -1.86$, $p = 0.35$) or both being overweight/obese ($\beta = -0.91$, $p = 0.30$) had no significant effect on stereotype ratings. In analyzing prejudiced attitudes, underweight participants showed no ingroup bias toward underweight targets ($\beta = -3.13$, $p = 0.14$). That is, underweight participants rating an underweight target were no less prejudiced toward them than other participants. However, there was a significant interaction for both participant and target being overweight/obese ($\beta = -3.41$, $p < 0.001$), indicating a three-point decrease in prejudiced attitudes. Lastly, for ratings of PQOL, again, neither underweight ($\beta = 0.52$, $p = 0.82$) nor overweight participants ($\beta = -0.85$, $p = 0.42$) showed any ingroup bias in their evaluations of their own ingroup in the form of a significant interaction. Participants who were underweight or overweight/obese did not think underweight or overweight/obese targets, respectively, had any better or worse quality of life than other participants. See Table 2.2 for results.

DISCUSSION

Weight has always been a salient status in evaluating others throughout time and place. These weight standards have been especially heavily placed on women to the detriment of their physical and mental wellbeing (Fikkan & Rothblum, 2012; Tsai et al., 2016; Wu & Berry, 2018). The increasing promotion of body diversity and acceptance, especially on social media, may be making progress in broadening beliefs about bodies and the people in them, but this effort has a long way to go in changing longstanding anti-fat cultural discourses. This study examined sentiments toward thin, average weight, and fat women to better understand how they compare in this context of shifting standards and trends.

Measures of negative stereotype attribution, prejudiced attitudes, and PQOL of thin, average weight, and overweight women were employed to make direct intergroup comparisons, a method frequently neglected by other research on weight biases. As hypothesized, across all three measures, overweight women were viewed most unfavorably, and average weight women most favorably, while thin women were in between the two. Though not the first study to find evidence of stigmatization of thin women, the finding here of significantly different evaluations of thin and fat women is important. Other studies, including those using forms of the Fat Phobia Scale (Bacon et al., 2001) used here, found no such difference. These previous studies found that both underweight and overweight women were rated less favorably than average weight women, but not significantly different from each other (e.g., Davies et al., 2020b). More research is needed to better understand if/how perceptions of thin and fat women differ in severity and content which will require better measures for doing so. Even when investigating evaluations of thin people, existing studies relied on general trait measures (e.g., Malloy et al., 2012) or anti-fat attitude measures (e.g., Tantleff-Dunn et al., 2009). But the limited existing evidence, including the findings here, suggests that stereotypes of thin and fat women are unique. Thin women are especially thought to be vain and highly concerned with their physical appearance (Dreisbach, 2012), assumptions already shown to be made of beautiful women (Dermer & Thiel, 1975; Han & Laurent, 2022). In this survey, the stereotypes associated most strongly with overweight/obese women included having poor eating habits, rarely exercising, and having low self-esteem, all averaging more than 3.75 on the 1–5 scale. For underweight/thin women, the highest-scoring negative stereotypes were uptight, controlling, and self-centered, averaging a bit lower around 3.25, illustrating the different themes of stereotypes based on target weight category.

I further investigated how participant gender influenced evaluations. Consistent with prior research (e.g., Elran-Barak & Bar-Anan, 2018; Latner et al., 2008; Lieberman et al., 2012; Schvey et al., 2013), men were significantly harsher in their ratings of overweight targets compared to women, except for ratings of PQOL. Though negative beliefs about fat and character or morality have always applied to both men and women, the association with beauty and attractiveness has been quite gendered (Chrisler, 2012; McKinley, 2011; Murnen, 2011). When we think of women, we cannot help but think of their bodies. Salient raced and gendered stereotypes include Black women having big butts and White and Asian women being petite. Meanwhile, men are mainly stereotyped in terms of abilities, like Black men being athletic, Asian men being intelligent, and White men being wealthy (Ghavami & Peplau, 2013). The widespread perception that fat women are unattractive has even been proposed as the underlying reason that, in the workplace, women see wage penalties associated with their weight (Gregory & Ruhm, 2011). In this study, men had no stronger stereotyping or prejudice toward underweight or average weight women, and they also did not think fat women had worse-quality lives. It was only when expressing their subjective dislike (prejudice) and unfavorable beliefs (stereotypes) about fat women that men demonstrated higher aversion. This reinforces the intensity of men's judgments of women's weight, particularly when they find it displeasing, in a way that does not occur in judgments of men's bodies (Chrisler, 2012; Smith, 2012). In rating fat women, men's strongest stereotypes included lazy, lacking self-control, and low self-esteem. Most telling of all, the prejudice items that men agreed with most strongly were that overweight/obese women are not sexually or physically attractive (both means around 5 on a 1–7 scale).

I also assessed effects of participant BMI category, and consistent with other evidence (e.g., Latner et al., 2008; Malloy et al., 2012; Tantleff-Dunn et al., 2009), neither underweight nor overweight participants showed any ingroup biases in the form of rating their own target group more positively, with one exception: overweight/obese participants expressed lower prejudice toward overweight/

obese targets. Some have proposed that fat ingroup stigmatization results from fat people considering others larger than themselves to be an outgroup rather than an ingroup (Brochu et al., 2020), and given that most of the overweight/obese participants were only overweight, this could be the case. That is, when prompted to evaluate overweight/obese targets, these participants may have envisioned people they consider different from themselves. Similarly, Elran-Barak and Bar-Anan (2018) found that higher weight, higher self-perception of obesity, and stronger feelings of being like fat people all predicted lower implicit and explicit anti-fat attitudes. This sort of bias has not been well-researched among thin or underweight people, but one study found that participants' own experiences being teased for their underweight was unrelated to their perceptions of underweight targets (Tantleff-Dunn et al., 2009). Again, further research is needed on perceptions that thinner people hold of other thinner people.

CONCLUSION

This study contributes to the slowly emerging evidence that body standards for women seem to be in a period of transition. This shift appears to primarily be marked by the depreciation of thinness though not accompanied by an increasing positivity toward fatness. Instead, both smaller and larger bodies for women are coming to evoke negative reactions relative to average size ones, but not to the same degree. Furthermore, the nature or content of the evaluations may differ quite a bit, an aspect inadequately captured by existing quantitative research. Thinness appears to conjure the same assumptions as physical attractiveness: we think women are vain and conceited when they achieve cultural ideals for beauty.

While this study makes several contributions to the literature, there are some limitations that restrict what can be learned here. First, this sample lacked the heterogeneity to allow for additional revealing subgroup comparisons, including by race, a status highly related to weight ideas. Black and Latina women often strive for curvier figures (large breasts, hips, bottoms) and recognize that thinness is more of a standard by and for White women (Awad et al., 2015; Capodilupo & Kim, 2014; Gruber et al., 2022; Overstreet et al., 2010). Still, dominant standards are strong and can create conflicting self-perceptions and desires for thinness even in women and girls of color (Cheney, 2011). Thus, while White women view average weight White bodies more favorably than both overweight and underweight, Black women may or may not judge Black bodies the same way (Davies et al., 2020b). But the underrepresentation by racially diverse participants made these comparisons unreliable statistically. Second, participants were not given any type of image representing each weight category. Rather, they were left to create their own mental images in terms of size and race. This makes it possible that they pictured extremes for both overweight and underweight targets. This could have widened disparities in evaluations, as attitudes toward very overweight people are worse than toward only slightly overweight people (Musher-Eizenman & Carels, 2009).

Future research should work to address these limitations, as well as the aforementioned weaknesses in current weight bias research. Understanding these in-flux body standards has implications for scholarship on topics related to bodies, beauty, the intersection of gender and race, the influence of the body positivity movement, and more. There are additionally the real-world implications of these issues that should shape approaches to fighting weight stigma and body dissatisfaction.

NOTES

1. BMI calculations are not designed to accommodate for racial and sex variation but are widely used regardless in diagnosing obesity. Experts have recommended raising BMI standards for categorizing Black women (Stanford et al., 2019).
2. The BMI scale uses the terms "normal" or "healthy" weight, but to avoid those more valued labels for targets, I opted for "average." Additionally, BMI is a medical rather than social classification that can only be ascertained through mathematical calculation, and many people are poor estimators of others' BMI (Vartanian & Germeroth, 2011). At the same time, the average US adult BMI is now in the overweight range, complicating the use of "average" as well (Ellison-Barnes et al., 2021).

REFERENCES

Albala, K. (2005). Weight loss in the age of reason. In C. E. Forth & A. Carden-Coyne (Eds.), *Cultures of the abdomen: Diet digestion, and fat in the modern world* (pp. 169–183). Palgrave Macmillan.

Alberga, A. S., Withnell, S. J., & von Ranson, K. M. (2018). Fitspiration and thinspiration: A comparison across three social networking sites. *Journal of Eating Disorders*, 6(1), 39. https://doi.org/10.1186/s40337-018-0227-x

Anderson, J. L., Crawford, C. B., Nadeau, J., & Lindberg, T. (1992). Was the Duchess of Windsor right? A cross-cultural review of the socioecology of ideals of female body shape. *Ethology and Sociobiology*, 13(3), 197–227. https://doi.org/10.1016/0162-3095(92)90033-Z

Andreyeva, T., Puhl, R. M., & Brownell, K. D. (2008). Changes in perceived weight discrimination among Americans, 1995–1996 through 2004–2006. *Obesity*, 16(5), 1129–1134. https://doi.org/10.1038/oby.2008.35

Aniulis, E., Sharp, G., & Thomas, N. A. (2021). The ever-changing ideal: The body you want depends on who else you're looking at. *Body Image*, 36, 218–229. https://doi.org/10.1016/j.bodyim.2020.12.003

Ata, R. N., & Thompson, J. K. (2010). Weight bias in the media: A review of recent research. *Obesity Facts*, 3(1), 41–46. https://doi.org/10.1159/000276547

Awad, G. H., Norwood, C., Taylor, D. S., Martinez, M., McClain, S., Jones, B., Holman, A., & Chapman-Hilliard, C. (2015). Beauty and body image concerns among African American college women. *The Journal of Black Psychology*, 41(6), 540–564. https://doi.org/10.1177/0095798414550864

Bacon, J., Scheltema, K., & Robinson, B. B. (2001). Fat phobia scale revisited: The short form. *International Journal of Obesity and Related Metabolic Disorders: Journal of the International Association for the Study of Obesity*, 25, 252–257. https://doi.org/10.1038/sj.ijo.0801537

Beggan, J. K., & DeAngelis, M. (2015). "Oh, my God, I hate you:" The felt experience of being othered for being thin. *Symbolic Interaction*, 38(3), 371–392. https://doi.org/10.1002/symb.162

Benton, C., & Karazsia, B. T. (2015). The effect of thin and muscular images on women's body satisfaction. *Body Image*, 13, 22–27. https://doi.org/10.1016/j.bodyim.2014.11.001

Bernard, M., Fankhänel, T., Riedel-Heller, S. G., & Luck-Sikorski, C. (2019a). Does weight-related stigmatisation and discrimination depend on educational attainment and level of income? A systematic review. *BMJ Open*, 9(11), e027673. https://doi.org/10.1136/bmjopen-2018-027673

Bernard, M., Riedel-Heller, S. G., & Luck-Sikorski, C. (2019b). Altruistic behavior depending on opponents' body weight: An experimental approach. *Obesity Facts*, 12(4), 448–459. https://doi.org/10.1159/000501318

Betz, D. E., & Ramsey, L. R. (2017). Should women be "All about that bass?": Diverse body-ideal messages and women's body image. *Body Image, 22*, 18–31. https://doi.org/10.1016/j.bodyim.2017.04.004

Boepple, L., Ata, R. N., Rum, R., & Thompson, J. K. (2016). Strong is the new skinny: A content analysis of fitspiration websites. *Body Image, 17*, 132–135. https://doi.org/10.1016/j.bodyim.2016.03.001

Bograd, S., Chen, B., & Kavuluru, R. (2022). Tracking sentiments toward fat acceptance over a decade on Twitter. *Health Informatics Journal, 28*(1), 14604582211065702. https://doi.org/10.1177/14604582211065702

Bozsik, F., Whisenhunt, B. L., Hudson, D. L., Bennett, B., & Lundgren, J. D. (2018). Thin is in? Think again: The rising importance of muscularity in the thin ideal female body. *Sex Roles, 79*(9–10), 609–615. https://doi.org/10.1007/s11199-017-0886-0

Brewis, A. (2017). Making sense of the new global body norms. In E. P. Anderson-Fye & A. Brewis (Eds.), *Fat planet: Obesity, culture, and symbolic body capital* (pp. 1–32). University of New Mexico Press.

Brewis, A., SturtzSreetharan, C., & Wutich, A. (2018). Obesity stigma as a globalizing health challenge. *Globalization and Health, 14*(1), 20. https://doi.org/10.1186/s12992-018-0337-x

Brewis, A. A., Wutich, A., Falletta-Cowden, A., & Rodriguez-Soto, I. (2011). Body norms and fat stigma in global perspective. *Current Anthropology, 52*(2), 269–276. https://doi.org/10.1086/659309

Broadbent, E. (2021, July 23). *No, skinny shaming and fat shaming are not the same*. Scary Mommy. https://www.scarymommy.com/skinny-shaming-and-fat-shaming-not-same

Brochu, P. M., Banfield, J. C., & Dovidio, J. F. (2020). Does a common ingroup identity reduce weight bias? Only when weight discrimination is salient. *Frontiers in Psychology, 10*, 3020. https://doi.org/10.3389/fpsyg.2019.03020

Capodilupo, C. M. (2015). One size does not fit all: Using variables other than the thin ideal to understand Black women's body image. *Cultural Diversity and Ethnic Minority Psychology, 21*(2), 268–278. https://doi.org/10.1037/a0037649

Capodilupo, C. M., & Kim, S. (2014). Gender and race matter: The importance of considering intersections in Black women's body image. *Journal of Counseling Psychology, 61*(1), 37–49. https://doi.org/10.1037/a0034597

Carden-Coyne, A., & Forth, C. E. (2005). Introduction: The belly and beyond. In C. E. Forth & A. Carden-Coyne (Eds.), *Cultures of the abdomen: Diet digestion, and fat in the modern world* (pp. 1–11). Palgrave Macmillan.

Cheney, A. M. (2011). "Most girls want to be skinny": Body (dis)satisfaction among ethnically diverse women. *Qualitative Health Research, 21*(10), 1347–1359. https://doi.org/10.1177/1049732310392592

Chrisler, J. (2012). "Why can't you control yourself?" Fat should be a feminist issue. *Sex Roles, 66*. https://doi.org/10.1007/s11199-011-0095-1

Cohen, R., Irwin, L., Newton-John, T., & Slater, A. (2019). #bodypositivity: A content analysis of body positive accounts on Instagram. *Body Image, 29*, 47–57. https://doi.org/10.1016/j.bodyim.2019.02.007

Cohen, R., Newton-John, T., & Slater, A. (2021). The case for body positivity on social media: Perspectives on current advances and future directions. *Journal of Health Psychology, 26*(13), 2365–2373. https://doi.org/10.1177/1359105320912450

Costin, C. (1997). *Your dieting daughter: Is she dying for attention?* Brunner/Mazel.

Cottom, T. M. (2019). *Thick: And other essays*. The New Press.

Culbert, K. M., Racine, S. E., & Klump, K. L. (2015). Research review: What we have learned about the causes of eating disorders – a synthesis of sociocultural, psychological, and biological research. *Journal of Child Psychology & Psychiatry, 56*(11), 1141–1164. https://doi.org/10.1111/jcpp.12441

Dacome, L. (2005). Useless and pernicious matter. In C. E. Forth & A. Carden-Coyne (Eds.), *Cultures of the abdomen: Diet digestion, and fat in the modern world* (pp. 185–204). Palgrave Macmillan.

Daufin, E.-K. (2020). Thick sistahs and heavy disprivilege: Black women, intersectionality, and weight stigma. In M. Friedman, C. Rice, & J. Rinaldi (Eds.), *Thickening fat: Fat bodies, intersectionality, and social justice* (pp. 160–170). Routledge.

Davies, A., Burnette, C. B., & Mazzeo, S. E. (2020a). Real women have (just the right) curves: Investigating anti-thin bias in college women. *Eating and Weight Disorders – Studies on Anorexia, Bulimia and Obesity, 25*(6), 1711–1718. https://doi.org/10.1007/s40519-019-00812-7

Davies, A. E., Burnette, C. B., & Mazzeo, S. E. (2020b). Black and White women's attributions of women with underweight. *Eating Behaviors, 39*, 101446. https://doi.org/10.1016/j.eatbeh.2020.101446

Dermer, M., & Thiel, D. (1975). When beauty may fail. *Journal of Personality and Social Psychology, 31*, 1168–1176. https://doi.org/10.1037/h0077085

Devine, S., Germain, N., Ehrlich, S., & Eppinger, B. (2022). Changes in the prevalence of thin bodies bias young women's judgments about body size. *Psychological Science, 33*(8), 1212–1225. https://doi.org/10.1177/09567976221082941

Dreisbach, S. (2012, May 2). *Weight stereotyping: The secret way people are judging you based on your body*. Glamour. https://www.glamour.com/story/weight-stereotyping-the-secret-way-people-are-judging-you-based-on-your-body-glamour-june-2012

Ellison-Barnes, A., Johnson, S., & Gudzune, K. (2021). Trends in obesity prevalence among adults aged 18 through 25 years, 1976–2018. *JAMA, 326*(20), 2073. https://doi.org/10.1001/jama.2021.16685

Elran-Barak, R., & Bar-Anan, Y. (2018). Implicit and explicit anti-fat bias: The role of weight-related attitudes and beliefs. *Social Science & Medicine, 204*, 117–124. https://doi.org/10.1016/j.socscimed.2018.03.018

Engel, J. (2018). *Fat nation: A history of obesity in America*. Rowman & Littlefield.

Fardouly, J., & Vartanian, L. R. (2016). Social media and body image concerns: Current research and future directions. *Current Opinion in Psychology, 9*, 1–5. https://doi.org/10.1016/j.copsyc.2015.09.005

Farrell, A. E. (2011). *Fat shame: Stigma and the fat body in American culture*. New York University Press.

Fikkan, J. L., & Rothblum, E. D. (2012). Is fat a feminist issue? Exploring the gendered nature of weight bias. *Sex Roles, 66*(9), 575–592. https://doi.org/10.1007/s11199-011-0022-5

Forth, C. E. (2019). *Fat: A cultural history of the stuff of life*. Reaktion Books.

Fraser, L. (2009). The inner corset: A brief history of fat in the United States. In E. Rothblum & S. Solovay (Eds.), *The fat studies reader* (pp. 11–14). New York University Press.

Ghavami, N., & Peplau, L. A. (2013). An intersectional analysis of gender and ethnic stereotypes: Testing three hypotheses. *Psychology of Women Quarterly, 37*(1), 113–127. https://doi.org/10.1177/0361684312464203

Gordon, A. (2020, September 1). *Please don't bring up 'skinny shaming' when we talk about fat shaming*. Self.Com. https://www.self.com/story/skinny-shaming

Gregory, C. A., & Ruhm, C. J. (2011). Where does the wage penalty bite? In M. Grossman & N. Mocan (Eds.), *Economic aspects of obesity* (pp. 315–347). University of Chicago Press. https://www.nber.org/books-and-chapters/economic-aspects-obesity/where-does-wage-penalty-bite

Gruber, E., Kalkbrenner, M. T., & Hitter, T. L. (2022). A complex conceptualization of beauty in Latinx women: A mixed methods study. *Body Image, 41*, 432–442. https://doi.org/10.1016/j.bodyim.2022.04.008

Han, D. E., & Laurent, S. M. (2022). Beautiful seems good, but perhaps not in every way: Linking attractiveness to moral evaluation through perceived vanity. *Journal of Personality and Social Psychology, 124*(2), 264–286. https://doi.org/10.1037/pspa0000317

Harper, A., & Power, M. (1998). Development of the World Health Organization WHOQOL-BREF quality of life assessment. *Psychological Medicine, 28*(3), 551–558. https://doi.org/10.1017/S0033291798006667

Harrison, D. L. (2021). *Belly of the beast – The politics of anti-fatness as anti-Blackness*. North Atlantic Books.

Hart, E. A., Sbrocco, T., & Carter, M. M. (2016). Ethnic identity and implicit anti-fat bias: Similarities and differences between African American and Caucasian women. *Ethnicity & Disease, 26*(1), 69–76. https://doi.org/10.18865/ed.26.1.69

Hawkins, N., Richards, P. S., Granley, H. M., & Stein, D. M. (2004). The impact of exposure to the thin-ideal media image on women. *Eating Disorders, 12*(1), 35–50. https://doi.org/10.1080/10640260490267751

Heckert, A., & Heckert, D. M. (2002). A new typology of deviance: Integrating normative and reactivist definitions of deviance. *Deviant Behavior*, *23*(5), 449–479. https://doi.org/10.1080/016396202320265319

Heckert, A., & Heckert, D. M. (2004). Using an integrated typology of deviance to analyze ten common norms of the U.S. middle class. *The Sociological Quarterly*, *45*(2), 209–228.

Himmelstein, M. S., Puhl, R. M., & Quinn, D. M. (2018). Weight stigma in men: What, when, and by whom? *Obesity*, *26*(6), 968–976. https://doi.org/10.1002/oby.22162

Hruschka, D. J. (2017). From thin to fat and back again: A dual process model of the big body mass reversal. In E. P. Anderson-Fye & A. Brewis (Eds.), *Fat planet: Obesity, culture, and symbolic body capital* (pp. 1–32). University of New Mexico Press.

Iter, A. Z. (2020, August 11). *Let's talk about a different type of body-shaming*. Medium. https://medium.com/live-your-life-on-purpose/lets-talk-about-a-different-type-of-body-shaming-e6e80d0d4f91

Jeon, Y. A., Hale, B., Knackmuhs, E., & Mackert, M. (2018). Weight stigma goes viral on the internet: Systematic assessment of YouTube comments attacking overweight men and women. *Interactive Journal of Medical Research*, *7*(1), e6. https://doi.org/10.2196/ijmr.9182

Karazsia, B. T., Murnen, S. K., & Tylka, T. L. (2017). Is body dissatisfaction changing across time? A cross-temporal meta-analysis. *Psychological Bulletin*, *143*(3), 293–320.

Kelley, C. C. (Galliger), Neufeld, J. M., & Musher-Eizenman, D. R. (2010). Drive for thinness and drive for muscularity: Opposite ends of the continuum or separate constructs? *Body Image*, *7*(1), 74–77. https://doi.org/10.1016/j.bodyim.2009.09.008

Kyrölä, K. (2014). *The weight of images: Affect, body image and fat in the media*. Ashgate.

Latner, J., O'Brien, K., Durso, L., Brinkman, L. A., & MacDonald, T. (2008). Weighing obesity stigma: The relative strength of different forms of bias. *International Journal of Obesity*, *32*, 1145–1152. https://doi.org/10.1038/ijo.2008.53

Lazuka, R. F., Wick, M. R., Keel, P. K., & Harriger, J. A. (2020). Are we there yet? Progress in depicting diverse images of beauty in Instagram's body positivity movement. *Body Image*, *34*, 85–93. https://doi.org/10.1016/j.bodyim.2020.05.001

LeBesco, K. (2004). *Revolting bodies? The struggle to redefine fat identity*. University of Massachusetts Press.

Lieberman, D. L., Tybur, J. M., & Latner, J. D. (2012). Disgust sensitivity, obesity stigma, and gender: Contamination psychology predicts weight bias for women, not men. *Obesity*, *20*(9), 1803–1814. https://doi.org/10.1038/oby.2011.247

Malloy, T. E., Lewis, B., Kinney, L., & Murphy, P. (2012). Explicit weight stereotypes are curvilinear: Biased judgments of thin and overweight targets. *European Eating Disorders Review*, *20*(2), 151–154. https://doi.org/10.1002/erv.1101

Marcus, S.-R. (2016). Thinspiration vs. thicksperation: Comparing pro-anorexic and fat acceptance image posts on a photo-sharing site. *Cyberpsychology: Journal of Psychosocial Research on Cyberspace*, *10*(2). https://doi.org/10.5817/CP2016-2-5

McCarthy, M. (1990). The thin ideal, depression and eating disorders in women. *Behaviour Research and Therapy*, *28*(3), 205–214. https://doi.org/10.1016/0005-7967(90)90003-2

McClure, S. (2017). Symbolic capital of an "other" kind: African American females as a bracketed subunit in female body valuation. In E. P. Anderson-Fye & A. Brewis (Eds.), *Fat planet: Obesity, culture, and symbolic body capital* (pp. 97–124). University of New Mexico Press.

McComb, S. E., & Mills, J. S. (2022). Eating and body image characteristics of those who aspire to the slim-thick, thin, or fit ideal and their impact on state body image. *Body Image*, *42*, 375–384. https://doi.org/10.1016/j.bodyim.2022.07.017

McDonnell, A., & Lin, L. (2016). The hot body issue: Weight and caption tone in celebrity gossip magazines. *Body Image*, *18*, 74–77. https://doi.org/10.1016/j.bodyim.2016.06.001

McKinley, N. M. (2011). Feminist perspectives on body image. In T. F. Cash & L. Smolak (Eds.), *Body image: A handbook of science, practice, and prevention* (pp. 48–54). Guilford Publications.

Mehdi, N., & Frazier, C. (2021). Forgetting fatness: The violent co-optation of the body positivity movement. *Debates in Aesthetics*, *16*(1), 13–28.

Morrison, T. G., & O'Connor, W. E. (1999). Psychometric properties of a scale measuring negative attitudes toward overweight individuals. *The Journal of Social Psychology*, *139*, 436–445.

Murnen, S. H. (2011). Gender and body images. In T. F. Cash & L. Smolak (Eds.), *Body image: A handbook of science, practice, and prevention* (pp. 173–179). Guilford Publications.

Musher-Eizenman, D., & Carels, R. A. (2009). The impact of target weight and gender on perceptions of likeability, personality attributes, and functional impairment. *Obesity Facts, 2*(5), 311–317. https://doi.org/10.1159/000235915

Ng, M., Fleming, T., Robinson, M., Thomson, B., Graetz, N., Margono, C., Mullany, E. C., Biryukov, S., Abbafati, C., Abera, S. F., Abraham, J. P., Abu-Rmeileh, N. M., Achoki, T., AlBuhairan, F. S., Alemu, Z. A., Alfonso, R., Ali, M. K., Ali, R., Guzman, N. A., ... Gakidou, E. (2014). Global, regional and national prevalence of overweight and obesity in children and adults 1980-2013: A systematic analysis. *Lancet (London, England), 384*(9945), 766–781. https://doi.org/10.1016/S0140-6736(14)60460-8

Nouri, M., Hill, L. G., & Orrell-Valente, J. K. (2011). Media exposure, internalization of the thin ideal, and body dissatisfaction: Comparing Asian American and European American college females. *Body Image, 8*(4), 366–372. https://doi.org/10.1016/j.bodyim.2011.05.008

Ogden, C. L., & Carroll, M. D. (2010). *Prevalence of overweight, obesity, and extreme obesity among adults: United States, trends 1960–62 through 2007–2008*. Center for Disease Control and Prevention: National Center for Health Statistics.

Ogden, J., Gosling, C., Hazelwood, M., & Atkins, E. (2020). Exposure to body diversity images as a buffer against the thin-ideal: An experimental study. *Psychology, Health & Medicine, 25*(10), 1165–1178. https://doi.org/10.1080/13548506.2020.1734219

Oliver, J. E. (2006). *Fat politics: The real story behind America's obesity epidemic*. Oxford University Press.

Overstreet, N., Quinn, D., & Agocha, V. (2010). Beyond thinness: The influence of a curvaceous body ideal on body dissatisfaction in Black and White women. *Sex Roles, 63*(1–2), 91–103. https://doi.org/10.1007/s11199-010-9792-4

Owen, P. R., & Laurel-Seller, E. (2000). Weight and shape ideals: Thin is dangerously in. *Journal of Applied Social Psychology, 30*(5), 979–990. https://doi.org/10.1111/j.1559-1816.2000.tb02506.x

Pool, R. (2001). *Fat: Fighting the obesity epidemic*. Oxford University Press.

Posner, J. (1976). The stigma of excellence: On being just right. *Sociological Inquiry, 46*(2), 141–144. https://doi.org/10.1111/j.1475-682X.1976.tb00759.x

Puhl, R. (2008). *Weight discrimination: A socially acceptable injustice*. OAC. https://www.obesityaction.org/resources/weight-discrimination-a-socially-acceptable-injustice/

Puhl, R. M., Andreyeva, T., & Brownell, K. D. (2008). Perceptions of weight discrimination: Prevalence and comparison to race and gender discrimination in America. *International Journal of Obesity, 32*(6), 992–1000. https://doi.org/10.1038/ijo.2008.22

Puhl, R. M., & Heuer, C. A. (2009). The stigma of obesity: A review and update. *Obesity, 17*(5), 941–964. https://doi.org/10.1038/oby.2008.636

Puhl, R. M., Latner, J. D., O'Brien, K., Luedicke, J., Danielsdottir, S., & Forhan, M. (2015). A multinational examination of weight bias: Predictors of anti-fat attitudes across four countries. *International Journal of Obesity, 39*(7), 1166–1173. https://doi.org/10.1038/ijo.2015.32

Purkiss, A. (2017, April 1). *(Re)examining fat stigma through Black women's history*. Food, Fatness and Fitness. https://foodfatnessfitness.com/2017/04/01/reexamining-fat-stigma-black-womens-history/

Rhode, D. L. (2010). *The beauty bias: The injustice of appearance in life and law*. Oxford University Press.

Ritenbaugh, C. (1982). Obesity as a culture-bound syndrome. *Culture, Medicine and Psychiatry, 6*(4), 347–361. https://doi.org/10.1007/BF00118882

Roberts, A., & Muta, S. (2017). Representations of female body weight in the media: An update of Playboy magazine from 2000 to 2014. *Body Image, 20*, 16–19. https://doi.org/10.1016/j.bodyim.2016.08.009

Rodgers, R. F., Ziff, S., Lowy, A. S., Yu, K., & Austin, S. B. (2017). Results of a strategic science study to inform policies targeting extreme thinness standards in the fashion industry. *International Journal of Eating Disorders, 50*(3), 284–292. https://doi.org/10.1002/eat.22682

Rubino, F., Puhl, R. M., Cummings, D. E., Eckel, R. H., Ryan, D. H., Mechanick, J. I., Nadglowski, J., Ramos Salas, X., Schauer, P. R., Twenefour, D., Apovian, C. M., Aronne, L. J., Batterham,

R. L., Berthoud, H.-R., Boza, C., Busetto, L., Dicker, D., De Groot, M., Eisenberg, D., ... Dixon, J. B. (2020). Joint international consensus statement for ending stigma of obesity. *Nature Medicine, 26*(4), Article 4. https://doi.org/10.1038/s41591-020-0803-x

Saguy, A. C. (2013). *What's wrong with fat?* Oxford University Press.

Saguy, A. C., & Almeling, R. (2008). Fat in the fire? Science, the news media, and the "obesity epidemic." *Sociological Forum, 23*(1), 53–83.

Sajbel, M. (1994, August 25). *Waif not: The modeling world is a fickle place. Waifs are out and glamour is in–again. Fashion writer Maureen Sajbel looks at the ever-shifting notion of what the ideal female form should be.* Los Angeles Times. https://www.latimes.com/archives/la-xpm-1994-08-25-ls-31141-story.html

Schvey, N. A., Puhl, R. M., Levandoski, K. A., & Brownell, K. D. (2013). The influence of a defendant's body weight on perceptions of guilt. *International Journal of Obesity, 37*(9), 1275–1281. https://doi.org/10.1038/ijo.2012.211

Simpson, C. C., & Mazzeo, S. E. (2017). Skinny is not enough: A content analysis of fitspiration on Pinterest. *Health Communication, 32*(5), 560–567.

Smirles, K. E., & Lin, L. (2018). Changes in anti-fat weight bias in women after exposure to thin and plus-sized models. *The Social Science Journal, 55*(2), 193–197. https://doi.org/10.1016/j.soscij.2018.02.002

Smith, C. A. (2012). The confounding of fat, control, and physical attractiveness for women. *Sex Roles, 66*(9–10), 628–631. https://doi.org/10.1007/s11199-011-0111-5

Sobal, J. (1995). The medicalization and demedicalization of obesity. In D. Maurer & J. Sobal (Eds.), *Eating agendas: Food and nutrition as social problems* (pp. 67–90). Aldine de Gruyter.

Sobal, J. (2001). Social and cultural influences on obesity. In P. Björntorp (Ed.), *International textbook of obesity* (pp. 305–322). John Wiley & Sons, Ltd. https://doi.org/10.1002/0470846739.ch21

Spahlholz, J., Baer, N., König, H.-H., Riedel-Heller, S. G., & Luck-Sikorski, C. (2016). Obesity and discrimination – a systematic review and meta-analysis of observational studies. *Obesity Reviews, 17*(1), 43–55. https://doi.org/10.1111/obr.12343

Stanford, F. C., Lee, M., & Hur, C. (2019). Race, ethnicity, sex, and obesity: Is it time to personalize the scale? *Mayo Clinic Proceedings, 94*(2), 362–363. https://doi.org/10.1016/j.mayocp.2018.10.014

Stearns, P. N. (2005). Fat in America. In C. E. Forth & A. Carden-Coyne (Eds.), *Cultures of the abdomen: Diet digestion, and fat in the modern world* (pp. 239–257). Palgrave Macmillan.

Stierman, B., Afful, J., Carroll, M. D., Chen, T.-C., Orlando, D., Fink, S., Fryar, C. D., Gu, Q., Hales, C. M., Hughes, J. P., Ostchega, Y., Storandt, R. J., & Akinbami, L. J. (2021). *National health and nutrition examination survey 2017–March 2020 prepandemic data files – development of files and prevalence estimates for selected health outcomes (No. 158; National Health Statistics Reports)*. National Center for Health Statistics.

Striley, K. M., & Hutchens, S. (2020). Liberation from thinness culture: Motivations for joining fat acceptance movements. *Fat Studies, 9*(3), 296–308. https://doi.org/10.1080/21604851.2020.1723280

Strings, S. (2019). *Fearing the black body: The racial origins of fat phobia.* University Press.

Swami, V. (2015). Cultural influences on body size ideals. *European Psychologist, 1*, 1–8. https://doi.org/10.1027/1016-9040/a000150

Swami, V., Frederick, D. A., Aavik, T., Alcalay, L., Allik, J., Anderson, D., Andrianto, S., Arora, A., Brännström, Å., Cunningham, J., Danel, D., Doroszewicz, K., Forbes, G. B., Furnham, A., Greven, C. U., Halberstadt, J., Hao, S., Haubner, T., Hwang, C. S., ... Zivcic-Becirevic, I. (2010). The attractive female body weight and female body dissatisfaction in 26 countries across 10 world regions: Results of the international body project I. *Personality and Social Psychology Bulletin, 36*(3), 309–325. https://doi.org/10.1177/0146167209359702

Sypeck, M. F., Gray, J. J., & Ahrens, A. H. (2004). No longer just a pretty face: Fashion magazines' depictions of ideal female beauty from 1959 to 1999. *International Journal of Eating Disorders, 36*(3), 342–347. https://doi.org/10.1002/eat.20039

Tantleff-Dunn, S., Hayes, S., & Braun, C. P. (2009). How did you get so thin? The effect of attribution on perceptions of underweight females. *Eating and Weight Disorders, 14*(1), 7.

Thompson, J. K., & Stice, E. (2001). Thin-ideal internalization: Mounting evidence for a new risk factor for body-image disturbance and eating pathology. *Current Directions in Psychological Science, 10*(5), 181–183. https://doi.org/10.1111/1467-8721.00144

Tiggemann, M. (2011). Sociocultural perspectives on human appearance and body image. In T. F. Cash & L. Smolak (Eds.), *Body image: A handbook of science, practice, and prevention* (pp. 12–19). Guilford Publications.

Tsai, S. A., Lv, N., Xiao, L., & Ma, J. (2016). Gender differences in weight-related attitudes and behaviors among overweight and obese adults in the United States. *American Journal of Men's Health, 10*(5), 389–398. https://doi.org/10.1177/1557988314567223

Tseëlon, E. (1992). What is beautiful is bad: Physical attractiveness as stigma. *Journal for the Theory of Social Behaviour, 22*(3), 295–309. https://doi.org/10.1111/j.1468-5914.1992.tb00221.x

Vartanian, L. R., & Germeroth, L. J. (2011). Accuracy in estimating the body weight of self and others: Impact of dietary restraint and BMI. *Body Image, 8*(4), 415–418. https://doi.org/10.1016/j.bodyim.2011.06.007

Vigarello, G., & Delogu, C. J. (2013). *The metamorphoses of fat: A history of obesity*. Columbia University Press.

Wan, S. (2021, March 16). *The truth behind skinny shaming*. The Just Girl Project. https://thejustgirlproject.com/blogs/news/the-truth-behind-skinny-shaming

West, C. M. (1996). Mammy, sapphire, and jezebel: Historical images of Black women and their implications for psychotherapy. *Psychotherapy: Theory, Research, Practice, Training, 32*(3), 458. https://doi.org/10.1037/0033-3204.32.3.458

Woolf, E. (2013, August 5). Why is skinny-shaming OK, if fat-shaming is not? *The Guardian*. https://www.theguardian.com/lifeandstyle/the-womens-blog-with-jane-martinson/2013/aug/05/skinny-shaming-fat-size-appearance

Woolf, E. (2014). *The ministry of thin: How the pursuit of perfection got out of control*. Soft Skull Press.

Wrench, J. S., & Knapp, J. L. (2008). The effects of body image perceptions and sociocommunicative orientations on self-esteem, depression, and identification and involvement in the gay community. *Journal of Homosexuality, 55*, 471–503.

Wu, Y.-K., & Berry, D. C. (2018). Impact of weight stigma on physiological and psychological health outcomes for overweight and obese adults: A systematic review. *Journal of Advanced Nursing, 74*(5), 1030–1042. https://doi.org/10.1111/jan.13511

Yager, S. (2010). *The hundred year diet: America's voracious appetite for losing weight*. Rodale.

CHAPTER 3

DOING BEAUTY, DOING HEALTH: EMBODIED EMOTION WORK IN WOMEN CANCER PATIENTS' NARRATIVES OF HAIR LOSS

Marley Olson

Social Sciences Department, Walla Walla Community College, USA

ABSTRACT

This chapter advances understandings of emotion work by examining how "doing gender" and "doing health" are implicated in the pursuit of emotional tranquility. The study examines the role of hair loss in women's illness narratives of cancer using in-depth interviews with 16 white women in the US Northwest who vary in age, marital status, diagnoses, and treatments. The absence of women's hair presents an appearance of illness that prevents them from doing femininity, which calls into question their health status because of Western beauty standards. To overcome this barrier, the women use emotion work to manage the effects of their appearance through necessarily co-occurring bodily, cognitive, and expressive strategies (Hochschild, 1979). The required emotion work during women's hair loss makes explicit the symbolic linking of the healthy body with the feminine body through women's head hair. Pursuing treatment for cancer is often seen as a "fight" or a "battle" against the disease and the bodily assaults of such treatments, including unwanted visible bodily changes. A substantial body of empirical work has established the complex web of social psychological problems associated with breasts and breast cancer, but less attention has been given to the side effect of hair loss that is common across cancer types and treatments.

Keywords: Beauty; body; gender; embodiment; emotion work, illness

> I would warmly encourage anyone interested in the social construction of gender to find some way of spending half a year or so as a totally bald woman. (Sedgwick, 1993, p. 12)

The nearly 81 billion USD global hair care industry (Grand View Research, 2022) reflects the considerable efforts women engage in to avoid a "bad hair day." The television network, TLC, even launched a series about bad hair days, aptly titled, *Bad Hair Day*, with episodes like, "Bye, Alopecia," and "Getting' Wiggy With It." Such media highlights the cultural relevance of head hair and reflects how we think about, talk about, and do head hair. Indeed, the symbolism and malleability of head hair make it a key site for gendered bodily practices (e.g., Kyle & Mahler, 1996; McAlexander & Schouten, 1989; Synnott, 1987; Weitz, 2001, 2004). Scholarship has largely assumed a healthy body and taken for granted the presence of hair, failing to consider what women's medically induced hair *loss* – the ultimate "bad hair day" – may teach us about both gender and health. Hair loss provokes an explicit and direct confrontation with the gender system and the complex dynamics underlying the accomplishment of proper femininity, including emotions and health. Through narrative analysis of 16 middle- to upper-class white women cancer patients' emotion talk about hair loss, I contend that gendered embodied emotionality is a driving force in women's navigation of involuntary bodily changes. It is essential to consider how emotion work – the emotional regulation one does in the private sphere to render feelings in a given situation as appropriate according to the social situation (Hochschild, 1979) – incorporates gender work and body work in cases of women's illness. Employing a theory of gendered embodied emotionality, this study demonstrates that women cancer patients' tactful management of their hair loss is primarily informed by feeling rules relating to gender and illness. By examining privileged[1] women's experiences of hair loss, the study shows that even with the most bodily, cultural, and financial resources, hair loss is a significant bodily change that is highly distressing and complicated to navigate due to the oft oppugnant ideological systems of gender and health. The varied gender strategies employed by the women in this study reveal the interdependence of successful emotion work and body work to convey gender and by extension, for women, health as well.

Emotions are gendered and emotion work is feminized; that is, it is more expected from and more often performed by women (Hochschild, 1979, 1983; Otis, 2012). This gendering is a learned phenomenon that then comes to be accepted as innate or natural, producing "[w]omen's bodies [as] vehicles for expressing nurture and care" (Otis, 2012, p. 17; see also Gimlin, 2007; Sulik, 2007). In this study, I use the experience of hair loss among women cancer patients to demonstrate the significance of embodied emotionality to the dependent projects of doing gender and doing health. I show how women manage confrontations with involuntary bodily changes through the concept of "affective gymnastics" – the cognitive, bodily, and expressive emotion work (Hochschild, 1979) that is done to navigate complex emotions not clearly guided by feeling rules. Bald women's bodies disrupt the expected emotional equilibrium as reminders of mortality. Even in perhaps the most justifiable of conditions not to, bald women cancer patients engage in affective gymnastics due to the lack of normalization around women's self-care; women who are fighting to survive cancer still feel strongly compelled to engage in intensive and multifaceted emotion work to "do gender" (West & Zimmerman, 1987) appropriately and avoid stigmatization from themselves and others. Women are taught to be emotion managers (Hochschild, 1983) and prioritize others' wellness, yet they also must do emotion work on themselves when faced with a cancer diagnosis. Care work remains immensely gendered today with women bearing a greater burden of caring for others, but, as patients, they are expected to prioritize care for oneself. How do bald women cancer patients navigate this antinomy? I argue that they carefully navigate the cultural politics of emotions, gender, and illness by employing complex bodily, expressive, and cognitive strategies.

METHODS

To understand gendered embodied emotion work, this study uses hair loss narratives from 16 heterosexual, white, middle- to upper-class women cancer survivors from the Northwest region of the United States. The study was approved by the institutional review board for human subjects research at the University of Colorado Boulder. All interviews were conducted by the author. Ten interviews were conducted in person and six via video chat due to geographical constraints. Respondents were initially recruited from the author's social network, followed by snowball sampling. In addition, four respondents were recruited from local cancer-related Facebook groups. Table 3.1 illustrates the study

Table 3.1. Interview Participants Demographic Data.

Pseudonym	Age	Married/Cohabitating	Dependent(s)	Employed
Cheryl	50	Yes	Yes	Yes
Theresa	48	No	Yes	Yes
Angie	66	Yes	No	No
Rebecca	60	Yes	No	Yes
Corissa	55	No	No	Yes
Sue	57	No	Yes	Yes
Karen	61	Yes	No	Yes
Denise	51	No	Yes	No
Kimberly	30	Yes	No	No
Samantha	31	Yes	Yes	No
Leslie	34	No	No	Yes
Jamie	29	Yes	No	Yes
Sheila	58	Yes	No	Yes
Hannah	19	No	No	No
Amelia	32	No	No	Yes
Grace	41	Yes	Yes	Yes

sample characteristics. Participants ranged in age from 19 to 66 years old, with 49 years being the median age. Age at first cancer diagnosis ranged from 8 to 64 years old. Most were married and about a third had dependent children living with them during cancer treatment.

Interviews lasted from 45 to 120 minutes, with most being approximately 75 minutes. Prior to the start of the interview, participants completed a brief survey for demographic information such as age, employment, and education, as well as their cancer diagnosis and treatment plan. Interviews began with the open-ended question, "Can you walk me through your cancer experience, starting with your cancer diagnosis?" The content of the interviews varied depending on how each woman constructed her hair loss narrative. In line with a grounded theory approach (Charmaz, 2003), such an open-ended question was critical to the interviewing process because it allowed the women to present their hair loss experiences according to the importance *they* placed on it, rather than presumptions about what was considered important by the researcher. Prepared questions for prompting conversation were rarely used as most women were eager to share their experiences.

All interviews were recorded, transcribed, and uploaded into the software NVivo (QSR International, Doncaster, Australia), a qualitative data analysis software, as a means for data organization and management, coding, and memoing. The analysis involved careful reading and rereading of each transcript. Preliminary themes were identified through line-by-line coding, and then clusters of codes and recurring patterns were identified. Themes were developed inductively and iteratively (Charmaz, 2003; Corbin & Strauss, 1990; Lofland et al., 2006). As analysis proceeded and themes of emotions emerged, additional deductive, theory-driven analysis was deployed to examine emotion work strategies in the narratives (Hochschild, 1979, 1983).

In this study, I use the case of acute, medically induced hair loss among women to explain how gender and emotion shape the strategies individuals employ to navigate involuntary bodily changes using affective gymnastics – the cognitive, bodily, and expressive emotion work (Hochschild, 1979) that is done to navigate complex emotions not clearly guided by feeling rules. Women cancer patients' precarious position of being a woman and a patient place them at the intersection of competing ideologies from the gender system and the institution of medicine. Managing a deviant appearance, particularly in an illness context, conveys care to others and is also a form of self-care. Caring for others and caring for oneself, however, are not always compatible. Thus, negotiating caring for others and caring for oneself sometimes necessitates affective gymnastics. I argue that women primarily orient themselves around emotions when making decisions about their hair loss management and, most often, prioritize others' feelings over their own. In the following sections, I describe how women holistically deploy the triad of emotion work strategies (i.e., expressive, cognitive, and bodily) in a complex process of affective gymnastics during chemotherapy-induced hair loss to reconcile competing health and gender ideologies for themselves and others, thereby maintaining emotional equilibrium.

BODILY STRATEGIES

Hair management is part of a larger configuration of body work (Kang, 2010; Lyon & Barbalet, 1994; Wolkowitz, 2002, 2006) practices[2] through which women work to produce feminine bodies and conform to dominant gender norms (Bartky, 1988; Bordo, 1993; Lorber, 1993; West & Zimmerman, 1987). Hair is a particularly visible part of the body, making it significant in the project of body work to accomplish a particular gendered appearance (Barber, 2008; Toerien & Wilkinson, 2003; Weitz, 2004). Hair management is one type of body work that the gender system encourages individuals to engage in to denote membership in a particular gender category. Women's hair management practices are sites for the commonplace production of normative femininity. Indeed, the presence and manipulation of head hair is so pervasive that it tends to go unnoticed (Weitz, 2004). Such gender normative expectations of women's hair promote a critical awareness among women of their appearances that results in heightened self-objectification (Fahs, 2011) and self-surveillance (Bordo, 1993; see also Boyle, 2005; Otis, 2012; Silva, 2008; Weitz, 2001). While women may question what specifically to do with their hair, they do not question that they ought to do something.

The women in the present study engaged in resisting and conforming body work practices to promote a positive affect for themselves and others. They experienced losing their hair as an intense, emotional process with baldness dramatically affecting their psychological well-being. This was, in part, because they felt under-gendered, ungendered, or even unhuman. For some, baldness made them feel *inadequately* gendered: "like a woman, but not like a *pretty* woman" (Jamie, 29). Other women felt genderless entirely. Cheryl (50) identified the deeply gendered hair norms saying, "For women, the normal is we have hair. It can be short, it can be long, it can be whatever, but we don't shave our heads *bald*." Grace (41) expanded on the importance of hair for doing gender by saying, "society has this expectation of how women should look – women should have hair – so I guess I figured not having my hair, I'd kind of look like a freak. I'd look different, and it would be *weird*." Grace's use of denigrating language to describe women without hair was not isolated. Others used language like "ugly," "unnatural," "mortifying," "scary," "terrible," and even "alien"; hair is a marker of humanness for women and is imbued with cultural value. Lucille (56), for example, said that she felt like "some kind of strange cyborg or monster without it [fake eyelashes, penciled eyebrows, and wig]." Thus, by practicing compensatory body work, like jewelry, clothing, or painted nails, women appear to be "normal." Hair makes women socially intelligible; it makes women look human.

To mitigate the associated distress of feeling under-gendered, ungendered, or unhuman, the women adopted three main strategies: avoiding, covering, and emphasizing. Women's own self-images contributed to the emotionality of hair loss. This caused them such anxiety that they avoided appearance reminders, like looking in the mirror, catching a glimpse of their reflections in windows, and viewing beauty magazines. They also avoided items associated with the hair they once had because these reminders negatively impacted their self-appraisals of femininity and beauty. Rebecca (60) explained that her avoidance tactics were attempts to protect her psychological well-being in the face of an external threat to her sense of self:

> I couldn't stand having my hair on my pillow and in my bed ... I just ... I couldn't handle my hair falling out ... So I sat there with a waste basket and I started pulling my hair out – just filling up the wastebasket with it. Then my friend came over and vacuumed the whole house and cleaned everything for me to get rid of any of the hair that was around because I didn't want to see the hair anymore. I just wanted it to be gone.

This, for her, was a way of "ignoring that [she] had cancer and trying not being upset that [she] had cancer." The women who chose to shave their heads preemptively did so to avoid experiences like Rebecca's. The women's very awareness of such stories indicates the emotional intensity of the hair loss process. Capturing this sentiment, Grace said, "I figured I would cry because... I had heard from people how hard it is to lose your hair." Baldness was a corporeal symbol of the realities of their diagnosis. Because longer head hair is strongly associated with femininity, baldness among women is believed to be a result of illness since the belief is that "no woman would ever choose to be bald." Studies on women's appearance work demonstrate the importance of hair for producing an appearance of health and normality (Dellinger & Williams, 1997; Hammer, 2012; Lyons, 2009). Thus, illness poses a great threat to women's gender performances. Without functioning bodies – including hair growth – women's routine performances of gender are disrupted (Peake et al., 1999). The failure to do femininity then has the potential to call into question a woman's health status.

Not only did the women worry about their own emotional well-being during the hair loss process, but they also worried about that of others. Evidence from verbal self-disclosures of cancer diagnoses provides further support of the gendered emotion work that disclosure entails for women who are concerned about the worrying of others and want to shield them from that emotional burden (Yoo et al., 2010). When Amelia (32) was considering shaving her head with her family, she spent hours debating whether it was "selfish" because it may be good for her but emotionally difficult for her family. She was particularly concerned with the effect it would have on the young children, stating, "I was very worried. I mean my hair was a little longer than shoulder length, and I thought it would be scary for – my nieces are pretty young – for them to see me go from having quite a bit of hair to being bald." With a similar concern about the distress that sudden hair loss could cause her or her young children, Grace chose to shave her head on the first day of treatment to avoid the unpredictability.

While some women avoided tangible reminders of hair, others tried to it cover by managing their appearances. Hannah (19) explained that the impact of being misgendered on her sense of identity was so great that, not unlike many of the women in this study, she introduced new body work practices and increased the frequency in which she practiced existing body work strategies during hair loss. She said, "I found ways to look girly-er so that people wouldn't mistake me for a boy. I got my ears pierced and I would paint my nails so that I would look like a girl." Sheila (58) similarly conformed to gender norms to elicit positive feelings about herself noting, "the wig and penciling in eyebrows and stuff helped with trying to look as normal as I could. When I thought I looked good, I felt good." Just like seeing herself as "normal" translated into positive emotions for Sheila, Samantha (31) similarly said, "With the wig, I didn't feel as self-conscious." Conforming to gendered appearance norms, whether for one's own pleasure or to avoid stigma from others, fostered a positive affect among the women. In an effort to protect others, the women tried to maintain normalcy so that their personal health crisis did not affect the lives of their loved ones. For example, to reduce the risk of others' detecting their baldness and identifying it as a marker of illness, some women picked out their wigs prior to experiencing hair loss to match the wig to their real hair. Denise (51) highlighted the strength of the norm that women have hair saying:

> It was looking thin and raggedy because I was losing it in patches. I could shave it all off and then put on the wig that would look more socially acceptable. Whenever I went out, I put on my wig and my fake eyelashes because I felt I was not the social norm. I tried faking it to try to fit in.

Her comments suggest that she could no longer "fake it," or "pass" (Goffman, 1963) without covering up "thin and raggedy" hair to gain social acceptance and "fit in." Women's management strategies were often chosen because of others' imagined responses. Women did not care just about their close intimates' emotional well-being but also that of strangers. Rebecca worried even about pedestrians walking by her apartment window:

> I didn't have it [the wig] on in the house, so I was careful that if I walked by my kitchen window – which looks out onto the parking lot – that I tried to cover up because I was always wondering if someone would come by and look in there and go, "Oh my god, that woman has no hair in that house!"

Similarly, Theresa (48) expressed the obligation she felt to wear her wig because it was what her friends wanted, and they had gifted her the wig. She also felt the wig could put her elementary school students at ease, so they would not "worry about what [she] was going through." Karen (61) chose to wear a wig because she thought that by wearing a scarf "in a way you're drawing attention to yourself about, 'Oh look, I have cancer.'" In this way, the wig became a means to maintain the emotional tranquility of the public sphere (Cahill & Eggleston, 1994) by using appearance management to pass as a healthy woman.[3] When managing their appearance based on their audience, the women considered how the emotional responses of each hair management technique may vary from individual to individual. Jamie explained how she regularly changed the type of head covering she wore depending on whom she was with.

> My sister preferred a scarf, but my husband couldn't stand the scarfs. He didn't like that reality of me looking like a cancer patient. He only liked hats, so if I was with him and we were doing just our basic everyday stuff I would wear hats. But then I'm also a dance teacher, and the hats would fall off a lot. My students liked the fun colors with the scarfs, so I'd wear a lot of scarfs to dance.

Other women chose bodily strategies that allowed them to address others' emotional responses solely as a means of protecting their own emotional well-being. Rebecca, who wore her wig while she was at work as a nurse, said, "I figured the wig would shut them up. I'd have the least amount of questions."

However, the use of wigs was not universally and unequivocally experienced positively; rather, some women expressed discord between how they thought they should feel with the wig and their experiences of wearing a wig. For example, Corissa (55) said, "It was hard for me to deal with. With the wig, I knew that the hair wasn't really mine. Certainly, it made me feel like I had cancer. It made me feel bald still." For this reason, a few women chose to make their bald heads publicly visible. Yet even these women engaged in other forms of heightened gender displays to compensate. As Leslie (34) said, "there are these other ways I can show that I'm trying to be feminine." Women's efforts to look feminine while bald included focalizing their head scarfs through the prints and colors, wearing more or more prominent jewelry, penciling in their eyebrows or having them tattooed on, and wearing makeup if they had not regularly done so before hair loss or wearing more of it.

The significance of head hair practices for gender and health is underscored by the fact head hair management concerns are observed among women (and, importantly, not men) who are fighting for their lives and experiencing physically exhausting treatments. Research consistently notes the serious mental, emotional, and social problems that hair loss poses for women, yet hair loss is often reduced to being considered a minor side effect of cancer treatment because it is not directly life-threatening (Hilton et al., 2008). The symbolism of hair is so powerful that the anticipated social injury from its loss is perceived as equal to or worse than physical harm. Women report wanting to refuse cancer treatment to ensure the preservation of their hair (Breed et al., 2011; Coates et al., 1983; Hansen, 2007; Münstedt et al., 1997). While men experience hair loss as an unavoidable and foreseen consequence of treatment, for many women, it is experienced as traumatic (Rosman, 2004; see also Breed et al., 2011). Because of this, women experiencing hair loss engage in a number of appearance work strategies, like prostheses, wigs, and makeup, to pass (Hansen, 2007; Kendrick, 2008; Rosman, 2004) – a strategy that has been packaged and promoted by the American Cancer Society's "Look Better, Feel Better" program (Kendrick, 2008).

EXPRESSIVE STRATEGIES

Women often fear burdening family and friends with their own troubles, including illnesses like cancer (Ashing-Giwa et al., 2004; Kagawa-Singer et al., 1997). Research among breast cancer patients finds that the fear of emotionally burdening one's family with their illness is second to none. Expectations as emotion managers are greater for women (Hochschild, 1983). Thus, women may feel burdened by and have great investments in doing both unpaid emotion work and paid emotional labor, from intimate relationships to the workplace (DeVault, 1999; Hochschild, 1983; Illouz, 2007; Kang, 2010). In the present study, this was not only evident in the women's attempts to camouflage their hair loss to avoid distressful emotions but also in the expressive strategies they deployed to mitigate failed bodily strategies. When the bodily strategies outlined above failed, the women used expressive emotion work strategies to restore emotional tranquility to the interaction. That is, the women added "talk" (e.g., warnings, humor, or body language) to their interactions to manage their own and others' emotions related to their hair loss.

One expressive strategy used to manage the emotions of others was prefacing. They often warned the future audiences of their appearance to facilitate positive interactions with others. Denise recalled that the parents in her neighborhood prepared their children for seeing her without hair so that it would not upset them. Before taking off her wig in the children's presence, Denise would first ask if they were ready. Similarly, Jamie recalled an instance when she had given her mother-in-law advance warning over the phone that she would not be wearing makeup or a head covering when she came to visit. Upon Jamie's arrival, her mother-in-law "looked at [Jamie] and she goes, 'Oh you *really* look like a cancer patient.'" Jamie's mother-in-law promptly apologized profusely for bothering her to come visit, offered to make a few prepared meals for her during the week, and would not accept her help in the kitchen as she usually had many times since Jamie's diagnosis.

Women also used collaboration strategies, involving others in their hair loss management to consider their preferences and foster connection. Some women invited others to participate in the purchasing of head coverings. Others asked what those around them preferred they wear or asked for permission to wear different head coverings (e.g., scarfs, beanies, and hats) or to go bald. For example, when visiting family for Christmas, Rebecca asked her siblings if they would be upset by her not wearing a head covering when she had a bit of "peach fuzz" growing back in and then asked each of their spouses, too.

If the women did offend or shock someone by their appearance accidently, they often used humor to minimize the emotional impact of their baldness on themselves and on others. For example, Cheryl's wig flew off in the wind while shopping for a car as a gift for her daughter's 16th birthday. When she noticed the salesperson and her family's facial reactions to the incident, she began laughing so as to "not make them feel bad" for her and to "make light of the situation." While Cheryl's comedic relief was retroactive and spontaneous, other women did so preemptively. Sue (57), for example, crafted a variety of "silly" head coverings, such as ladybug antennas for Valentine's Day and a Leprechaun hat for St. Patrick's Day, to infuse comedic relief into her appearance. She said,

> A lot of times people didn't know how to approach us. Breaking that ice, taking the awkwardness out of the moment, is one of the harder parts. If you had silly hats on and silly scarves, it broke that ice by making someone laugh.

For these women, defining situations as laughable helped mitigate the emotional confusion and discomfort (Cahill & Eggleston, 1994).

COGNITIVE STRATEGIES

Women often avoid burdening their families while experiencing an unfulfilled need for emotional support themselves (Ashing-Giwa et al., 2004). The women in this study negotiated their roles as women and patients through "self-talk" to justify to themselves the bodily and expressive emotion work strategies they used. Such cognitive strategies were grounded in care for others and themselves and were framed by medicine and gender. The women's inclusion of others into their hair management strategies suggests that they were as concerned with the emotional well-being of others as they were with their own. For example, Grace conveyed how concern for others' emotional responses to her baldness engendered intensive self-talk. She recalled an instance at the grocery store when a four-year-old girl asked Grace why she had no hair:

> I told her I had to take medicine that made my hair fall out. Later that night though, I was kicking myself because I thought, "Oh no, did I just give this little girl a complex that if she takes medicine her hair is going to fall out?" Maybe I should have just said, "Oh, I'm taking medicine that makes me grow *new* hair," instead, but I was just trying to be honest.

After Grace told this story, she sighed, slumped back into her chair, and said, "I can't beat myself up about it." Thus, deep caring about others' emotional responses to their hair loss prompted negative emotions for them, like grievance, regret, guilt, and worry, which then required additional emotion work in the form of self-talk.

Not unusual in cases of illness, the women commonly reported feelings of lost personal control. The presence of head hair provides a medium through which to express individualism and exercise agency. Rebecca used an emotionally powerful comparison, saying she felt like the "women that got their heads shaved in the Holocaust." There have been several examples in global history of the cutting and shaving of women's hair being used as means of social control through humiliation and dehumanization. In addition to Holocaust victims, head-shaving in France and hair-cutting in Greece were used as forms of gendered punishment for fraternizing with Germans during World War II. Virgili (2002) argues that the practice of head-shaving as punishment in France during the Liberation was a gendered punishment because, while some men's heads were shaved, it was mostly women who comprised the estimated 20,000 individuals who received this form of punishment. A similar punishment was imposed on women in Greece who had their hair cut violently with razors, knives, or scissors for violating traditional gender norms by participating in the resistance. Reflective of the deep social importance of head hair to women, the impact of this punishment was so great that it was touted as a great success for achieving social order (Vervenioti, 2000). For the women in this study, during a time when they could suddenly no longer control something as seemingly mundane as their hair, controlling their gender performances became a project of individual agency. The women framed each of their hair decisions, whether wearing a wig, wearing nothing, or shaving their heads *a priori*, as *choices* – acts of reclaiming their bodies and their identities. They were not going to *let* cancer *take* anything else from them when it had already taken their health *and* their hair, which "was like pouring salt on the wound" (Karen). Having a different emotional experience than anticipated further contributes to emotional distress. Angie (66) captured this sentiment in saying, "Losing your hair is like losing your virginity. You never know quite what to expect." Grace captured the unanimous sentiment among the women that reframing the hair loss process was a way to employ agency:

> That was one thing I could control – when I was going to lose my hair – and I was going to lose it because *I* chose to lose it, not because it fell out, which would be something that I wouldn't have control over. You'd go to bed one night and your hair is there, and then you wake up in the morning and now there's a clump of hair on your pillow. It's like I said – so much of what was going on was out of my control, and so that would have been one more thing that was happening *to me*, instead of me choosing it.

The uncertainty that engendered the hair loss process evoked anxiety in the regrowth process as well because the potential change in texture, thickness, or color could "be another one of those things to attribute to cancer; one more *big* thing" (Jamie). These women, who would never have *chosen* to be bald, developed a heightened appreciation for individual agency as they navigated controlling systems of gender and medicine.

However, the women could not control the conflicting self-appraisals they faced and, as such, sought to censor ones that did not fit within their preferred schemas. Women experienced emotional strain as they negotiated negative self-appraisals for vanity and positive ones for engaging in appearance management and avoiding appearance reminders. Kimberly (30) addressed her frustration with the conflict between social norms and moral values related to hair stating,

> It shouldn't be a big deal but it is a big deal. Those clashing feelings inside me that I shouldn't be that petty and appearance focused .... But at the same time, it [baldness] is a reminder of everything that I've been through.

All the women reported negative self-appraisals for their appearance management strategy, whether it was conforming or not, which then resulted in women's self-censoring of "inappropriate" emotions. Women felt ashamed that their hair loss upset them because they perceived it as being vain, which has a generally negative societal evaluation. For example, Rebecca said, "I know I should be grateful to just be alive, but I don't know if [being concerned about one's appearance] is *all* vanity. How you look and how you perceive yourself is a really big thing for women." To mediate this dissonance, the women engaged in practices of deception. For example, Samantha engaged in intensive emotion work to prevent depressive symptoms even though "it might be a completely deceptive thing," favoring the benefits those deceptions provided. One technique some women used was imagining emotional memories (Hochschild, 1983) by using past experiences with positive associations as cues to change their feelings. For example, head coverings served as a physical cue for many women. Illustrating this cognitive technique, Angie said of a brimmed sunhat she bought while visiting Disneyland, "it helped remind me of that good memory every time I put it on." This cognitive emotion work strategy served as a coping mechanism to support their gender strategy by aligning their feelings with their behavior of exposing their baldness and rejecting beauty norms to create a sense of genuineness.

The final cognitive strategy women engaged in was avoidance. They often achieved this by using technology as a mediator to remove themselves from situations where they anticipated others reacting negatively to their baldness. In doing so, the women simultaneously avoided internal emotion work (e.g., recounting and reliving the negative effects hair loss had on them) while also relinquishing them from expectations of interactional emotion work. For example, Kimberly utilized a blog to share updates with her family and friends as an alternative to synchronous communication modes. Explaining why she did this, she said, "I would be trying to cheer them up while at the same time I was talking about things that were really negatively impacting me. It was just exhausting." Thus, technology eased emotional strain by disembodying the interaction and removing the appearance cue of baldness from interaction. This highlights the importance and complexities of emotionality existing in the space between two or more bodies (Burkitt, 2002). Appearance work is not a zero-sums game, however. The women understood that the reactions their appearance elicited reflected societal norms that constructed them as (insert denigrating adjective: wrong, ugly, alien, weird, etc.). The very appearance work they did to mitigate distressful emotions simultaneously reminded them of their stigma which required cognitive emotion work to manage the shame they experienced as bald women.

CONCLUSION

By examining cases where women are more sensitive to head hair's ubiquitous importance by no longer having it, this study captures the gendered embodied emotionality of hair. While previous research has established the emotionality of hair loss (e.g., Breed et al., 2011; Cash, 2001; Coates et al., 1983; Hansen, 2007; Hilton et al., 2008; Münstedt et al., 1997; Weitz, 2004), it has not clarified the motivations behind women's responses to hair loss. This study offers a description of how women choose hair loss management strategies and, in doing so, illustrates how emotion work is deeply framed by gender. The women in this study primarily orient themselves around emotions when making decisions about their hair loss management. They practice great care for others' feelings about their hair loss by using expressive strategies. To mediate the cognitive dissonance resulting from the belief that concern about their appearance is incompatible with concern about their health, the women engage in cognitive strategies of emotion work. Emotion work is necessary for women's successful performance of femininity, making it central to their gender strategy. In this study, the women navigate the gender system's bodily and emotional expectations by holistically deploying the triad of emotion work strategies – bodily, expressive, and cognitive (Hochschild, 1979) – for both themselves and others because using only one or two strategies is ineffective, being perceived as inauthentic or ingenuine.

Importantly, while there are many head hair management strategies for women to choose from, there is no option simply to ignore the social forces encountered. This begs the question of whether or not women really *choose* their hair management practices, as they must choose *something*. However, the women's choices also serve as forms of self-care because it allows them to shape interactions in ways that may minimize emotional burn out and avoid negative feelings from violating feeling rules. Most often, the women prioritize others' feelings over their own. Failing to do so may be seen as an "act of political warfare" (Lorde, 1988) against our gender system by violating gendered norms of appearance and gendered emotion work expectations. In this way, a woman's choice to display her bald head is a radical act because it releases her from the burden of worrying about the emotional well-being of others and instead allows her to focus on that of her own. Existing scholarship provides evidence of the consequences of emotion work, including emotional exhaustion, disconnection from one's own emotions, and emotional burnout (Wharton & Erickson, 1995). Paradoxically, by attending to others' emotional well-being, women compromise their own as their attention to others' feelings prompts grief, regret, guilt, worry, and more.

Some women conform to gender scripts through their hair to pass as healthy women to avoid attention from others, while others seek to portray a consistent appearance to preserve their sense of self. Adhering to dominant gendered appearance norms enables the women to conceal their health as women's baldness is taken to be indicative of illness due to feminine body norms. These women value the benefit that adhering to gender norms provides over those privileges gained through the sick role as they engage in and, in many cases, even intensify their extensive, expensive, and exhausting hair management efforts despite their life-threatening condition. While some gender scholars argue conforming practices that appear empowering to the individual women who practice them nonetheless serve to maintain the gender system (Acker, 1990; Bordo, 1993; Kwan & Trautner, 2009; Lorber, 1994; Weitz, 2001), it would be unsound to assume that women's adherence to gender scripts is due to a lack of agency or because they are "cultural dopes" (Garfinkel, 1964). Resistance is not the singular form of agency. Rather, other feminist scholars argue that women's conformity to sexist cultural scripts can serve as sources of empowerment for individual women in some contexts, ranging from Muslim women who wear the hijab (Ahmed, 2011; Mahmood, 2001) to women in male-dominated occupations like funeral directing (Pruitt, 2018). A similar recoding of gender is evident in the present study of women with medically induced hair loss who redeployed what has been argued to be oppressive feminine bodily expectations for their own self-care in acts of empowerment.

Even the women who participated in resistance practices by not passing continued to manage their bodies in other ways. These women are resisting one part of the social order – gendered expectations of head hair that rest on assumptions of health – while accepting many others. This is highlighted by the fact that none of the women in this study, even those who predominantly engage in resistance practices, ultimately say they would ever *choose* to shave their heads. Additionally, the deployment of resistance practices depends on the temporality of a non-normative appearance. Under "normal" or healthy circumstances, these resistance practices would not be acceptable (Williams, 1998). Consequently, the women in this study maintain a gender system that presumes health by reinforcing the normativity of women's hair under healthy conditions. It is this intersection of gender and health that problematizes the assumption of a "normal" healthy body in theories of doing gender (West & Zimmerman, 1987) and, inversely, the absence of gender in theorizing performances of health (Williams, 1998).

The body elicits emotions while also being a tool for emotion work – both that conforms to and resists feeling rules. The accounts of embodied emotion work in the women's hair loss stories further problematize the mind/body dualism that continues to dominate the emotion scholarship. Other scholars (Chandler, 2012; Otis, 2012) have critiqued Hochschild's (1979) the formulation of bodily strategies of emotion work for its focus on the movements or gesturing of bodies. This study expands on such critiques by demonstrating how emotion work occurs on the surface of the body – or its esthetic – in the case of women's baldness. These findings help us to understand how doing femininity relies holistically on the three emotion work strategies to present a coherent, or seemingly genuine, presentation of self. In doing so, this study furthers our understanding of the social and personal importance of hair *loss* for women, as opposed to the more studied symbolism of the variations in hair. The women who resist normatively feminine hair practices report receiving positive responses from other current and former patients, suggesting that their hair loss management practices may help to normalize women's baldness, thereby minimizing stigma and relieving significant emotional distress for women experiencing hair loss during cancer treatment. Normalizing diverse hair styles, including baldness, for women would relieve significant emotional distress for women when losing their hair from cancer treatment.

This study demonstrates that doing gender and doing health are interdependent for women; the successful appearance of health requires successfully doing femininity, and doing femininity is predicated on an appearance of health. Since beauty norms vary by ethnicity and socioeconomic status (Black, 2004), women with different intersecting identities may experience and respond to hair loss differently. Thus, a more intersectional approach in theorizing the performance of health (Williams, 1998) is needed. While this study permits insight into white and middle- to upper-class experiences of chemotherapy-induced hair loss, further research is needed to investigate how this varies across other intersecting identities since ideals of color, length, style, and gender-distinction vary by age, geographical location, class, religion, race, ethnicity, and occupation (Bellinger, 2007; Craig, 2002; Dash, 2006; Delaney, 1994; Gimlin, 1996; Rooks, 1996; Scott, 2007; Synnott, 1987; Weitz, 2001, 2004). Finally, health status may also be an important variable in women's emotion management of hair loss since the women in this study often referenced the temporality of their baldness as important to their cognitive strategies. Permanently bald women, like those with autoimmune-related cases of alopecia, may, therefore, experience hair loss and baldness differently.

NOTES

1. This is the most privileged group of women in the context of hair loss because they have the resources to access products and services that enable them to manage their hair loss – such as wig stores, race appropriate makeup, and social services. Moreover, they have white privilege since qualities defining what is "good hair" and generally conventionally attractive align with those characteristics most typically describing Anglo hair (Bellinger, 2007; Robinson, 2011).

2. Such practices include, among others, striving for thinness despite negative consequences (e.g., Bordo, 1993; Fraser, 1997), cosmetic surgery (e.g., Davis, 1995; Fraser,

2003; Sullivan, 2001), daily applications of makeup (e.g., Dellinger & Williams, 1997), the removal of body hair (e.g., Fahs, 2011; Toerien et al., 2005), and the styling of head hair (e.g., McAlexander & Schouten, 1989; Mercer, 1994; Weitz, 2001, 2004).

3. This is according to specifically white beauty culture. It is important to note that scarfs are normative in other beauty cultures (Bellinger, 2007) and would not necessarily bring suspicion of a woman's health status.

ACKNOWLEDGMENT

The author thanks Dr. Sanyu Mojola (Princeton University) for feedback on this manuscript and mentorship.

REFERENCES

Acker, J. (1990). Hierarchies, jobs, bodies: A theory of gendered organizations. *Gender & Society*, *4*(2), 139–158.

Ahmed, L. (2011). *A quiet revolution: The veil's resurgence, from the Middle East to America*. Yale University Press.

Ashing-Giwa, K. T., Padilla, G., Tejero, J., Kraemer, J., Wright, K., Coscarelli, A., Clayton, S., Williams, I., & Hills, D. (2004). Understanding the breast cancer experience of women: A qualitative study of African American, Asian American, Latina and Caucasian cancer survivors. *Psycho-Oncology*, *13*(6), 408–428.

Barber, K. (2008). The well-coiffed man: Class, race, and heterosexual masculinity in the hair salon. *Gender & Society*, *22*(4), 455–476.

Bartky, S. L. (1988). Foucault, femininity, and the modernization of patriarchal power. In R. Weitz (Ed.), *The politics of women's bodies: Sexuality, appearance and behavior* (pp. 25–45). Oxford University Press.

Bellinger, W. (2007). Why African American women try to obtain "good hair." *Sociological Viewpoints*, *23*, 63–72.

Black, P. (2004). *The beauty industry: Gender, culture, pleasure*. Rutledge.

Bordo, S. (1993). *Unbearable weight: Feminism, Western culture, and the body*. University of California Press.

Boyle, L. (2005). Flexing the tensions of female muscularity: How female bodybuilders negotiate normative femininity in competitive bodybuilding. *Women's Studies Quarterly*, *33*(1/2), 134–149.

Breed, W., van den Hurk, C., & Peerbooms, M. (2011). Presentation, impact and prevention of chemotherapy-induced hair loss. *Expert Reviews Dermatology*, *6*(1), 109–125.

Burkitt, I. (2002). Complex emotions: Relations, feelings, and images in emotional experience. *The Sociological Review*, *50*(2_suppl), 151–167.

Cahill, S. E., & Eggleston, R. (1994). Managing emotions in public: The case of wheelchair users. *Social Psychology Quarterly*, *57*(4), 300–312.

Cash, T. F. (2001). The psychology of hair loss and its implications for patient care. *Clinics in Dermatology*, *19*(2), 161–166.

Chandler, A. (2012). Self-injury as embodied emotion work: Managing rationality, emotions, and bodies. *Sociology*, *46*(3), 442–457.

Charmaz, K. (2003). Grounded theory. In J. A. Smith (Ed.), *Qualitative psychology: A practical guide to research methods* (pp. 81–110). Sage Publications, Inc.

Coates, A., Abraham, S., Kaye, S. B., Sowerbutts, T., Frewin, C., Fox, R. M., & Tattersall, M. H. (1983). On the receiving end – Patient perception of the side-effects of cancer chemotherapy. *European Journal of Cancer & Clinical Oncology*, *19*(2), 203–208.

Corbin, J., & Strauss, A. (1990). Grounded theory research: Procedures, canons, and evaluative criteria. *Qualitative Sociology*, *13*(1), 4–21.

Craig, M. (2002). *Ain't I a beauty queen?: Black women, beauty, and the politics of race*. Oxford University Press.
Dash, P. (2006). Black hair culture, politics and change. *International Journal of Inclusive Education*, *10*(1), 27–37.
Davis, K. (1995). *Reshaping the female body: The dilemma of cosmetic surgery*. Routledge.
Delaney, C. (1994). Untangling the meanings of hair in Turkish society. *Anthropological Quarterly*, *67*, 159–172.
Dellinger, K., & Williams, C. L. (1997). Makeup at work: Negotiating appearance rules in the workplace. *Gender & Society*, *11*(2), 151–177.
DeVault, M. (1999). Comfort and struggle: Emotion work in family life. *The Annals of the American Academy of Political and Social Science*, *561*, 52–63.
Fahs, B. (2011). Dreaded "otherness": Heteronormative patrolling in women's body hair rebellions. *Gender & Society*, *25*(4), 451–472.
Fraser, L. (1997). *Losing it: America's obsession with weight and the industry that feeds on it*. Dutton.
Fraser, S. (2003). *Cosmetic surgery, gender and culture*. Palgrave MacMillon.
Garfinkel, H. (1964). Studies of the routine grounds of everyday activities. *Social Problems*, *11*(3), 225–250.
Gimlin, D. (1996). Pamela's place: Power and negotiation in the hair salon. *Gender and Society*, *10*(5), 505–526.
Gimlin, D. (2007). What is 'body work'? A review of the literature. *Sociology Compass*, *1*(1), 353–370.
Goffman, E. (1963). *Stigma: Notes on the management of spoiled identity*. Simon and Schuster, Inc.
Grand View Research. (2022). *Hair and scalp care market size report, 2021-2028*. https://www.grandviewresearch.com/industry-analysis/hair-care-market#
Hammer, G. (2012). Blind women's appearance management: Negotiating normalcy between discipline and pleasure. *Gender & Society*, *26*(3), 406–432.
Hansen, H. P. (2007). Hair loss induced by chemotherapy: An anthropological study of women, cancer, and rehabilitation. *Anthropology & Medicine*, *14*(1), 15–26.
Hilton, S., Hunt, K., Emslie, C., Salinas, M., & Ziebland, S. (2008). Have men been overlooked? A comparison of young men and women's experiences of chemotherapy-induced alopecia. *Psychooncology*, *17*(6), 577–583.
Hochschild, A. R. (1979). Emotion work, feeling rules, and social structure. *American Journal of Sociology*, *85*(3), 551–575.
Hochschild, A. R. (1983). *The managed heart*. University of California Press.
Illouz, E. (2007). *Cold intimacies: The making of emotional capitalism*. Polity Press.
Kagawa-Singer, M., Wellisch, D. K., & Durvasula, R. (1997). Impact of breast cancer on Asian American and Anglo American women. *Culture, Medicine and Psychiatry*, *21*, 449–480.
Kang, M. (2010). *The managed hand: Race, gender and the body in beauty service work*. University of California Press.
Kendrick, K. (2008). 'Normalizing' female cancer patients: *Look good, feel better* and other image programs. *Disability & Society*, *23*(3), 259–269.
Kwan, S., & Trautner, M. N. (2009). Beauty work: Individual and institutional rewards, the reproduction of gender, and questions of Agency. *Sociology Compass*, *3*, 49–71.
Kyle, D. J., & Mahler, H. I. M. (1996). The effects of hair color and cosmetic use on perceptions of a female's ability. *Psychology of Women Quarterly*, *20*(3), 447–455.
Lofland, J., Snow, D., Snow, L., & Lofland, L.H. (2006). *Analyzing social settings: A guide to qualitative observation and analysis*. Wadsworth.
Lorber, J. (1993). Believing is seeing: Biology as ideology. *Gender & Society*, *7*(4), 568–581.
Lorber, J. (1994). Night to his day: The social construction of gender. In J. Lorber (Ed.), *Paradoxes of gender* (pp. 13–36). Yale University Press.
Lorde, A. (1988). *A burst of light: Essays*. Firebrand Books.
Lyon, M. L., & Barbalet, J. M. (1994). Society's body: Emotion and the 'somatization' of social theory. In T. J. Csordas (Ed.), *Embodiment and experience: The existential ground of culture and self* (pp. 48–66). Cambridge University Press.
Lyons, A. C. (2009). Masculinities, femininities, behaviour and health. *Social and Personality Psychology Compass*, *3*(4), 394–412.

Mahmood, S. (2001). Feminist theory, embodiment, and the docile agent: Some reflections on the Egyptian Islamic revival. *Cultural Anthropology, 16*(2), 202–236.
McAlexander, J. H., & Schouten, J. (1989). Hair style changes as transition markers. *Sociology and Social Research, 74*(1), 58–62.
Mercer, K. (1994). *Welcome to the jungle: New positions in Black cultural studies*. Routledge.
Münstedt, K., Manthey, N., Sachsse, S., & Vahrson, H. (1997). Changes in self-concept and body image during alopecia induced cancer chemotherapy. *Supportive Care in Cancer, 5*(2), 139–143.
Otis, E. (2012). *Markets and bodies: Women, service work, and the making of inequality in China*. Stanford University Press.
Peake, S., Manderson, L., & Potts, H. (1999). 'Part and parcel of being a woman': Female urinary incontinence and constructions of control. *Medical Anthropology Quarterly, 13*(3), 267–285.
Pruitt, A.-S. (2018). Redoing gender: How women in the funeral industry use essentialism for equality. *Gender, Work & Organization, 25*(2), 144–158.
Robinson, C. L. (2011). Hair as race: Why 'good hair' may be bad for Black females. *Howard Journal of Communications, 22*(11), 358–376.
Rooks, N. M. (1996). *Hair raising: Beauty, culture, and African American women*. Rutgers University Press.
Rosman, S. (2004). Cancer and stigma: Experience of patients with chemotherapy-induced alopecia. *Patient Education and Counseling, 52*(3), 333–339.
Scott, J. (2007). *The politics of the veil*. Princeton University Press.
Sedgwick, E. K. (1993). *Tendencies*. Duke University Press.
Silva, J. M. (2008). A new generation of women? How female ROTC cadets negotiate the tension between masculine military culture and traditional femininity. *Social Forces, 87*(2), 937–960.
Sulik, G. A. (2007). The balancing act: Care work for the self and coping with breast cancer. *Gender & Society, 21*(6), 857–877.
Sullivan, D. (2001). *Cosmetic surgery: The cutting edge of commercial medicine in America*. Rutgers University Press.
Synnott, A. (1987). Shame and glory: A sociology of hair. *The British Journal of Sociology, 38*(3), 381–413.
Toerien, M., & Wilkinson, S. (2003). Gender and body hair: Constructing the feminine woman. *Women's Studies International Forum, 26*(4), 333–344.
Toerien, M., Wilkinson, S., & Choi, P. Y. L. (2005). Body hair removal: The 'mundane' production of normative femininity. *Sex Roles, 52*, 399–406.
Vervenioti, T. (2000). Left-wing women between politics and family. In M. Mazower (Ed.), *After the war was over: Reconstructing the family, nation, and state in Greece, 1943–1960* (pp. 105–121). Princeton University Press.
Virgili, F. (2002). *Shorn women: Gender and punishment in liberation France* (J. Flower, Trans). Bloomsbury Publishing.
Weitz, R. (2001). Women and their hair: Seeking power through resistance and accommodation. *Gender & Society, 15*(5), 667–686.
Weitz, R. (2004). *Rapunzel's daughters: What women's hair tells us about women's lives*. Farrar, Straus, and Giroux.
West, C., & Zimmerman, D. H. (1987). Doing gender. *Gender & Society, 1*(2), 125–151.
Wharton, A. S., & Erickson, R. J. (1995). The consequences of caring: Exploring the links between women's job and family emotion work. *The Sociological Quarterly, 36*(2), 273–296.
Williams, S. J. (1998). Health as moral performance: Ritual, transgression and taboo. *Health, 2*(4), 435–457.
Wolkowitz, C. (2002). The social relations of body work. *Work, Employment and Society, 16*(3), 497–510.
Wolkowitz, C. (2006). *Bodies at work*. Sage Publications.
Yoo, G. J., Aviv, C., Levine, E. G., Ewing, C., & Au, A. (2010). Emotion work: Disclosing cancer. *Supportive Care in Cancer, 18*, 205–215.

CHAPTER 4

"HOW DO THEY REALLY SEE ME?": THE SEXUAL POLITICS OF MULTIRACIAL DESIRABILITY

Julia Chin

Independent Scholar, USA

ABSTRACT

How do participants navigate the sexual politics of multiracial dating and how does this relate to belonging? The results of this study illustrate that the 21 participants interviewed faced internal and external struggles and triumphs due to their mixed-race identity. For participants, trying to situate themselves into just one racial identity when they straddled both became a point of contention with romantic partners and themselves. Moreover, participants struggled with feeling like they were "enough" and if they belonged. Furthermore, mixed-race women and non-binary people were forced to navigate the racial expectations of others as well as the fetishization of their mixed-race identity. In turn, this impacted confidence levels, self-esteem, and sense of belonging and authenticity. The findings contribute to research on desirability and critical mixed-race studies by examining how mixed-race women and non-binary people perceive their own desirability.

Keywords: Mixed race; gender; desirability; dating; self-esteem; stereotyping

---

They want, like, the exoticism of being Asian, but they also want it to be tempered by whiteness. So, like, you know, you're kind of stuck in the middle (…). I still have white features, but at the end of the day, I'm also Asian. So it's like, how do they see me? Like, do they see me as a, like, more interesting white person?

Kayla illustrates how mixed-race people, in this case, white and Asian, straddle two racial identities and the challenges being in this *middle* state causes. Previous research suggests that multiracial individuals are already viewed as very desirable romantic and sexual partners (Curington et al., 2015; Sims, 2012). Previous research has not sufficiently explored how multiracial people perceive their own desirability. Desirability has traditionally been studied through a lens of dating, romance, "hookup culture," long-term relationships, and marriage (Chou, 2012; Demarest & Allen, 2000; Hill Collins, 2004; Jones, 2020; Wiederman & Hurst, 1997). The mixed-race population in the United States is growing three times as fast as the total US population (Parker et al., 2015). In 2013, 9 million Americans chose two or more races when asked to describe their race. As this booming generation of multiracial young adults grows up, their experience with identity formation and self-esteem are essential voices to honor in research. Their experience adds to flourishing and expansive literature on multiracial people and desirability in dating, sex, and love. This study addresses this gap in how mixed-race women and non-binary people interpret their own desirability. It also seeks to address how mixed-race women and non-binary people navigate belonging and self-esteem in response to having multiple racial identities.

These findings from this study provide a crucial expansion and new take on dating, self-esteem, and marginalization. The sample offers a new lens to Storrs (1999) previous research on multiracial women distancing themselves from a white identity and illustrates how instead participants embraced a multiracial identity. The analysis confirms the previous work of Ivory Roberts-Clarke et al. (2004) and Jennifer Sims (2012) that multiracial people are viewed as more attractive than monoracial individuals. The findings also offer an alternative take on Leigh Wilton et al. (2013) work on marginalization and belonging by showing how mixed-race people fit into group membership and identities. The analysis also adds to the work of Saskia Forster et al. (2019) and Alicia Cast and Peter Burke (2002) on self-esteem.

This chapter proceeds as follows. I detail the relevant literature using a framework of sexual politics, multiraciality, and "enoughness." I walk through the key data and methods of 21 interviews with multiracial women and non-binary people, including my "ideal case" approach. I analyze my data, focusing on how sexual politics shapes the mixed-race experience. I explain how the significance of "enoughness" in the sexual politics of multiracial dating has for the fields of multiraciality and desirability in sociology.

LITERATURE REVIEW

Multiracial Studies in the US Context

The concept of mixed-race identity in the United States is based on the strict Black–white color line historically enforced, including the one-drop rule that considers even a small amount of non-white heritage to make an individual non-white (Omi & Winant, 2014). However, not all countries view race as a dichotomy, as seen in Brazil where mixed-race identities are viewed as more fluid and may even have their own names like "mulatto" (Winant, 2001). This is explored in Howard Winant's (2001) "The World is a Ghetto," which compares post-World War II racial dynamics in four different countries. The rise of critical mixed-race studies in the United States can be traced back to the growing public awareness of mixed-race identity, which was fueled by the increase in interracial relationships in the 1970s and beyond. This movement peaked in the late 1990s, particularly around the 2000 census, and challenged racial and ethnic studies to consider the fluidity of race in a new way (Curington, 2016; Daniel et al., 2014; Lundquist & Lin, 2015; Rockquemore et al., 2009; Sims, 2012; Storrs, 1999). Today's research on critical mixed-race studies is a result of the formation of a more defined field of study in the early 2000s (Daniel et al., 2014).

Sexual Politics Shapes Desirability

Scholarship on gender and race in sexual politics explores how gender, race, and sexuality shape treatment and perceptions of individuals. Patricia Hill Collins (2004) explains how these factors contribute to the reproduction or reinforcement of racial hierarchies and oppressions in African American communities. Rosalind Chou (2012) extends this analysis to include Asian Americans and acknowledges historical contexts that produce different renditions of controlling images of sexualization and femininity such as the role of orientalism in exoticizing Eastern culture. Gloria González-López and Salvador Vidal-Ortiz (2008) examine the connection between sexuality and Latinx individuals, exploring how sexual politics affect their everyday lives and relationships.

How Sexual Politics Shapes Gender, Sexuality, and Multiraciality

The existing literature implies that a more intersectional perspective is required to investigate interracial relationships involving multiracial individuals, particularly concerning sexuality and gender. Jennifer Lundquist and Ken-Hou Lin (2015) have found that men of color are avoided by white gay and straight daters, while women of color are viewed as more desirable. Shantel Buggs (2020) studied how transgender, immigrant multiracial individuals may have to sacrifice aspects of their identity to be seen as desirable partners. Lawrence Stacey and TehQuin Forbes (2022) found racial fetishization on gay dating apps can lead to objectification, stereotyping, and hindered interpersonal relations for men of color.

How Sexual Politics Shapes Interracial Relationships of Multiracial People

Studies show how multiracial daters desire other partners, with some preferring their multiracial counterparts and others preferring monoracial identities (Bonam & Shih, 2009; Curington et al., 2020; McGrath et al., 2016). Multiracial individuals are generally more comfortable in interracial relationships than monoracial white individuals, with the biggest comfortability gap in marriage rates. However, the way multiracial daters still internalize and reproduce dominant racial hierarchies can lead to Black monoracial daters being viewed as least desirable (Bonam & Shih, 2009). Jennifer Sims (2012) examined the "biracial beauty stereotype," which views mixed-race people as more attractive, and how some multiracial people with white identities are viewed as more attractive than others.

How the Sexual Politics of Multiracial People's Desirability Shapes "Enoughness"

Self-esteem
Researchers have studied the impact of self-esteem on resilience and self-concept, drawing on Erving Goffman's theory (1959) of social life which involves a front stage and backstage. Goffman's theory, as well as studies by Michael Hughes and David Demo (1989) and Charles Jaret et al. (2005), helps explain how people of color and mixed-race individuals view themselves and their identities. Saskia Forster et al. (2019) conducted a study on how females perceive themselves and how they believe others view them, finding that both self-appraisals and interpretations of how others view them affect their self-concept. Studies have explored mixed-race desirability and self-esteem, including Ivory Roberts-Clarke et al. (2004), who found that multiracial women were open to partners of other races. Vanessa Bing (2004) and Monica Ghabrial (2019) examined how queer women and gender diverse people of color or multiracial identity perceive others' desirability toward themselves and how this affects their mental health and self-esteem. However, a wider range of mixed races, sexuality, and gender needs to be examined.

Marginalization
Self-esteem is tied to how mixed-race people experience marginalization, and building positive self-esteem can protect against negative social invalidation or marginalization. When individuals cannot verify their identities, their self-esteem declines (Cast & Burke, 2002; Eccleston & Major, 2006). France Winddance Twine (1996) illustrated how mixed-African descent women become socially constructed as white or white-identifying in an effort to decrease marginalization with their largely white community. Stigma consciousness is the constant awareness of the microaggressions and oppression faced by marginalized communities (Kellogg & Liddell, 2012; Wilton et al., 2013). Leigh Wilton et al. (2013) found that biracial individuals feel a greater sense of belonging around other marginalized racial communities. In contrast to the sample of the present study, Kevin Binning et al. (2009) found that multiracial individuals who identify with only one racial group have a worse sense of belonging, psychological well-being, and social engagement compared to those who identify with multiple racial groups. Angela Kellogg and Deborah Liddell (2012) found college-aged mixed-race individuals seek solace and belonging among other mixed-race people (Kellogg & Liddell, 2012).

The literature on multiracial identities, desirability, and dating often overlooks the experiences of non-binary and queer women with multiple marginalized identities. Monica Ghabrial (2019) discusses how bisexual women and gender-diverse people of color with multiple minority identities may feel pressure to "pass" as one identity, leading to conflicts and stress related to their racial identities and sexualities. This can be compared to the complicated feelings of light-skinned individuals passing as white and mixed-race individuals who may also be able to pass as white.

Present Study's Contributions
What these scholars miss, however, is an intersectional lens into critical mixed-race studies that spans race, sexuality, and gender. In the same way, it may be impossible for mixed-race people to choose a singular racial identity, and it is imprudent to just study how a mixed-race identity affects desirability without considering gender and sexual orientation. Gaps in results between mixed race, gender, and sexuality identities cause further identity erasure and marginalization; in turn, this gap impacts identity formation and self-esteem. Multiracial people who identify with different genders and sexualities may experience desirability in different ways. The literature observes how other people desire multiracial people compared to how multiracial people perceive their own desirability; even so, examining how multiple identities, such as gender, race, and sexuality, operate within the sexual politics of dating for multiracial people remains missing.

DATA AND METHODS

From January to April 2021, I examined how multiraciality, sexuality, and gender impact self-perceived desirability among women and non-binary individuals of three multiracial combinations (Black/white, Asian/white, and Latinx/white) at a Southern California public university. Recruitment efforts targeted departments and organizations that interact with multiracial and/or LGBTQ+ students. Participants were selected based on their self-identification as multiracial or biracial women and non-binary individuals. By holding white racial identity constant, I aimed to uncover how multiracial individuals in this sample experience whiteness. The goal was to recruit equal and/or representative numbers of cis, trans, and gender non-binary/non-conforming individuals and straight and queer participants. Queer includes a range of sexualities including lesbian, gay, bisexual, pansexual, two-spirit, asexual, and aromantic sexual orientation identities. I conducted interviews with participants who responded to my outreach until I could no longer proceed. I conducted 21 interviews, consisting of 4 white/Black, 8 white/Asian, and 9 white/Latinx or Chicanx-identified participants. Eighteen participants were women and three participants were non-binary or agender. Thirteen people were straight/heterosexual, three people were bisexual, two were pansexual, one person was demisexual, one person was asexual, and one person was queer. Twelve were pursuing social science degrees, four were humanities majors, and four were STEM majors.

Main topics of discussion in the interview centered around when participants were first aware of their intersecting and sometimes conflicting identities such as race, gender, and sexuality.[1] This section included more questions about their multiracial identities and identity formation. Another major set of question covered how they viewed their own desirability and if their experiences with dating, sex, and love were grounded in it or juxtaposed to it. The last part of the interview was structured around how their views on their own desirability affected their self-esteem and overall confidence. The semi-structured interviews were conducted over Zoom and all interviewees were given pseudonyms. The transcripts were transcribed using Otter.ai software and manually reviewed before being uploaded into ATLAS.ti coding software to identify common themes from this sample such as marginalization, first dates, body image, and insecurity. The participants in this sample explicitly mentioned feeling "exoticized" or "fetishized" rather than implicitly showing this through their dating experiences.

ANALYSIS

The 21 participants interviewed faced internal and external struggles and triumphs due to their mixed-race identity. For participants, trying to situate themselves into just one racial identity when they straddled both became a point of contention with romantic partners and themselves. Participants struggled with feeling like they were "enough" and if they belonged. From first dates to long-term partnership, mixed-race people received many messages about marginalization that affected belonging.

Navigating Racialized Expectations from Others

Many participants described experiences where strangers, dates, partners, parents, and friends placed their racialized expectations upon them. These encounters created conflict for them, as they grappled with fitting into these predetermined racial norms. This section of analysis is distinct from the fetishization theme, as it explores broader experiences of race, such as the pressure to conform to racial expectations or being told that they are not "enough" of a particular race due to their mixed identity.

> So, like, you know, being Asian makes me more interesting, but at the end of the day, I look like you know, their Eurocentric standards of beauty.... And I think like, a lot of the time, like, when people compliment me or when they, you know, say anything about my facial features, they only really comment on like, the Eurocentric, like the white features.

Kayla provides a nuanced understanding of "interesting" by breaking down that although she may be viewed as unique due to her Asian identity, it is only her white features that people find desirable enough to compliment her on. Specifically, referring to eye and nose shape was a common theme throughout interviews with white and Asian mixed individuals. By complimenting the Eurocentric beauty ideals in mixed white and Asian participants, this reveals the way that, although having an identity of color makes a person more captivating, it is still their whiteness that gives them value as objects of desire. Ivory Roberts-Clarke et al. (2004) reported that multiracial women were often perceived to hold a white identity and that their Eurocentric features and straight hair were viewed as "exotic or attractive" (p. 108). This perception of multiracial women as having white features may have increased their desirability. Participants from each of the three multiracial groups often brought up unique "compliments" or comments they received about how desirable different aspects of their physical appearance were. W. E. B. Du Bois's (2018 [1902]) essay on double consciousness from "The Souls of Black Folk" contributes a nuanced understanding to self-conceptualization by examining how, at all times, one is viewing themselves through the lens of how others view them.

Black and white mixed women and non-binary people, like Naomi, often brought up their type of curly hair or less textured hair.

> I feel like multiracial people who have kind of curly hair like mine, where it's not necessarily, like super tight curls ... like this is my natural hair, but it's not natural hair in terms of what people think of when it comes to like Black natural hair ... I feel like multiracial people in the media, like their natural hair is more embraced. And it's kind of like, they're considered lucky for having this type of hair. And like, having white people as well, like always wanting curls, like the kind multiracial people have.

Naomi illustrates this idea of enoughness because her hair is more represented in the media as attractive hair versus other portrayals of Black natural hair. By saying that her hair does not conform to Black natural hair, it actually conforms more to these mixed-race beauty standards, which is more embraced by white people. It is this tension between not feeling Black enough and also accepting that Naomi's hair is more acceptable to white people as a result. All of the Black and white mixed people I interviewed brought up their hair in some capacity which aligns with multiple studies such as Ginetta E. B. Candelario (2007) and Ingrid Banks (2000) who suggest that hair is a prominent hallmark of desirability for Black and Latina women. Based on these findings, it appears not only that "good" hair is one of the most desirable traits a woman can have but also that a certain type of hair is the racialized expectation from Black and white mixed women and non-binary people.

For many Latinx and white women and non-binary people, body type also had racially coded expectations. For Leah, a white and Latinx woman, friends and her mother both affected her desirability about her body through comments such as this one:

> Growing up she called me skinny. A lot. But said it in Spanish as if to say like, I lack Latina curves, at least that's the way I interpreted it. I've been told that by my Latino friends growing up too.

It is interesting how Leah's friends and mom are communicating that there is only one right way to be Latina, as if being Latina is a monolith. Transitioning from discussing perceptions of beauty to perceptions of personality traits, Leah had one last thought she wanted to say about her mixed-race identity and desirability.

> I feel like there's this perception of the fiery Latina that I guess has made me hold back from getting angry because I don't want to. I don't want to fulfill the stereotype, or even fiery as in like kinkier which I've found to be offensive.

Leah clearly had struggled with self-worth surrounding her desirability as she was not seen as being able to live up to these expectations. She struggles with the stereotypes of being a "fiery Latina"' and the expectations from dates that she does not fulfill. This can change how young women of color see themselves as explained by Julie Bettie (2000), Rosalie Rolón-Dow (2004), and Lorena Garcia and Lourdes Torres (2009).

Participants detailed numerous experiences where they were told by others how they did or did not meet racialized expectations of being mixed. For some, their physical appearance was seen as more interesting due to their mixed-race heritage, but still close enough to whiteness that they fulfilled European beauty standards. For others, many had to negotiate not being "enough" of a racial stereotype, such as not fulfilling the racialized trope of a "fiery Latina."

Experiencing Fetishization Based on Racial Stereotypes

The overwhelming majority of participants had received comments from dating apps, first dates, partners, and even friends that fetishized their mixed-race identities. I distinguish this from the previous section "racial expectations" due to the overt sexualization of mixed-race people in each scenario presented. Family and friends served as moderating factors in how these exotifying comments affect self-esteem as well. Lauren, a white and Asian woman, relayed her dismay to the attention or strange compliments centered around her multiracial identity saying:

> In those times, it's been a little uncomfortable. Because it felt like they're stereotyping what it means to be mixed. They're like, "Oh, this means you're, you're exotic," or you're, I don't know, you can do things differently.

All things considered, participants reported fetishization on first dates at higher frequencies than in long-term relationships. The majority of participants reported feeling fetishized or exoticized due to their mixed-race identities; however, all eight mixed-race Asian and white participants specifically mentioned being perceived as more "exotic" due to their race. Rosalind Chou (2012) posits that orientalism "serves to 'exoticize' what is seen as Eastern culture in a patronizing way" (p. 11). Marissa, a white and Asian woman, most succinctly describes her dating experience on Tinder saying:

> There definitely are guys that have the whole Asian fetish and explicitly ask, like, "oh, are you half Asian, half white? Like, I love wasians." And I'm like, okay, like, that's a little like, you don't need to tell me that.

By essentializing Marissa due to her race, this potential date evoked the stereotype and fetishization of Asian women due to being objectified as sexually submissive while still being viewed as desirable due to their whiteness. Rosalind Chou (2012) documents the societal construction of Asian American women as hypersexual docile bodies ready for conquest, which is an idea that helps explain Marissa's experience. The narrative gets more extreme as she recounts another person asking which parent was the Asian one replying to him "I was like, my mom, and he was like, I bet your mom's a MILF,'" which is an acronym for slang used to describe a physically attractive mother that has a sexual connotation. Not only does Marissa experience the marginalization of being desired as a sexual object, but also her mother's desirability is being exoticized as well. It is a catch-22 where mixed-race people are not seen as enough to fit into the mold but also fetishized for this difference.

Proximate to Lauren's experience on dating apps, Madison, a white and Asian bisexual woman, shared the sexualization she experienced both as a multiracial person *and* queer person. Madison again illustrates how even though there is pressure to exist in specific boxes rather than in-between, women face fetishization for not fitting into racial, gendered, or sexual orientation binaries.

> At the same time it, [mixed race identity], kind of shared like similar problems of people like sexualizing my bisexuality ... There was a while where I kind of like stopped telling my guy friends that I'm bisexual because I was like, I don't need more people like sexualizing who I am.

Madison illustrates the exotification experienced as the result of her two marginalized identities even from friends. Madison not only indicated her frustration with this but also appeared frustrated at the practice of hiding her sexuality. The price that many queer mixed-race people all paid for being open about their identities was potential rejection or even fetishization from friends, family, and dates as illustrated by studies of Vanessa Bing (2004) and Monica Ghabrial (2019).

The data from this sample clearly show that mixed-race people experienced fetishization or exotification on the basis of their race, often exacerbated by a queer sexuality, and participants were very conscious of this. The majority of participants all mentioned this and all eight Asian/white mixed-race participants mentioned this as well. Instances of participants receiving fetishizing comments via dating apps were common, but also could be found even from friends, proving that no matter the proximity of relationships, being fetishized and stereotyped followed participants wherever they were.

Negotiating Confidence and Body Image

In this section, I analyze how perceptions of "enoughness" and fetishization impact self-esteem. Multiracial participants, when asked about first dates, reported the lowest levels of self-esteem compared to long-term partners. In this case, first dates are delineated as those who went on first dates with a new partner or were "asked out" in a romantic or sexual context such as over a dating app. For instance, Ariana, a white and Chicanx woman, explained how first dates were so nerve wracking for her, she often canceled:

> The confidence that I lack comes from it. It does come from being mixed. I feel like, too, they think, Oh, am I not enough? Like Mexican [enough]?

Many participants lacked confidence in how they would be perceived on a first date. Often, like Ariana, this was rooted in participants' fears that their mixed-race identity would not be enough, especially for monoracial dates who shared one of the same mixed-race identities. Concurrently, low self-esteem because of their mixed-race identity was also due to not meeting expectations of physical attractiveness, whether that be due to being not monoracial, or not living up to a perfect idea of mixed women. Charles Cooley's (1994) "Looking-Glass Self" explores that what moves the self is the perceived reaction from another individual's perception of them. Cooley states "there is no sense of 'I' without its correlative sense of you, or he, or they" (p. 255). As adults, Cooley argues that people become unable to separate what people think and how they interpret their visible reactions to this thought.

Lauren, a white and Asian woman and member of one of the multi-ethnic clubs on campus, was one of the few exceptions to people who got nervous for first dates saying if there was a disconnect, "It's not something that is necessarily wrong with either of us. It's just that we're just not clicking or something." What is key to Lauren's experience and indicative of high self-esteem is that if the date sours, this is not taken as a reflection of herself or her date. While Ariana shoulders the success of the date in terms of whether they are enough for their dates, Lauren chalks it up to poor connection. This variation between participants could be due to Lauren's security in herself and her identity as a leader in an organization for multi-ethnic students on campus. Alicia Cast and Peter Burke (2002) proposed that the act of validating one's identity generates a sense of confidence and value, resulting in an elevation of self-esteem. Lauren has this outlet to explore and come to terms with her identity alongside people who can empathize with her experience, whereas Ariana did not reveal any such connections.

When it comes to multiracial women and non-binary people perceiving their own desirability, there were more instances of positive self-esteem when discussing the context of long-term relationships than on first dates. For instance, Viviana, a white and Asian woman, noted that the compliments paid to her by her partner were not "geared towards, I guess, stereotypical features of either side" and that because they never affected her negatively, "it made me feel better about my biraciality, I guess, in a sense." What I heard from Viviana confirmed that not perceiving their own desirability in a racially stereotypical or fetishizing way boosts their self-esteem. This could potentially be explained because when participants have higher self-esteem, they can interpret others' self-appraisal more positively, but when a participant experiences low self-esteem, the inverse is true (Forster et al., 2019). As Viviana is an Asian and white woman, her partner not commenting on her Asian or white features in a "stereotypical way" could be viewed as a counter due to the fetishization that Asian women often experience (Chou, 2012; Mukkamala & Suyemoto, 2018). By not being complimented on stereotypically "Asian" or "white" features, Viviana is interpreting her multiracial identity as positive, but also separate from her desirability.

In contrast to Viviana's experiences where long-term partners positively impacted self-esteem, sometimes, the inverse was true. When Ally's partner mentioned that he had "only ever dated white blonde girls … that obviously kind of caused some insecurities in me." Here, Ally displays diminished self-esteem as a mixed white and Chicanx person when it comes to her multiracial desirability because she does not look like this idealized white blonde. This most likely would not have been the case if Ally heard this on a first date, but because it came from an esteemed partner, their opinion cut to her insecurities more. This further explains Saskia Forster et al. (2019) point that when a woman has low self-esteem, they are more likely to appraise themselves lower based on others opinions of themselves.

Many participants reported extensively worrying about first dates, conveying a lack of confidence in how they would be perceived or whether they would meet their dates expectations. This appeared to be rooted in fears that their mixed-race identities may reflect poorly on their physical appearance; opposingly, for others who experienced higher confidence and more positive images of themselves, the success of the date or whether they were viewed as attractive was a reflection of their connection or their partner's personal preferences, not their racial identities. For some, the absence of comments linked to race could affirm the participant that they were desirable for more reasons than just racially stereotypical features. Lastly, a partner's dating history, specifically the race of their previous partners, could also diminish or boost confidence in themselves, depending on the relationship.

Cultivating Belonging and Authenticity

This section examines how mixed-race people find belonging and authenticity in their romantic and social lives. David Grazian (2018) defines authenticity as "a variety of aesthetic, moral, or cultural traits, including credibility, originality, sincerity, naturalness, genuineness, innateness, purity, or realness" (p. 191). One way participants cultivated authenticity was by embracing *all* identities they held. Sexuality cannot be understated as another unique layer that mixed-race participants were forced to navigate. Lilly, a white and Chicanx person who uses she and they pronouns, best explains the challenges of being mixed-race and pansexual as "I've sort of felt really divided down the middle with like, pretty much everything." By being fully open in one identity, Lilly may lose another.

> Um, and, like, you know, obviously, like my being biracial as well ... that has sort of caused like, a separation because I feel like if I come out, I'm going to lose my Latino side.

Lilly is an example of how being mixed race and queer can cause more marginalization when one side of the family is culturally and religiously conservative. For the queer and non-binary participants interviewed, the majority when referencing their family referenced further marginalization of the queer identity. This was on top of the marginalization of their mixed race and queer identities faced from society (Collins, 2000; Todd et al., 2016).

For others like Kennedy, a white and Asian mixed demisexual person who uses she and they pronouns, they could also relate to this divide between their mixed race and queer identities.

> Oh, no, I feel like I've always felt very invisible, I guess, as a result of being multiracial. Like, in dating, and also in general ... Especially because, like, I feel like a lot of times in queer circles, it's very, like, I've mostly interacted with white people so I'm like, do they get that I'm not one of them?. Like, how are they perceiving me in relation to their race?

While Kennedy did not mention her relationship with her family, she experienced a similar experience as Lilly, where in seeking to embrace one queer identity, they felt like their Asian mixed-race identity was rendered invisible. This is consistent with Shantel Buggs (2020) research on how individuals who are transgender, multiracial immigrants may need to compromise certain aspects of their identity to be perceived as attractive to potential partners. Kennedy tried to counter this by engaging in online dating spaces, but they still were worried about how they were being perceived. Queer and multiracial people potentially have multiple sites of marginalization. Therefore, they are forced to seek belonging in multiple ways, with sometimes contradictory processes like Kennedy and Lilly.

Alex, a white and Black non-binary person who uses all pronouns, explains a lack of authenticity and belonging in dating due to feeling the obligation to code switch between racial identities to fit in, depending on the date's race.

> I am not able to really show my true, authentic self, and if I'm always putting up somewhat of a front, like, even if I am showing a bit of my identity, like I'm not showing what is me as this mixed individual, but instead, what is me as if Alex was a white person, or as if Alex was a Black person?

Alex explains marginalization, regardless of the date's race, due to being a multiracial person and unable to be real and authentic as a result. Race is a core element of Alex's personality, but what is abundantly clear, due to Alex's experience, is that the lack of belonging experienced as a multiracial person is more salient than being Black or white. This is consistent with previous research on theories of group membership and marginalization (Cast & Burke, 2002; Eccleston & Major, 2006; Wilton et al., 2013). Mixed-race non-binary people and women experienced marginalization universally. Sometimes, this was due to their multiracial identity being fetishized by dates or seen as less desirable or also feeling like they are forced to live less authentically due to their multiracial identity.

As exposed by the previous narratives shared, variation in belonging and authenticity occurs across gender, sexuality, mixed races, and even within groups. Parents and friends served as key guides for building, or not building, a sense of belonging. Moreover, Leah explains how not only a lack of conversations about her mixed-race identity but even a lack of acknowledgment to others about her mixed-race status from her mom makes her feel untethered to either side.

> My mom will acknowledge with me that I'm Latina ... I haven't heard her, say to her friends when she's talking about me that I am Latina ... I've questioned whether she does see me as Latina ... (pause). Yeah, I just, I feel like I don't really have that connection with that side of me. Or my white side, either, for that matter. It's kind of in-limbo.

By briefly acknowledging to Leah that she is also Latina but leaving out that same detail to her friends, Leah's mom is sending her contradictory signals about the openness she should have in her racial identity. The implication of hiding, or conveniently not mentioning, Leah's mixed race, is that she is treating her daughter's race like it does not belong outside the home or in certain environments. Yet, at the same time, she was the one who said, in Spanish, that she lacked "Latina curves." France Winddance Twine's (1996) study provides another instance of how the desirability and self-esteem of multiracial women were monitored. Twine's research highlighted how mixed-race African women expressed feelings of being excluded when their white mothers were hurt and felt rejected by them if they pursued a romantic relationship with someone who identified as Black. Society displays unease toward mixed-race individuals who do not conform to a particular racial category, yet they are also stigmatized, sometimes by their own mothers, for failing to do so. That leaves mixed people to feel like the only place they belong is "in-limbo."

Despite the external challenges resulting from larger social networks in a stable, long-term partnership, Leah and others also acknowledge the sense of belonging felt from being understood as a person of color or other shared identities with their partners. When asked what her partner finds desirable about her, Leah replied:

> He loves that we can talk about being people of color. Which I love too. I think I couldn't be in a relationship without that factor. I think that's important for me to have my partner, really see who I am.

While her partner may not have been mixed race, having a shared racial identity in Leah's case magnified the feelings of belonging as people of color and Chicanx people. Alicia Cast and Peter Burke (2002) suggest that validating identities associated with a particular group, such as Chicanx, is likely to enhance self-esteem, leading to an increased sense of belonging. This is because the confirmation of group identities represents acknowledgment and endorsement of the self within that group. This common understanding binds the couple together in a deeper, more authentic way so that even a clash with her partner's parents could not shake the solid foundation their long-term relationship was built on.

While many participants were still coming to terms with their racial identity, embracing a mixed-race identity at the end of a struggle resulted in stronger feelings of belonging and self-acceptance. For Renee, a white and Chicanx mixed woman, discovering a multiracial identity, came with a sense of belonging and comfort.

> I think my multiracial identity has actually helped me feel more comfortable in my own skin. Because I was like, "What? Like, what am I?"... But after I found out, I was like, Oh my god, I love it. And I felt more beautiful.

Embracing a multiracial identity for Renee meant that the identity puzzle she was struggling with as an adolescent was finally completed and she felt more whole, beautiful, and confident than ever. This is consistent with further research on self-esteem, such as the conclusions reached by Collette Eccleston and Brenda Major (2006), which indicate that when an individual encounters discrimination against their group identity, in this instance, being multiracial, they are more likely to strengthen their sense of belonging to that group.

From early life experiences from family and friends shaping belonging, to feeling the need to code switch to navigate two racial worlds, participants are often contending with external signals about belonging. The concept of racial "enoughness" or a feeling of belonging was mentioned in some form in every interview. Internally, participants who are queer have extra or compounding experiences with their sexuality and race. Moreover, having a partner to talk about race with or embracing a mixed-race identity for the first time can be key factors in increasing the feeling of authenticity as a mixed-race person. It is clear from listening to the participants of this study that they all just wanted to find their place in the world where they felt they belonged, were accepted, and experienced love, not in spite of their identities, but because of their identities. Maybe this place was with their families, their friends, their partners, or even within themselves.

CONCLUSION

Key Findings

The major finding from this study is this idea that mixed-race women and non-binary people all experience some degree of struggle in their romantic relationships resulting from perceptions of their multiple racial identities. Upon review of these findings, this idea of racial "enoughness" or a sense of belonging was brought up in some variation in every single interview. Members of each mixed-race group (e.g., Black/white, Asian/white, and Chicanx/white) dealt with different racially coded expectations regarding physical appearance. The majority of participants, including each Asian/white participant, mentioned being mixed race in itself was considered "exotic" or fetishized by romantic interests. The experience of fetishization is compounded by the addition of queer sexuality.

Mixed-race women and non-binary individuals have unique experiences when it comes to confidence and body image. Some individuals experience intense anxiety before a first date, while others do not. This may be because they tie their physical and racialized appearance to the success of the date. Some individuals in certain relationships feel more validated and experience a boost in self-esteem from their partners, who offer compliments unrelated to race. In the absence of this support, partners can become a source of negativity, causing self-esteem to decline rapidly.

Participants negotiated what it meant to live authentic lives as mixed-race people and, if relevant, queer people. The definition of belonging can be summed up as the desire to be accepted and heard. Some individuals had distinct experiences while seeking acceptance in the dating world. Black and white participants had to engage in code-switching to present themselves in a particular racial manner that their date could identify with, thereby obscuring their multiracial identity. Participants found joy when accepting their identity or being able to talk positively with partners about race.

Contributions

Storrs (1999) suggested that mixed-race women tend to distance themselves from their white identities and lean toward non-white identities. However, this study indicates that participants did not necessarily identify with either white or non-white racial identities. Contrary to Storrs' findings, many participants in this study embraced a multiracial identity and only felt marginalized when a monoracial partner wished they were monoracial rather than multiracial. These findings are important in understanding the complexities of multiracial identity as it suggests that individuals can hold multiple identities simultaneously rather than in opposition to one another. It is possible that this cohort of younger, multiracial participants holds distinct perspectives compared to mixed-race participants in Storrs (1999) study. These results also align with previous research on self-esteem, which suggests that when an individual's group identity is discriminated against, they are more likely to strengthen their group membership identity (Eccleston & Major, 2006).

Roberts-Clarke et al. (2004) reported that multiracial women were often perceived to have a white identity and that their straight hair and Eurocentric features were viewed as "exotic or attractive" (p. 108). These findings are consistent with the results of the present study. However, this study provides a novel perspective by exploring the compliments received by individuals with different mixed-race identities. The specific compliments given often varied depending on the individual's mixed-race identity. For instance, Black and white mixed-race participants reported that their partners complimented their straighter or wavy curls, while Asian and white mixed-race individuals were frequently praised for their eye and face shape.

Participants from various mixed-race groups expressed concerns about not feeling like they belonged, which led to feelings of inadequacy and the need to code-switch. This study provides a fresh perspective on Leigh Wilton et al. (2013) findings that mixed-race individuals tend to feel more comfortable with other marginalized racial communities. Many participants in this study described feeling insecure and having to code-switch regardless of whether their romantic interests were white or from a marginalized racial group. They reported experiencing rejection or a sense of not belonging when their monoracial partners did not fully accept their mixed-race identity. Mixed-race individuals often struggled to conform to the body image and cultural expectations associated with the marginalized racial identity they identified with.

Generalizations

Although this study was conducted at a mid-size four-year university in Southern California, the findings may be relevant to individuals with multiple marginalized identities who struggle to navigate how others perceive them. This study could be replicated at similar-sized and composed universities since the campus population of mixed-race individuals was only about two percent. This topic is relevant to any company, organization, or university that values racial justice and diversity, given the subject of racial stratification and struggles. As the United States becomes increasingly racially mixed, this information is becoming more critical. While multiracials or multiracial identities cannot single-handedly solve racial inequality, various studies indicate that multiracials have a keen awareness of these inequities (Daniel, 2021). Nevertheless, the insights gained from this study suggest that mixed-race individuals will continue to experience pervasive racism, even in the context of love and relationships, for the foreseeable future.

Limitations

There are several limitations to this study that should be acknowledged. First, the study did not include interviews with men-identified participants, as the focus was on the experiences of women and non-binary individuals. Additionally, by only examining three mixed-race groups, the study may not capture the diverse perspectives of individuals with two or more identities of color. Lastly, the study recruited participants primarily from social science listservs, sociology and feminist studies, as well as student organizations composed of mixed-race individuals. Therefore, it is possible that the participants may have been more knowledgeable or comfortable discussing their mixed-race identity and desirability, potentially limiting the generalizability of the findings.

Future Findings
Future findings surrounding this topic should aim to more heavily include or solely center non-binary, queer, and trans populations about their experiences with mixed-race desirability. All genders, including men, should be studied and compared against each other to explore the maximum variation in experiences. Scholars could study a larger swatch of the general population instead of just college-aged students to widen the age and experiences discussed. All mixed-race identities can be interviewed or even surveyed about their mixed-race desirability experience. Ultimately, the breadth of critical mixed-race studies and sexuality remains incomplete without speaking to the dynamic and essential relationship between the two fields.

NOTE

1. Information regarding the recruitment email, consent form, and interview guide is available from the author upon request.

REFERENCES

Banks, I. (2000). *Hair matters: Beauty, power, and Black women's consciousness.* New York University Press.
Bettie, J. (2000). Women without class: Chicas, cholas, trash, and the presence/absence of class identity. *Signs, 26*(1), 1–35.
Bing, V. M. (2004) Out of the closet but still in hiding. *Women & Therapy, 27*(1–2), 185–201.
Binning, K. R., Unzueta, M. M., Huo, Y. J., & Molina, L. E. (2009). The interpretation of multiracial status and its relation to social engagement and psychological well-being. *Journal of Social Issues, 65*(1), 35–49.
Bonam, C., & Shih, M. (2009). Exploring multiracial individuals' comfort with intimate interracial relationships. *Journal of Social Issues, 65*(1), 87–10.
Buggs, S. (2020). (Dis)owing exotic: Navigating race, intimacy, and trans identity. *Sociological Inquiry, 90*(2), 249–270.
Candelario, G. E. B. (2007). *Black behind the ears: Dominican racial identity from museums to beauty shops.* Duke University Press.
Cast, A., & Burke, P. (2002). A theory of self-esteem. *Social Forces, 80*(3), 1041–1068.
Chou, R. (2012). *Asian American sexual politics: The construction of race, gender, and sexuality.* Rowman and Littlefield Publishers.
Collins, F. J. (2000). Biracial-bisexual individuals: Identity coming of age. *International Journal of Sexuality & Gender Studies, 5*(3), 221–253.
Cooley, C. H. (1994). Looking-glass self. In J. O'Brien (Ed.), *The production of reality: Essays and readings in social psychology* (pp. 266–268). Pine Forge Press.
Curington, C. V. (2016). Rethinking multiracial formation in the United States: Toward an intersectional approach. *Sociology of Race and Ethnicity, 2*(1), 27–41.
Curington, C. V., Lin, K., & Lundquist, J. K. (2015). Positioning multiraciality in cyberspace: Treatment of multiracial daters in an online dating website. *American Sociological Review, 80*(4), 764–788.

Curington, C. V., Lundquist, J. K., & Lin, K. (2020). Tipping the multiracial color-line: Racialized preferences of multiracial online daters. *Race Social Problems, 12*, 195–208.

Daniel, G. R. (2021). Sociology of multiracial identity in the late 1980s and early 1990s. *Journal of Ethnic and Cultural Studies, 8*(2), 106–125.

Daniel, G. R., Kina, L., Dariotis, W. M., & Fojas, C. (2014). Emerging paradigms in critical mixed race studies. *Journal of Critical Mixed Race Studies, 1*(1), 6–65.

Demarest, J., & Allen, R. (2000). Body image: Gender, ethnic and age differences. *The Journal of Social Psychology, 140*(4), 465–472.

Du Bois, W. E. B., & Alexander, S. (2018 [1902]). *The souls of black folk: Essays and sketches*. University of Massachusetts Press.

Eccleston, C., & Major, B. (2006). Attributions to discrimination and self-esteem: The role of group identification and appraisals. *Group Processes & Intergroup Relations, 9*(2), 147–162.

Forster, S., Drueke, B., Britz, S., Gauggel, S., & Mainz, V. (2019). How females think about themselves and how they assume that significant others think about them: The influence of perspective taking on self-referential processing. *PloS One, 14*(5), e0217870.

Garcia, L., & Torres, L. (2009). New directions in Latina sexualities studies. *NWSA Journal, 21*(3), 7–16.

Ghabrial, M. (2019). We can shapeshift and build bridges: Bisexual women and gender diverse people of color on invisibility and embracing the borderlands. *Journal of Bisexuality, 19*(2), 169–197.

Goffman, E. (1959). *The presentation of self in everyday life*. Bantam Doubleday Dell Publishing Group.

González-López, G., & Vidal-Ortiz, S. (2008). Latinas and Latinos, sexuality, and society: A critical sociological perspective. In H. Rodríguez, R. Sáenz, & C. Menjívar (Eds.), *Latinas/os in the United States: Changing the face of América*. Springer. https://doi.org/10.1007/978-0-387-71943-6_20

Grazian, D. (2018). *Demystifying authenticity in the sociology of culture*. Routledge.

Hill Collins, P. (2004) *Black sexual politics: African Americans, gender and the new racism*. Routledge.

Hughes, M., & Demo, D. (1989). Self-perceptions of Black Americans: Self-esteem and personal efficacy. *American Journal of Sociology, 96*, 132–159.

Jaret, C., Reitzes, R., & Shapkin, N. (2005). Reflected appraisals and self-esteem. *Sociological Perspectives, 48*(3), 403–419.

Jones, A. (2020). *Camming: Money, power, and pleasure in the sex work industry*. New York University Press.

Kellogg, A. H., & Liddell, D. L. (2012). Not half but double: Exploring critical incidents in the racial identity of multiracial college students. *Journal of College Student Development, 53*(4), 524–541.

Lawrence, S., & Forbes, T. D. (2022). Feeling like a fetish: Racialized feelings, fetishization, and the contours of sexual racism on gay dating apps. *The Journal of Sex Research, 59*(3), 372–384.

Lundquist, J. K., & Lin, K. (2015). Is love (color) blind? The economy of race among white gay and straight daters. *Social Forces, 93*(4), 1423–1449.

McGrath, A. R., Tsunokai, G. T., Schultz, M., Kavanagh, J., & Tarrence, J. A. (2016). Differing shades of colour: online dating preferences of biracial individuals. *Ethnic and Racial Studies, 39*(11), 1920–1942.

Mukkamala, S., & Suyemoto, K. (2018). Racialized sexism/sexualized racism: A multimethod study of intersectional experiences of discrimination for Asian American women. *Asian American Journal of Psychology, 9*(1), 32–46.

Omi, M., & Winant, H. (2014). *Racial formation in the United States* (3rd ed.). Routledge.

Parker, K., Horowitz, J. M., Morin, R., & Lopez, M. H. (2015). *Multiracial in America: Proud, diverse and growing in numbers*. Pew Research Center.

Roberts-Clarke, I., Roberts, A. C., & Morokoff, P. (2004). Dating practices, racialidentity, and psychotherapeutic needs of biracial women. *Women & Therapy, 27*(1–2), 103–117.

Rockquemore, K. A., Brunsma, D. L., & Delgado, D. J. (2009). Racing to theory or retheorizing race? Understanding the struggle to build a multiracial identity theory. *Journal of Social Issues, 65*(1), 13–34.

Rolón-Dow, R. (2004). Seduced by images: Identity and schooling in the lives of Puerto Rican girls. *Anthropology and Education Quarterly, 35*(1), 8–29.

Sims, J. P. (2012). Beautiful stereotypes: The relationship between physical attractiveness and mixed race identity. *Identities, 19*(1), 61–80.

Storrs, D. (1999). Whiteness as stigma: Essentialist identity work by mixed race women. *Society for the Study of Symbolic Interaction, 22*(3), 187–212.
Todd, M., Oravecz, L., & Vejar, C. (2016). Biphobia in the family context: Experiences and perceptions of bisexual individuals. *Journal of Bisexuality, 16*(2), 144–162.
Wiederman, M. W., & Hurst, S. R. (1997). Physical attractiveness, body image, and women's sexual self-schema. *Psychology of Women Quarterly, 21,* 567–580.
Wilton, L., Sanchez, D., & Garcia, J. (2013). The stigma of privilege: Racial identity and stigma consciousness among biracial individuals. *Race and Social Problems, 5*(1), 41–56.
Winant, H. (2001). *The world is a ghetto: Race and democracy since World War II.* Basic Books.
Winddance Twine, F. (1996). Brown skinned white girls: Class, culture and the construction of white identity in suburban communities. *Gender, Place and Culture: A Journal of Feminist Geography, 3*(2), 205–224.

CHAPTER 5

BODY IMAGE AND SEXUAL PLEASURE IN WOMEN AND GENDERQUEER INDIVIDUAL'S SEXUAL EXPERIENCES

Spencier R. Ciaralli

Augustana University, USA

ABSTRACT

Past research has shown there is a relationship between body image, sexual behavior, and pleasure. However, the majority of this research has centered on heterosexual participants. In this analysis, the author considers how this relationship between body image, sexual behavior, and pleasure may look within women and genderqueer individuals who are all AFAB (assigned female at birth) with 26 out of 30 participants identifying as LGBTQIA+. The author examines perceptions of body size, body hair, and genitals to consider how intersections of social structures – specifically internalized sexism, racism, and misogyny – influence the participants' experience of sexual interactions. Both resistance and embodiment of traditional gender norms, even as queer women and genderqueer individuals, were examined in these narratives. The majority of the moments where traditional gender norms are examined describe situations when the participants were sexually interacting with cis-gendered men.

Keywords: Body image; LGBTQ+; sexuality; queer; pleasure; sexual behavior; gender; embodiment

Previous research such as Sanchez and Kiefer (2007) and Gillen and Markey (2019) find that there is a relationship between body shame, sexual pleasure, and sexual problems that are mediated by sexual self-consciousness during physical intimacy. More recently, Kendall Poovey et al. (2022) sought to understand the processes by which body image influences sexual well-being and found that body dissatisfaction was associated with weaker self-focused approach motives, stronger avoidance motives, and overall more distraction which led to less pleasure. Other research finds that women who are more satisfied with their body image report higher rates of sexual activity, orgasm, and trying new sexual behaviors (Ackard et al., 2000; Faith & Schare, 1993; Murstein & Holden, 1979). However, these studies look at heterosexual cis-gendered men and women. This analysis will center women and genderqueer[1] individual's (who were AFAB) sexual experiences as they pertain to body image, as well as how their embodiment or resistance of gender norms may influence their sexual behavior.

INTRODUCTION
Body Image and Sexuality

Most research finds that poor body image influences sexual outcomes in negative ways such as fewer or complete lack of orgasms, less desire and arousal, or even pain (Bramwell & Morland, 2009; Carvalheira et al., 2017; Dosch et al., 2016; Gillen & Markey, 2019; Poovey et al., 2022; Quinn-Nilas et al., 2016; Sanchez & Kiefer, 2007; Silva et al., 2016). In the select research on the topic of queer women and body image, there are contrasting views as to whether one's sexuality impacts the experience of body image. Some researchers have suggested that lesbians may be less likely to have poor body image due to the tendency to occupy more inclusive spaces that promote gender fluidity and diverse body presentation, as well as a rejection of the male gaze (Hill & Fischer, 2008; Rothblum, 1994). Studies by Lisa M. Alvy (2013) and Anne-Maree Polimeni et al. (2009) support this theory, suggesting that lesbian women may have lower rates of poor body image. However, Sari H. Dworkin (1988) has argued that lesbian women are influenced by the same processes of heteronormativity and gender socialization as straight women are. Select studies support Dworkin's theory, with results showing no significant difference between sexual orientation and its relation to body dissatisfaction (Peplau et al., 2009; Yean et al., 2013). All these studies, however, examine lesbian women and forgo any analysis as to how this may impact bisexual, pansexual, and other queer-identified women, let alone genderqueer individuals. This is not surprising, as researchers often create monosexual, binary, static identities (gay/lesbian/heterosexual) that invalidate the bisexual and/or pansexual identity and consequently perpetuate bisexual/pansexual erasure (Barker & Langdridge, 2008; Gonzalez et al., 2017).

There are select studies, however, such as the research conducted by Nikki Hayfield et al. (2013) which address this gap in the literature. Hayfield et al. (2013) explore a spectrum of sexual orientations and their relationship to their body hair, body image, and use of cosmetics. They found no significant differences in body satisfaction between individuals of varying sexual orientations but found that lesbian and bisexual women maintained more positive attitudes toward body hair. Another study by Susan Kashubeck-West et al. (2018) investigated potential factors that may contribute to the quality of relationships for bisexual women and found that body dissatisfaction and relationship satisfaction mediated the relations of objectified body consciousness[2] with self-consciousness during sexual interactions. Additionally, they found that as objectified body consciousness increased, relationship satisfaction decreased. All in all, research on the relationship between sexual orientation and body image remains conflicting and at times unclear.

Genital Panic

In sexual interactions, perceptions of body image may oftentimes pertain to perceptions of genitals. A qualitative study by Breanne Fahs (2014) found their sample of women evoked descriptions of anxiety, need for control, and internalized sexism when describing their relationship to their genitals. Fahs (2014) notes that this relationship between sexuality and body image has connections to internalized racism, sexism, and homophobia. Interestingly, they discuss that the participant's perceptions of their vagina were less overtly understood as disgusting or gross and oftentimes were perceived to be in constant need of "maintenance" and frustrating. In other words, the participants found themselves perceiving their vagina as a part of their body that required a lot of "work" to meet esthetic standards (e.g., maintenance of pubic hair) or that caused them anxiety as it was largely "unknown" if their vagina met standards of smell, taste, or overall appearance (Fahs, 2014).

Importantly, Fahs (2014, p. 215) remarks that a meta theme was found throughout all their themes: "men's appraisals of vaginas as central to women's feelings about their own vaginas." The participant's descriptions of anxiety pertaining to their vagina as dirty, unnatural, or needing maintenance (whether in terms of smell, hair, shape, or color) is what Fahs (2014) calls genital panic. It is clear in Fahs (2014, p. 215) data that there is "immense and cultural baggage for women" as it pertains to their vagina.

Sexual Scripts and Gender

Sexual scripts provide a way to make sense of behavior and perceptions of the self throughout a sexual interaction. John Gagnon and William Simon (1973) proposed a script theory of sexuality, which, instead of understanding humans as being born sexual, posits that sexuality is socially learned. They theorized that we are taught by society what desires, feelings, and emotions count as sexual and which may be considered appropriate scripts for sexual behavior. Steven Seidman (2010, p. 26) remarks: "Sexual scripts tell us where, when, and with whom we are supposed to have sex, and what it means when we do." In essence, sexual scripts are cognitive schema that permeate the interpersonal and intrapersonal levels and influence an individual's sexual behaviors and beliefs (Gagnon, 1990; Parker & Gagnon, 1995; Simon & Gagnon, 1984).

Sexual scripts perpetuate gender inequality. In fact, upholding gender scripts of women being sexually submissive creates a lack of communication and inability to express themselves sexually (Sanchez et al., 2012), as well as internalizes the demure, submissive role (Impett & Peplau, 2003; Kiefer et al., 2006). Furthermore, sexual scripts are a point of interaction between gender structures and the individual, shaping beliefs, behaviors, and even desires (Gavey, 2005; Jackson & Cram, 2003; Tolman, 2002). For example, traditional sexual scripts for men encompass having high sex drives, initiating sex, desiring for recreational sex over relationships, and being sexually skilled (Byers, 1996; Seal & Ehrhardt, 2003; Ward et al., 2022). Such gendered sexual scripts give us meaning behind how to understand and act in sexual situations (e.g., men want sex and women want love; men pursue sex at all times and women are gatekeepers) that frame and reify traditional gender norms and heterosexuality (Connell, 2002; Hamilton & Armstrong, 2009; Jackson & Cram, 2003). Consequently, gendered sexual scripts are powerful tools that shape how people choose to sexually interact with one another, while maintaining traditional gender expectations (Laws & Schwartz, 1977; Ward et al., 2022; Wiederman, 2005).

Sexual scripts not only organize interactions between men and women but specifically privilege men over women (Gagnon, 1990; Lips, 1981; Wiederman, 2005). As a result, sexual scripts create a sexual double standard (men are encouraged to be sexually promiscuous while women are expected to be selective and sexually demure), as well as pose outright danger to women's safety (men have a "right" or "entitlement" to sex) (Armstrong et al., 2010; Sanchez et al., 2012).

Embodiment

Embodiment is a key player in emotions, and it is important to be reminded that the physiological and cognitive are elements in this ability to label. We may externalize and internalize an emotion by which roles we play, and which emotions are appropriate for that role. For example, a woman may feel gendered obligations to embody and preform sexual pleasure since their male partner "deserves" and is "entitled" to give them an orgasm to properly perform their masculinity.

Stevi Jackson and Sue Scott (2007) suggest that we have *to learn* to recognize an orgasm and also learn its cultural definitions, similar to Howard Becker's (1953) argument that marijuana users must learn to relate their "symptoms" not only to the action of the drug but also to deem them enjoyable and comparable to the "symptoms" experienced by other users and, thus, appropriate. A similar process is necessary for women to learn to "do" orgasm. Women's sexual pleasure, as Jackson and Scott (2007) argue, is so embedded in cultural scripts of gender that one must acquire the cultural competencies that enable one to "know" what it is and to "recognize" it in ourselves and others. "Feeling" then requires reflexive decoding of our own sensate embodiment (Jackson & Scott, 2007). That is, one does not solely "feel" sensations but, perhaps most importantly, interprets them. In turn, our interpretations of sensations give them meaning.

Akin to work by Hannah Frith (2013), my feminist study is built on a premise that sex is socioculturally produced and, therefore, is interested in exploring the meanings through which sexual behavior and perception of self is constructed. Consequently, larger social, cultural institutions shape the ways actors make sense of their own behavior within seemingly private, intimate spaces. Again, akin to Frith (2013, p. 495):

> These accounts can be deconstructed to expose power operating through the enabling or constraining of material practices (what we actually do in bed – or elsewhere) and opening up or closing down of sexual subjectivities (what kind of sexual being it is possible to be).

This in mind, the role of embodiment is significant in this analysis, as it considers how meanings are produced and reproduced in day-to-day interactions; that a close look at meaning-making in sexual behavior elucidates the role of traditional gender constructs, particularly as this has been understudied within LGBTQIA+ participants. Consequently, this study aims to add to the growing body of work on queer, nonheteronormative sexuality and examine how women and genderqueer individuals navigate body image and sexual pleasure in light of cultural norms surrounding gender and sexuality.

METHODS

This research employed qualitative data gathered from a group of 30 adults identifying as women and genderqueer, all of whom were AFAB. The recruitment of participants took place in 2019 and 2020 across the Midwest region of the United States, primarily utilizing social media platforms and focusing on "women/femme" Facebook support groups. The recruitment process targeted women aged 18 and above, inviting them to contribute to a study focused on capturing narratives and experiences related to their sexual lives and pleasures.

Given that the study specifically explored sexual behavior in connection to vaginal stigma and self-image, possessing a vagina was a prerequisite for participation. It is important to note, however, that the researcher recognizes the diversity of gender identities and acknowledges that not all women have vaginas and not all individuals with vaginas identify as women. The age range of participants varied from 23 to 51. In terms of self-identified race and ethnicity, the sample consisted of 21 white participants, 1 Chinese/Taiwanese participant, 1 Palestinian participant, 1 Syrian participant, 3 Black participants, 1 Latinx participant, 1 Vietnamese participant, and 1 Filipino participant. For self-reported sexual identity, the sample included 4 straight/heterosexual participants and 26 participants who identified within the LGBTQIA+ community.

For gender identity, my sample included 23 cis-gender women participants, 4 questioning participants, 2 nonbinary participants, and 1 agender participant. Five of these participants shifted their gender identity after the interview was conducted, whereas two of these participants already identified as nonbinary when they participated in the study. Every genderqueer participant expressed interest in joining the study due to their experiences of being labeled as girls and having vaginas during their upbringing. For the remainder of this research, the term "women and genderqueer individuals" will be used in the analysis, as unanimously agreed upon by the participants.[3] Participants reported a wide range of occupations, familial status, educational backgrounds, and religious affiliation (see Table 5.1).

Table 5.1 Participant Demographics.

Name	Age	Race/Ethnicity	Gender Orientation	Sexual Orientation	Education	Occupation	Family Status
Parker	35	Latinx	Questioning	Pansexual/polyamorous	Master's degree	Unemployed	Single, one child
Estelle	23	Black	Cis-gendered	Fluid sexuality/heteroromantic	Some college	Bartender	Single, no children
Judith	32	White	Cis-gendered	Straight	Master's degree	Speech language pathologist	Married, no children
Anne	28	Filipino-American	Cis-gendered	Straight	Some graduate school	Student	Relationship, no children
Olivia	25	Black	Cis-gendered	Pansexual	Some college	Nanny	Relationship, no children
Morgan	33	White	Cis-gendered	Ambiguous	Some college	Service industry	Relationship, no children
Gail	23	White	Agender	Bisexual/queer/homoflexible	Master's degree	Hospice social worker	Relationship, no children
Phoebe	49	White	Cis-gendered	Bi-light	Bachelor's degree	Customer service	Single, no children
Emily	32	White	Cis-gendered	Homoromantic/bisexual	Bachelor's degree	Administrative assistant	Single, no children
Valerie	36	White	Cis-gendered	Bisexual	Bachelor's degree	Software technician	Married, one child
Cam	41	White	Cis-gendered	Bisexual	Master's degree	Health/life coach	Relationship, one child
Riley	25	Vietnamese	Nonbinary	Pansexual/polyamorous	Some college	Bartender	Relationship, no children
Liz	32	White	Cis-gendered	Bisexual	Some college	Bartender	Relationship, no children
Brianna	27	White	Cis-gendered	Bisexual	Bachelor's degree	Behavioral therapist/technician	Single
Taylor	27	White	Cis-gendered	Bisexual/queer	Some graduate school	Social worker	Relationship, no children
Quinn	26	White	Questioning	Bisexual/demi sexual	Some college	Real estate agent	Relationship, one child
Sawyer	30	White	Cis-gendered	Bisexual	Some college	Unemployed	Married, no children
Emory	25	White	Cis-gendered	Queer/bisexual/gay	Culinary cert., no college	Service industry	Single, no children
Fin	30	White	Questioning	Queer/homoromantic	Master's degree	Service industry and community outreach	Single, two children

Body Image and Sexual Pleasure

Name	Age	Race/Ethnicity	Gender	Sexuality	Education	Occupation	Relationship
Pat	30	White	Questioning	Pansexual	Bachelor's degree	Unemployed	Single, no children
Mack	28	Syrian	Cis-gendered	Bisexual	Some college	Service industry	Single, no children
Westley	30	African American/Black	Cis-gendered	Bisexual	Master's degree	Artist	Single, two children
Gina	30	white	Cis-gendered	Bisexual	Some college	User interface designer	Engaged, no children
Jamie	27	White	Cis-gendered	Bisexual	Some college	Service industry	Relationship, no children
Sam	27	Palestinian	Cis-gendered	Straight	Associates	Health care worker	Divorced, no children
Felix	24	Chinese/Taiwanese	Nonbinary	Bisexual	No college	Tech company worker	Relationship, no children
Kai	33	White	Cis-gendered	Bisexual/pansexual	Some college	Freelance photographer	Divorced, no children
Jorden	51	White	Cis-gendered	Straight	Master's degree	Self-employed (ed. consultant)	Divorced, one child
Aiden	33	White	Cis-gendered	Bisexual	Bachelor's degree	Unemployed	Married, two children
Charlie	32	White	Cis-gendered	Bisexual	Some college	Payroll coordinator	Married, no children

The author conducted all interviews in compliance with an Institutional Review Board-approved study (STUDY20190494). Prior to participation, all individuals provided both verbal and written consent, allowing their interviews to be recorded and transcribed in full. To safeguard anonymity, identifiable information was excluded, and participants were assigned pseudonyms. The interview sessions, lasting approximately 1–2.5 hours, involved respondents responding to semi-structured prompts related to their sexual history, practices, pleasures, and their sentiments toward their sexuality and body.

Employing a life history method, the study emphasized participants' voices and utilized narratives to uncover the social processes under discussion (Erdmans, 2007). This approach enabled participants to guide conversations and actively contribute to the construction of knowledge (Geiger, 1986). Respondents had the autonomy to choose the day, time, and location for interviews, including virtual sessions via Zoom during the COVID-19 pandemic (13 interviews were conducted this way). Considering the sensitivity of the subject matter, a resource list containing mental health resources, LGBTQ+ Centers, and Women's Centers was provided at each interview.

I had a set of questions in this study that asked about participants' body image, such as: "(1) What are your thoughts or feelings about your body?" and "(2) What are your thoughts or feelings about your vagina? Body hair near your vagina?" Prior to these questions, there were prompts asking participants about their thoughts and feelings about their kinks and sexual play, descriptions of their pleasure with their selves and with sexual partners, as well as the history of their sexual behavior. Although the interview prompts were pre-scripted and guided, the interviews were conducted in such a manner that encouraged conversation, probes, follow-up questions and clarifications, and dialog that transitioned into other areas of interest. In short, the interviews were a space of co-construction of knowledge, where both the researcher and participant engaged in free-flowing, active conversation (Fontana, 2002; Holstein & Gubrium, 2000). This interview style acknowledges the researcher's collaborative construction of the story, while creating intentional space and a platform for respondents to tell their narratives.

I coded the interviews line by line and assigned codes to chunks of data to preserve the narrative using NVivo, a qualitative software service. I examined the ways in which participants portrayed themselves in connection to their bodies and partners, searching for discernible patterns. It is crucial to note that the codes were generated using the respondents' own language, preserving their voice within their narratives. As I refined and broadened these codes, I observed trends and recurring patterns in their accounts of sexual behavior, bodies, and self-perception.

Throughout the findings, I will focus on five particular participants. Using life story narratives provides a "panoramic" yet deep, contextual perspective of participants lives. Akin to Ciaralli and Vercel (2023, p. 15), this study aims to: "prioritize presenting a few participants' stories ... across their lives, in considerable depth and in context, rather than presenting isolated and abbreviated quotations from many participants." This is a practice that has been utilized in material culture studies through approaches such as "follow-the thing" (Cook, 2004; Evans, 2020; Mayr, 2021), or in the study by Ciaralli and Vercel (2023) a "follow-the-body." By focusing on select narratives, I am afforded more space to illustrate the rich, deep connections participants make and build upon throughout their narration, across their experiences – which shape their current realities and relationship to their bodies.

RESULTS

Genital Panic in Queer Women and Genderqueer Individual's Sexual Behavior

In this current study, anxiety was found in queer women and genderqueer individual's perceptions of their bodies, particularly when focalized around their vaginas,[4] and that this anxiety impacted their fulfillment in sexual experiences. Twenty-seven out of 30 participants brought up some form of displeasure, anxiety, or distaste in relation to their vagina, inclusive of genital hair, smell, taste, and image. Consequently, "genital panic" was a theme that arose in the current study. Mack (28, Syrian, cis, bisexual), for example, refuses to receive oral from her partners if she feels that she isn't "ready," which (to her) means shaved and freshly showered:

[Spencier]: How often would you say you give oral in comparison to the amount of oral you receive?
[Mack]: Mm, that's a good question. Definitely a big difference, I'd say, but I think that's more on my part.
[Spencier]: Difference in what?
[Mack]: In me giving more than receiving, and I'm saying it's on me mostly because I'm not always comfortable with myself down there. And if I feel like I'm not prepared or I'm not ready, like I didn't shave or I didn't – I worked all day. *I usually don't let someone perform oral on me if I'm not feeling up to par on my standards for my vagina.* [emphasis added]

Keep in mind that earlier in the interview, Mack admitted that her primary way to experience an orgasm with a partner is through oral sex. Mack, then, is denying herself an orgasm due to the anxiety of how her vagina will be perceived. Why? Select research argues that women's perception of their bodies, particularly their genitals, as "unfresh" or "unclean" is an internalized byproduct of the objectification of women (Roberts & Waters, 2008). As for why women may internalize and exhibit a self-surveillance of their bodies, Tomi-Ann Roberts and Patricia Waters (2008, p. 10) remark that: "Habitual body monitoring is actually a survival strategy in a sexually objectifying culture." As for the constant performance of femininity, Dorothy Smith (1988) notes that there is an incredibly large amount of labor that goes into the presentation of self as "feminine" and, therefore, an ideal, desirable body. Mack seems to be prioritizing the presentation of self and her sexual partners' interpretation of her body over her own potential sexual gratification. However, Mack's prioritization of the presentation of self is embedded within a system of patriarchal power.

Mack continues to criticize her body:

[Spencier]: What are your feelings or thoughts about your body?
[Mack]: I'm very insecure. I'm still working on self-esteem. I have a lot of problems with that, mostly because of my childhood. I'm starting to like myself, but I've always been insecure about weird little things like my feet or my big veiny hands or my nose or my hairiness. It was a lot of little things like that, that collectively just made me really insecure, but it's a work in progress.
[Spencier]: So, what are your feelings and thoughts about your vagina, vulva, clitoris, the entire area down there, and body hair near your vagina or things like that?
[Mack]: Hm-hmm. [Affirmative] I remember the first time I actually saw my vagina in a mirror. I was really young. I was a kid. This is so funny. I don't know why I didn't have underwear on, and I was in one of those kid nightgowns where they're – they have cartoons on them. And I was swinging on this door. It was a door like this. There was a mirror on it, and I was a little monkey, so I was swinging on it like this with my feet on the door, on the mirror, and me holding on to the handle. *And, boop! I took a peep, and there she was. That was the first time I saw it, and I was enamored.* I was like, oh my God, is that what it looks like? I never thought to look before.

But it took me a long time to even get comfortable with someone performing oral on me. I just feel like some of the guys that I've been with early on made it seem like vaginas aren't the best thing to look at, so I always felt insecure about that. And now that I'm 28, I'm realizing they all look the same. They're all beautiful. I don't know why guys were so scared of them besides sticking their penis in them. When it comes to hair, I am really hairy, and that is one thing that I'm pretty insecure about because I usually, when I do have sex, hopefully, I shave my hair down there. And it grows back really fast, and there's always that awkward, stubbly, prickly part of the growth that I hate so much. I have to shave it. I can't let it go loose. It's way too much. And I shave my butt, my butthole. [emphasis added]

Mack mentions that her concerns and anxiousness surrounding the perception of her vagina stem from formative sexual experiences with men. In her narrative, you can trace her first experience seeing her vagina and being "enamored," to being uncomfortable and "insecure" as men convey it isn't the best thing to look at, to now re-learning her body (and perhaps, other women's bodies), to feel that all vaginas are "beautiful." Despite Mack's work toward self-love of her vagina, she still admits to consistent maintenance of her body hair before sexual interactions. The insecurity Mack feels around her body hair aligns with what current research finds on attitudes toward women's body hair – that there is an expectation for women to be hairless (Tiggemann & Hodgson, 2008; Tiggemann & Kenyon, 1998; Tiggemann & Lewis,

2004; Toerien et al., 2005; Toerien & Wilkinson, 2003). In addition to her concern over her body hair, Mack's negative image of her body and vagina align with what Fahs (2014) has found to be a "genital panic" among women. Furthermore, this genital anxiety is not surprising, as Janet Holland et al. (1994, p. 33) remark that:

> Letting particular aspects of the body emerge, as in "letting oneself go," with lank hair, chipped nails, blemished skin, visible body hair in the "wrong, places," "fat," evidence of menstruation, body odour, is to be unfeminine. Women's material (e.g., hairy, discharging) bodies are taken socially to be unnatural. In sexual situations there can be a particularly complex and unstable tension between the material body and what is social inscribed on the body, rather than either unity or a balanced dualism.

Participants such as Mack bring an understanding into their sexual encounters of how their material body is expected to appear, smell, and behave in comparison to "the" ideal feminine body. Similar to Holland et al.'s (1994) description, Mack determines that her body requires "tending to" before being perceived as desirable, or perhaps deserving of sexual pleasure – an embodiment of traditional femininity, despite her comment that she appreciates and finds all vaginas beautiful.

Fin (30, white, questioning, queer/homoromantic[5]) describes a similar development of her body image throughout the years akin to Mack:

[Spencier]: What are your feelings or thoughts about your vagina, and body hair near your vagina?

[Fin]: Mm-hmm. I feel like, now, I'm very confident. I feel good about my body. *I feel good about my body hair, which is something that was a source of stress when I was younger.* I remember the first time that it had ever struck me that I needed to do anything about it – I was so young. It's so weird to think about it. I was in sixth or seventh grade, and I remember walking into the bathroom at school, and my friend was talking to my other friend about this girl they know who had gotten fingered for the first time. And they were like, "I can't believe that she let that happen when she hadn't even cleaned up down there. It was like a jungle. Isn't that so gross?" And I was like, oh, no. This is something that I'm supposed to be aware of and making sure that that doesn't ever happen. So, then I was hyper-aware about shaving, and it was also weird because I got armpit hair very, very young. *I think I was probably in fourth or fifth grade, and my mom was adamant that I needed to do something to remove it. But I also had really sensitive skin there, so I would always have razor bumps, and it would be broken out. Growing up, it was so important to me that I was removing this body hair, and now, I just don't.* Sometimes, I shave my legs, but that's about it. But I remember – remembering that and then hearing my friend make this comment about how *you cannot have your first sexual experience while you have hair or everyone in the school is going to know about it, and everyone's going to think it's gross, so I had this crazy feeling. But at the time, I had also never looked at my vagina. It was a thing that was supposed to be off limits, and nobody's supposed to touch that, and I, for some reason, thought that that extended to myself.* So, it was just this thing that was down there that I had never looked at, and I hoped it was normal, but I also felt like it would be weird to check it out. After I had kids, I definitely – I think it's probably due to the partner that I had kids with, but I definitely have a lot of nervousness about having sexual interactions after having children. So, it's like, does it look different? Is it weird compared to what women's bodies look like before they have kids? *Is it less able to be pleasurable for another person?* But since then, I've kind of gotten over all of that. And my last partner and I, we're still really good friends, and they're actually my roommate, but they were very helpful to me *in coming to terms with the fact that my body's still a good body and that it still performs the things that it's supposed to do. And it also gave me a lot of space to explore myself.* We were in an open relationship, so I just had a lot more space to do things about myself, and I think that I learned a lot about my body not only by being with them but by the space that I was given by being with them.

[Spencier]: Yeah. Did you ever take a mirror and investigate or look at it or –

[Fin]: Probably not until after I had kids. I don't think that it's something that I did before that. I don't know. I feel like even as I started to become a sexual being, I still was very worried about doing things that were weird or not normal, and it wasn't until I mean, once I had kids, it was like most of the shame was gone. Thirty people have been in a doctor's office staring at my vagina while I gave birth, so it was just like, oh, now I guess I can look at it. The weirdness has already happened.

[Spencier]: What about having people go down on you in your first formative experiences?

[Fin]: *I was definitely nervous about smell, and I also had this weird thing when I was like 17 and I was just starting to experience sexuality. Something that I was very nervous about was vaginal discharge and just any kind of moisture down there. I felt like it was not normal, and it wasn't supposed to be there, and I thought that people would think it was weird.* I remember being – before I had had a sexual experience but once I had started to recognize myself as a sexual being, not only would I be really intentional about shaving and everything, but I would use baby powder and stuff to make sure that I wasn't moist down there. Now, I look back at it, and that's so weird. Vaginas are supposed to be moist. I thought that's what they do. So I remember that being a huge source of stress was that I had too much discharge or that it wasn't normal to be wet. [emphasis added]

Fin speaks to experiencing shame, anxiety, and being nervous around her body hair and vagina. The management of body hair and vaginal discharge, which includes constant pain (razor bumps, burns) and vaginal discomfort (baby powder) were mechanisms for Fin to manage a source of stress about herself.

Therefore, traditional gendered constructions of beauty are influencing many of these women and genderqueer individual's sexual behaviors; particularly the presentation of self for others approval and comfort, even at the expense of one's own comfort or sexual pleasure.

Where do these participants learn and embody these negative perceptions about their body hair and perception of their vagina? Fin gleaned information from their school peers in the bathroom, and their friend remarking on the importance of shaving before their first sexual interaction with a boy. Fin lacked educational information to use from either her family or her school system to make informed judgments about her body – to the point of worrying over the moistness of her vagina, and consequently throwing baby powder on it. Throughout Fin's struggles and anxiety over their vagina and body over the years, their most recent partner serves as a point of resistance in her narrative.

Fin's last relationship illustrates a way in which a social relationship assisted Fin in forming a healthier relationship with her body, particularly as she works through her anxieties of having a vagina that has birthed two children and its ability to pleasure others. Interestingly, this healthy past relationship Fin refers to is with a queer-identified, nonbinary individual. Consequently, it seems participants feel more comfortable communicating their needs and desires with other queer-identified individuals, which can be seen even as they navigate their multifaceted feelings toward their own bodies. Nevertheless, past research shows that women consistently perceive their vagina in a negative light, or at the minimum, in need of constant maintenance (Berman & Windecker, 2008; Braun & Wilkinson, 2001; Crann et al., 2017). As Fin and Mack exemplify, the vagina may be a source of great anxiety that leads to body modification and denial of oral sex that extends into not just heterosexual women's experiences but also queer women and genderqueer individual's lives.

Genital Panic and White Beauty Standards

This anxiety or "genital panic" extends beyond sexist distaste for the vagina or body hair: it also encompasses embodied racism, and in particular, distaste with one's own skin color. Sam (27, Palestinian, cis, straight) sits crossed-legged on my couch in her work clothes, sipping a cup of water, and, in a low, quiet voice, quickly provides a narrative of her self-image with respect to her body and genitals:

[Spencier]: What are your feelings or thoughts about your body?
[Sam]: I don't – my body from a distance like, in a mirror or whatever, like ... I like my body. I don't like my skin. I have bacne.[6] And whenever I shave, like, I get really bad bumps, no matter what. But I'm also too lazy to go get it waxed or whatever. *And then like, my perineum like, vaginal/anal area because I'm Middle Eastern is dark. And I find that, like ... I know that that is like that because I'm Middle Eastern or whatever. But I just don't find it attractive. I get nervous when like, Jason wanted to like, go down on me. Because I didn't want him to like, look at*

[Spencier]:   *that area. I just ... I Googled, if there was like, bleaching I could do, or like, laser or something. Because, like, I'm uncomfortable with it. But I know that's just, you know ... but then you watch porn, the misconception of bodies. Like, their bodies all look clear. And their little areas are pink, and like – you know what I mean?*
[Spencier]: Hm-hmm. [affirmative] When did you first look and investigate and explore your vagina?
[Sam]: A long time ago. When I was like, 14, I took a mirror and looked down there. Because that's when I was starting to talk to dudes on the internet and they would ask for fucked up pictures. And I'm like, no, I'm not doing that. *Like, it doesn't look good. I'm like, I don't know what you think you're going to see, but it doesn't look good down there. [Laughs] And I have, I guess, bigger labia that like, stick out and stuff. It, like, that makes me uncomfortable.*
[Spencier]: And then, what about your thoughts about how your vagina smells or tastes?
[Sam]: *I used to be afraid that I smelled.* But I started taking this thing called like, lactobacillus acidophilus which is like, a probiotic. And it's because I used to take a lot of antibiotics. So, that would like, throw off my pH and give me a lot of yeast infections. So, I started taking that. And I feel like that's helped. And then like, sexually, Jason and I would like, talk dirty and stuff like that. He'd be like, yeah, touch yourself. Yeah. Taste yourself. I don't think I taste bad, I guess. And that turned me on when he would do that shit. [Laughs] So, I get, like, I'm getting more comfortable. Still don't want to see it. But, like, you can look. [emphasis added]

    Sam compares her vagina to what she sees online in porn, reflecting that her genitals are too dark, her labia too large, and, therefore, considers it unattractive. Sam's point of vaginal comparison, porn, idealizes hairlessness and labias that are tucked away, essentially prepubescent (Cokal, 2007; Rodrigues, 2012; Schick et al., 2011). What is not addressed in this research, however, is that these representations of vaginas are not only objectifying but almost exclusively representing white bodies. Sam has internalized the racism displayed in porn that an attractive vagina looks a very particular way: hairless, tucked in, and white.

    Like Fin, Sam discusses extreme measures to "manage" her body to appease others, inclusive of investigating bleaching. Research by Tami Rowen et al. (2018) shows that in a nationally representative survey of nonincarcerated individuals within the United States, women were less likely to report genital dissatisfaction if they were older, identified as Black, and lived within the Northeastern or Midwestern United States. Interestingly, there was no association found between genital dissatisfaction and gender of sexual partner.

    Participants in this current study are from the Midwest of the United States, and for many participants, they tell me a story of working toward "overcoming" majority of their anxiety surrounding their genitals. What fails to be considered in these representative surveys, however, is that women such as Mack and Sam are

Middle Eastern and, indeed, live an existence as a person of color, yet, in many representative surveys, they are considered white. Sam and Mack both tell stories of struggling with their body hair and self-image about their genitals in a way that may be unique to their experiences as self-identified brown women navigating a society that privileges white women's bodies. Consequently, it is important to consider the ways that bodily anxieties extend inequality beyond traditional gendered scripts, into systems of racism and white privilege as well.

Grappling with the Cult of Thinness in the Bedroom

As the narratives show, genital panic included smell, taste, color, body hair, and shape. However, another factor that is brought up consistently in participant's stories is body size. Parker (35, Latinx, questioning, pansexual) is a former professional dominatrix and single mother, who is currently unemployed due to medical health reasons and the COVID-19 pandemic. Throughout their sexual history, Parker weaves body image as a central theme that impacts their sexual experiences. When I asked them about the first time they had sex, Parker volunteers that they refused oral sex due to their body image:

[Spencier]: What about the first time then?
[Parker]: He was huge. It was incredibly painful. It was missionary style.
[Spencier]: Was there any foreplay?
[Parker]: Not really. All the lights were on. It was not what I would hope for. *I never ever, ever wanted anybody to go down on me. I had huge fears of that. Huge. Even when I was in the best shape of my life, maybe a buck ten, solid muscle, I was terrified of somebody seeing me from that angle. Absolutely terrified. I was a very chubby kid. I still have huge body dysmorphia issues.* I was called pig, whale. Every fat shaming name in the book from the time I was very little. My mom had me go on diets and exercise plans from the time I was ten on. Oh yeah. There was a lot. Oral sex was never something I was interested in.
[Spencier]: So oral at that point, you weren't interested because …
[Parker]: *My belly. I was afraid of someone having to look up at me past my belly. Or my fupa being the biggest part of that experience. I told myself I didn't like it even though I didn't know if I liked it or not. And I would just tell people, oh I don't like that. So, I would be in control of it instead of me just being deathly afraid they would think I was fat.* [emphasis added]

Parker denies oral sex from many of their formative sexual partners, and admits to telling them that they "didn't like it," despite admitting later in our interview that it is the primary way for them to achieve an orgasm with another partner. Research shows that body image is known to be related to sexual satisfaction, in that healthy body image correlates to both higher rates of, and more satisfying sex (Sanchez & Kiefer, 2007; Træen et al., 2016; van den Brink et al., 2018; Woertman & van den Brink, 2012). This finding makes sense, as many sexual acts typically entail an intimate moment where people are commonly unclothed and very close, touching bodies. One could guess that the more confident and satisfied one feels about their body image, the higher likelihood they feel comfortable allowing another person to explore and experience their body without added anxieties about the perception of their body.

This relationship between sexual satisfaction and body image is found in both men and women,[7] however, and appears most prevalent within women (Satinsky et al., 2012; Traen et al., 2016). Why? A theory by Barbara Fredrickson and Tomi-Ann Roberts (1997) coined "objectification theory," suggests that society treating women as sexual objects results in women treating themselves as an object to be scrutinized and evaluated by others (self-objectification). For example, Parker's consistent monitoring of their body and how it is perceived by others, even if it meant literally denying themselves sexual pleasure or satisfaction.

Participant's narratives show an understanding of their own body – enough to understand the mechanisms necessary to reach climax, yet, continue to establish sexual interactions from a heteronormative lens. That is, as others have found, that sex encompasses shorter bouts of foreplay (oral, petting, kissing) which are precursors to penetrative sex, with the intention of male orgasm (Bryan, 2001; Fahs & Swank, 2016; Frith, 2013; McClelland, 2010). What is surprising (or perhaps not surprising) is that this remains true with the current participants who are queer-identified women and genderqueer individuals when interacting with cis-gendered men.

Consequently, the body objectification Parker experiences trickles into their current sex life despite their work toward self-love and care. They had just finished showing me their professional dominatrix toy collection they use on clients, and their face lights up as they described the sincere love they have for teaching bondage and discipline, dominance and submission, sadism and masochism (BDSM) courses. They go into a poetic, passionate trance when describing the uses of sexual play for working through trauma, and the ways ethical, safe, BDSM play has transformed their life in a way clinical therapy never could. Yet, as we re-center their story on their own sexual experiences of pleasure, they sigh and physically deflate – their shoulders sag back down, and their brow furrows – and they begin to tell me a recent sexual interaction they had with a current casual sex partner when smoking weed:

[Parker]: So, when I finally got the dress off ... I'm never embarrassed of my body when I'm a submissive. That's a lie. *I never admit that I'm embarrassed of my body as a submissive. When I was high, oh my God. The dysmorphia came out of my mouth like an unending sewer stream.* I refused to come out from behind the door of his closet, behind which I took the dress off. He's like, what are you doing?

[Spencier]: And this is when you two have had multiple sexual interactions already?

[Parker]: This was at like the five-month mark. He's clearly seen me naked. But because I was high as balls I refused to come out from behind the door and he had to come over and be like, "okay, come on." And I was like, "ugh, fine." [Laughs] So I went over and laid on the bed and he's trying to be sexy with me. *I just looked at him and I was like, "no, you need to stop." He's trying to play with my clit and I'm like, no. I fully looked up and I said "when you and I are together, I get off on our interaction, on the dynamic. But I get to show you what will actually make me cum and how I make myself cum because you aren't doing it right." He was like "uh, okay."* [Laughs] *Full shock. Of course, in his mind I made him feel like a sex god because I faked every orgasm. I'm totally into him. The fantasy and everything is fantastic and I find him incredibly physically attractive. But man, that whole fakery was gone. All faking of anything was gone. Also I had not shaved. With him, I make sure I'm always super trimmed, it was full on 70s porn star bush. Glorious. It was curly. I had conditioned it.* I'm just like spread on his bed and I'm playing with myself and he's looking down at me and he's shocked. He's in full shock. He doesn't know what to do with himself. He's touching while I'm playing with myself, he's like, "oh my God, you are soaked." I'm like, "welcome to what it's supposed to feel like." He's like, "have you been faking?" I was like, maybe. Anyway. [Laughs] When I'm in character, he like throat fucks me. It's a violent, it's all about the gag, it's all about the drool. Down girl. But when I was super high I was like, "look, you need to not go past my hard palate." I showed him, right here. This is where you need to be. And he's like, "oh, okay, so don't thrust?" He was shocked at how good it felt when I was just having him in my mouth. *He was like, that feels really good. Yep, for me too. It doesn't hurt. He's like, "have I been hurting you?"* What sends him over the edge is when I do both hands with a lot of spit and it's very tantric and he can't control himself. So, whenever I have to take control of the situation with him I just start doing that. *But yeah, you have to understand, when I let you do what you want to do it hurts. And that's part of what I want. That's part of what I'm into with you. But right now, I don't want to gag. I just want to suck on your dick like a lollipop.* So that's what we're going to do.

But at one point, the dysmorphia really came flying out of my mouth. I was naked and he was naked. He wanted me to suck his dick but then to be on all fours and his face was back here and I was like, mm mm, no. *There's no way you'll enjoy the view from back there.* And he's like, what the fuck are you talking about? I was like, I don't think I want to do this. And he's like, "we've literally done this twenty times, what is wrong?" And he wasn't angry about it. He was just like, what the fuck is going on? Finally, after we had sex I'm like, pulling the covers up over me and he's like, what are you doing? *I'm like, dude, do you have a fat fetish? Are you a chubby chaser? I was still super high and it just came out. Is that your thing?* He's just staring at me. He's just had the most amazing orgasm of his life. He's like, no. Not at all. Usually I like very thin women, very athletic physiques. And I was like, then what the fuck are you doing? [Laughs] *It did not compute in my head, in my state of not having a filter, without having this guise of sexual power and weaponized sexuality. It did not compute and all the insecurity came flying out. Look at this pendulous fucking fat, how can you like this? What the fuck? I was angry.* He looked at me and he was like, "it's your personality." *It's the fat girl with the great personality? He went, "number one, that's awful. Number two, yeah I like your personality." Okay.* [emphasis added]

Parker's story is both reflective and critical of their own simultaneous resistance and tolerance of patriarchal beauty standards that ebb and flow throughout their sexual encounters. Parker leads me through an interaction where they are in a constant state of body dysmorphia and anxiety – one that leads them to admit that they perhaps are always feeling this way, but never willing to communicate that to their sex partner. However, within this same scene, they describe moments of agency and communicating their needs; Parker tells their sexual partner what they do or don't like, and how to properly satisfy them sexually. Consequently, although Parker embodies shame and anxiety over their weight, they also choose to weaponize their feelings to establish a conversation that results in their sexual gratification. An entitlement to sexual pleasure.

As Parker ends their sexual "scene" on a negative note (telling me that they cover their own body in a blanket and asks their partner if he has a fat fetish), I consider how Parker may not notice their own acts of resistance and agency. By refusing to shave their genital hair, and describing their hair as glorious and conditioned. By masturbating to show their partner what they prefer. Through talking out what method and style they would like to perform oral sex.

Smoking weed broke down many boundaries of communication for Parker that were otherwise closed off in previous sexual interactions with their partner, but it also broke down so many boundaries that their internalized negative body image came spewing along with it. Parker admits that their low self-image of their body is always present, so one may argue that breathing life into their feelings through communication may be the first step in working through them. This process may be understood as "naming" emotion, which allows one to interpret and legitimize their emotions and feelings (Stets, 2005). If we can label it, it helps us understand, interpret, and categorize it.[8]

For Parker, they may feel traditionally gendered obligations to embody and perform sexual pleasure since their male partner "deserves" and is "entitled" to give them an orgasm to properly perform their masculinity. However, during this scene, Parker resists this traditional gendered embodiment, poor body image withstanding, to communicate and establish boundaries with their own pleasure in mind.

Jorden (51, white, cis, straight), on the other hand, seems to be cognizant of her resistance to body shame and her entitlement to pleasure. Jorden explains how being a woman over six feet tall and "large" is unable to "be invisible," in that she is always noticed and taking up space. After working through her formative feelings about her body, she depicts her recent transformation in body image, telling me how if she was going to take up space, she might as well embrace it.

One of the ways Jorden resists traditional gender norms surrounding women's bodies is by wearing heels, "Because I'm going to be taller than most men anyways, so why not allow myself to wear the shoes I want?" It seems ironic that by wearing heels, Jorden is resisting gender norms (i.e., heels have often been associated with traditional standards of feminine beauty) – but Jorden formerly stifled her wardrobe choices because she was frequently taller than men. Jorden enacts agency and resistance in her entitlement to pleasure as well when I inquire about a form of oral sex. Jorden comments that she often feels "passive" in receiving oral sex, so I ask if she has ever experienced a more participatory form of oral sex:

[Spencier]: Have you ever sat on your partner's face?
[Jorden]: Yes, and I liked that too. But that was a – that was probably the latest thing, experience that I had that I liked. I mean, that was like after my divorce, so within the last five years.
[Spencier]: I feel like that may be a more engaging way to receive oral. You're also still kind of in control, in a way.
[Jorden]: Yeah, which definitely is a thing for me. But, see, prior to that, you know, *I'm six feet tall and I'm not thin, I have never been thin. So, I think there was always a discomfort with sitting on someone's face, that like it would be awful for them, you know? And that I could hurt them or that they would be like – I don't know, well, you know, I have no idea specifically.* Like, you know, when I think about it from a physiological standpoint, I'm like, "That doesn't make any sense." But, you know, that was where my emotional, you know, where my emotions went around that act. *And so, I would not even try it for like most of my life. You know? And I think that there were – like when people would bring it up, that was like a hard stop for me, like no.* But yeah, after my divorce I dated someone who was 16 years younger and he was – and we were a terrible match outside of bed but we were a great match in bed. And with him that came, like I just – *you know, he really loved that, convinced me that he really loved it. And then, I was like, "All right, well let's try this." And yeah, then I was sort of hooked. So, now, yeah, you know, so sad if you get smothered, oh well.* [emphasis added]

Jorden reflects on how she denied herself a more participatory, engaged form of oral sex due to her body-image, and how this has changed in more recent years. It seems that a partner who encouraged and expressed loving the activity is what impacted her change of heart. With this in mind, did a male partner's approval or desires still determine whether or not Jorden permitted herself to explore a sexual activity that she now enjoys? Perhaps this is what started her venture into more participatory forms of oral sex, but she ends her thought on a particularly emboldened note: "So sad if you get smothered, oh well."

CONCLUSION

The patriarchy is enacted and embodied through gendered sexual scripts, and these narratives illustrate how these scripts are shaped by perceptions of body image, body hair, genital appearance, and body size. These narratives touched on ways that women and genderqueer individuals, inclusive of those within the LGBTQIA+ community, navigate traditional gender structures as they permeate other identities that intersect with their body and their sexual behavior.

Perceptions of body size, body hair, and genitals were closely examined, to consider how intersections of social structures – specifically internalized sexism, racism, and misogyny – influence the participants' experience of sexual interactions. Both resistance and embodiment of traditional gender norms, even as queer women and genderqueer individuals, were examined in these narratives. Interestingly, many of the moments where traditional gender norms are examined describe situations when the participants were sexually interacting with cisgendered men. One may ask, then, *why* were participants more likely to embody traditional gender norms and sexual scripts around cis men – is it due to safety? More "work" to teach cis-gender men their sexual needs or desires? Assumptions around what cis men may desire in their partners? These questions remain unanswered and are worthy of further exploration.

The experiences of the participants are rooted in the Midwest region of the United States. Discussions on sexual behavior, gender, and sexuality in the United States are multifaceted and influenced by various factors such as religion, age, and education. However, the absence of standardized sex education across the nation (Goldfarb & Lieberman, 2020; Lindberg & Kantor, 2022) results in many young individuals exploring their bodies (and potential partners) with limited information (Kantor & Lindberg, 2020) or resorting to the Internet for answers (Jones & Biddlecom, 2011). In instances where sex education is provided in schools, it often leans toward an abstinence-only curriculum (Santelli et al., 2017) and offers restricted information focused solely on heterosexual, risk reduction, and cis-gendered sexual practices (Guttmacher Institute, 2023). This sociocultural context informs my participants experiences – many, which tell a story of unlearning a culture of "silence" around sexual behavior that also carries with it a gendered sexual script (i.e., women's purity; penetrative, procreative sex; prioritization of cis male ejaculation; and women's bodies looking a certain way).

Akin to previous research (Ackard et al., 2000; Faith & Schare, 1993; Murstein & Holden, 1979; Poovey et al., 2022), the participants' perception of their bodies influenced their sexual behavior and sexual satisfaction. In line with work by Fahs (2014), many participants find themselves beholden to the patriarchal standards and expectations of men, regardless of their sexual orientation or gender identity. Similar to previous research, participants oftentimes find themselves perceiving their bodies and sexual pleasure through the lens of traditional femininity, thereby increasing rates of anxiety, particularly in relation to the presentation of their body (Bramwell & Morland, 2009; Carvalheira et al., 2017; Dosch et al., 2016; Gillen & Markey, 2019; Poovey et al., 2022; Quinn-Nilas et al., 2016; Sanchez & Kiefer, 2007; Silva et al., 2016). Consequently, this study builds upon the gender, body image, and sexual behavior literature to consider the role of sexual orientation and gender identity.

This research serves as an analysis of the pervasiveness of patriarchy as manifested through traditional gendered scripts that are prevalent in many queer women and genderqueer individual's lives. Many of the participants' self-worth, entitlement to pleasure, and enactment of sexual behavior were influenced by the heteronormative standard of female beauty and behavior. Again, sexual scripts are an intersection of gender structures and the individual that as previous scholars have noted perpetuates traditional gender norms, heterosexuality, and gender inequality (Gavey, 2005; Impett & Peplau, 2003; Jackson & Cram, 2003; Kiefer et al., 2006; Tolman, 2002). As illustrated throughout the findings, one cannot discuss women and genderqueer individual's sexual behaviors, even those within the LGBTQIA+ community, without also talking about power. Sexual scripts are seemingly inescapable (or at the very least, are in a constant process of unlearning), even to those who are aware of them.

The participants' stories of their sexual experiences provide a unique perspective, in that it allows us to see the embodiment of larger social institutions play out in a seemingly private, interactional way. The impacts of gender, race, and body size are examined through how these participants navigate and experience sexual interactions. Perhaps most interestingly, queer individuals recognize and are conscious of an unjust patriarchal system with its unattainable standards that shape their views and behaviors. Nevertheless, they often end up conforming to these standards themselves. That is, participants are both resisting notions of ideal feminine beauty, while reckoning with its tight hold on their actions. This in mind, these narratives allow me to contemplate questions such as how do participants perpetuate gendered sexual scripts when they don't prioritize their own sexual pleasure, and how may they be simultaneously deconstructing, or queering, forms of sexual pleasure when they love their bodies? This dualistic tension participants navigate as they reflect on their sexual life history reminds us to hold space for the continual, nonlinear process of unlearning problematic systems of oppression and the slow but restorative process of building our true selves. Finally, these narratives speak to the importance of work that needs to be done within larger institutions of education and media, to deconstruct the images of ideal femininity that finds itself creeping into queer women and genderqueer individuals' intimate sexual spaces.

NOTES

1. Genderqueer is used to describe a person whose gender identity does not correspond to conventional (western-colonial) binary gender categories. It may be used as an umbrella term to encompass various gender fluid identities (the genderqueer community such as agender, nonbinary, and genderfluid) or as a particular gender identity in it of itself (e.g., "I am genderqueer").

2. To self-objectify, view one's own body as an object to be looked at and evaluated by others.

3. All participants were asked after the interview what gender identity term(s) they felt comfortable with the author using in their analysis and writing. AFAB and genderqueer were some of the terms provided by all participants (among those who are not cis-gendered). Select participants use she/they pronouns. To honor their pronouns, I use them interchangeably.

4. When using the term vagina, I am using it in laymen's terms. This was discussed with each participant, in that it was inclusive of the vaginal canal, labia (lips), clitoris, and so forth.

5. Fin is "queer/pansexual" in terms of sexual interaction, but is homoromantic, in that she is only interested in romantic relationships with other queer-identified individuals, primarily other femme-identified individuals.
6. Acne on the back.
7. These studies primarily look at cis men and women and, therefore, leave out the trans and genderqueer community. If this study was gender inclusive, I suspect the results may look different.
8. However, social locations such as gender, race, social class, and other forms of power stratification define how emotions are *interpreted* (e.g., women being understood as too emotional and, thus, inferior or not taken seriously).

REFERENCES

Ackard, D., Kearney-Cooke, A., & Peterson, C. (2000). Effect of body image and self-image on women's sexual behaviors. *International Journal of Eating Disorders*, 28, 422–429.

Alvy, L. M. (2013). Do lesbian women have a better body image? Comparisons with heterosexual women and model of lesbian-specific factors. *Body Image*, 10(4), 524–534.

Armstrong, E., England, P., & Fogarty, A. (2010). Orgasm in college hookups and relationships. *American Sociological Review*, 77(3), 435–462.

Barker, M., & Langdridge, D. (2008). Bisexuality: Working with a silenced sexuality. *Feminism & Psychology*, 18(3), 389–394.

Becker, H. (1953). Becoming a marihuana user. *American Journal of Sociology*, 59, 235–242.

Berman, L., & Windecker, M. A. (2008). The relationship between women's genital self-image and female sexual function: A national survey. *Current Sexual Health Reports*, 5, 199–207.

Bramwell, R., & Morland, C. (2009). Genital appearance satisfaction in women: The development of a questionnaire and exploration of correlates. *Journal of Reproductive and Infant Psychology*, 27, 15–27.

Braun, V., & Wilkinson, S. (2001). Socio-cultural representations of the vagina. *Journal of Reproductive and Infant Psychology*, 19(1), 17–32.

Bryan, T. S. (2001). *Pretending to experience orgasm as a communicative act: How, when, and why some sexually experienced college women pretend to experience orgasm during various sexual behaviors* [Unpublished doctoral dissertation]. University of Kansas, Lawrence, KS.

Byers, E. S. (1996). How well does the traditional sexual script explain sexual coercion? Review of a program of research. *Journal of Psychology & Human Sexuality*, 8(1–2), 7–25.

Carvalheira, A., Godinho, L., & Costa, P. (2017). The impact of body dissatisfaction on distressing sexual difficulties among men and women: The mediator role of cognitive distraction. *Journal of Sex Research*, 54, 331–340.

Ciaralli, S., & Vercel, K. (2023). Affording pleasure: The role of objects in women's and AFAB individuals' sexual self-knowledge and pleasure. *Consumption Markets & Culture*. https://doi.org/10.1080/10253866.2023.2222657

Cokal, S. (2007). Clean porn: The visual aesthetics of hygiene, hot sex, and hair removal. In A. C. Hall & M. J. Bishop (Eds.), *Pop-porn: Pornography in American culture* (pp. 137–153). Praeger.

Connell, R. W. (2002). *Gender*. Blackwell.

Cook, I. (2004). Follow the thing: Papaya. *Antipode*, 26(4), 642–664.

Crann, S. E., Jenkins, A., Money, D. M., & O'Doherty, K. C. (2017). Women's genital body work: Health, hygiene and beauty practices in the production of idealized female genitalia. *Feminism & Psychology*, 27(4), 510–529.

Dosch, A., Ghisletta, P., & der Linden, M. V. (2016). Body image in dyadic and solitary sexual desire: The role of encoding style and distracting thoughts. *Journal of Sex Research*, 53, 1193–1206.

Dworkin, S. H. (1988). Not in man's image: Lesbians and the cultural oppression of body image. *Women & Therapy*, 8(1–2), 27–39.

Erdmans, M. (2007). The personal is political, but is it academic? *Journal of American Ethnic History*, 26(4), 7–23.

Evans, D. M. (2020). After practice? Material semiotic approaches to consumption and economy. *Cultural Sociology*, 14(4), 340–356.

Fahs, B. (2014). Genital panics: Constructing the vagina in women's qualitative narratives about pubic hair, menstrual sex, and vaginal self-image. *Body Image, 11*(3), 210–218.
Fahs, B., & Swank, E. (2016). The other third shift?: Women's emotion work in their sexual relationships. *Feminist Formations, 28*(3), 46–69.
Faith, M. S., & Schare, M. L. (1993). The role of body image in sexually avoidant behavior. *Archives of Sexual Behavior, 22*, 345–356.
Fontana, A. (2002). Postmodern trends in interviewing. In J. Holstein & J. Gubrium (Eds.), *Handbook of interview research: Context and method* (pp. 161–175). Sage.
Fredrickson, B. L., & Roberts T.-A. (1997). Objectification theory: Toward understanding women's lived experiences and mental health risks. *Psychology of Women Quarterly, 21*(2), 173–206.
Frith, H. (2013). Labouring on orgasms: Embodiment, efficiency, entitlement and obligations in heterosex. *Culture, Health & Sexuality, 15*(4), 494–510.
Gagnon, J. H. (1990). The explicit and implicit use of the scripting perspective in sex research. *Annual Review of Sex Research*, 1, 1–44.
Gagnon, J. H., & Simon, W. (1973). *Sexual conduct: The social sources of human sexuality*. Aldine.
Gavey, N. (2005). *Just sex? The cultural scaffolding of rape*. Routledge.
Geiger, S. N. G. (1986). Women's life histories: Method and content. *Signs, 11*(2), 334–351.
Gillen, M. M., & Markey, C. H. (2019). A review of research linking body image and sexual well-being. *Body Image, 31*, 294–301.
Goldfarb, E. S., & Lieberman, L. D. (2020). Three decades of research: The case for comprehensive sex education. *Journal of Adolescent Health, 68*(1), 13–27.
Gonzalez, K. A., Ramirez, J. L., & Galupo, M. P. (2017). 'I was and still am': Narratives of bisexual marking in the #stillbisexual campaign. *Sexuality & Culture, 21*(2), 493–515.
Guttmacher Institute (2023). *Sex and HIV education*. Retrieved March 22, 2023, from https://www.guttmacher.org/state-policy/explore/sex-and-hiv-education
Hamilton, L., & Armstrong, E. A. (2009). Gendered sexuality in young adulthood: Double binds and flawed options. *Gender & Society, 23*(5), 589–616.
Hayfield, N., Clarke, V., Halliwell, E., & Malson, H. (2013). Visible lesbians and invisible bisexuals: Appearance and visual identities among bisexual women. *Women's Studies International Forum, 40*(1), 172–182.
Hill, M. S., & Fischer, A. R. (2008). Examining objectification theory: Lesbian and heterosexual women's experiences with sexual and self-objectification. *The Counseling Psychologist, 36*(5), 745–776.
Holland, J., Ramazanoglu, C., Sharpe, S., & Thomson, R. (1994). Power and desire: The embodiment of female sexuality. *Feminist Review, 46*(1), 21–38.
Holstein, J., & Gubrium, J. (2000). *The self we live by: Narrative identity in a postmodern world*. Oxford University Press.
Impett, E. A., & Peplau, L. A. (2003). Sexual compliance: Gender, motivational, and relationship perspectives. *Journal of Sex Research, 40*, 87–100.
Jackson, S., & Cram, F. (2003). Disrupting the sexual double standard: Young women's talk about heterosexuality. *British Journal of Social Psychology, 42*(1), 113–127.
Jackson, S., & Scott, S. (2007). Faking like a woman? Toward an interpretive theorization of sexual pleasure. *Body and Society, 13*(2), 95–116.
Jones, R. K., & Biddlecom, A. (2011). Is the internet filling the sexual health information gap for teens? An exploratory study. *Journal of Health Communication, 16*(2), 112–123.
Kantor, L. M., & Lindberg, L. (2020). Pleasure and sex education: The need for broadening both content and measurement. *American Journal of Public Health, 110*(2), 145–148.
Kashubeck-West, S., Zeilman, M., & Deitz, C. (2018). Objectification, relationship satisfaction, and self-consciousness during physical intimacy in bisexual women. *Sexual and Relationship Therapy, 33*(1–2), 97–112.
Kiefer, A., Sanchez, D. T., Kalinka, C. J., & Ybarra, O. (2006). How women's nonconscious association of sex with submission relates to their subjective sexual arousability and ability to orgasm. *Sex Roles, 55*, 83–94.
Laws, J. L., & Schwartz, P. (1977). *Sexual scripts and the social construction of female sexuality*. Dryden Press.

Lindberg, L. D., & Kantor L. M. (2022). Adolescents' receipt of sex education in a nationally representative sample, 2011–2019. *Journal of Adolescent Health, 70*(2), 290–297.
Lips, H. M. (1981). *Women, men, and the psychology of power*. Prentice Hall.
Mayr, C. (2021). *The material vibrancy of sex: An analysis of consumption and the meaning of vibrators* [PhD dissertation, Alpen-Adria-Universität Klagenfurt].
McClelland, S. (2010). Intimate justice: A critical analysis of sexual satisfaction. *Social and Personality Psychology Compass, 2*(9), 663–680.
Murstein, B. I., & Holden, C. C. (1979). Sexual behavior and correlates among college students. *Adolescence, 14*, 625–639.
Parker, R. G., & Gagnon J. H. (1995). *Conceiving sexuality: Approaches to sex research in a postmodern world* (pp. 3–16). Routledge.
Peplau, L. A., Frederick, D. A., Yee, C., Maisel, N., Lever, J., & Ghavami, N. (2009). Body image satisfaction in heterosexual, gay, and lesbian adults. *Archives of Sexual Behavior, 38*(5), 713–725.
Polimeni, A. M., Austin, S. B., & Kavanagh, A. M. (2009). Sexual orientation and weight, body image, and weight control practices among young Australian women. *Journal of Women's Health, 18*(3), 355–362.
Poovey, K., de Jong, D. C., & Morey, K. (2022). The roles of body image, sexual motives, and distraction in women's sexual pleasure. *Archives of Sexual Behavior: The Official Publication of the International Academy of Sex Research, 51*(3), 1577–1589.
Quinn-Nilas, C., Benson, L., Milhausen, R. R., Buchholz, A. C., & Goncalves, M. (2016). The relationship between body image and domains of sexual functioning among heterosexual, emerging adult women. *Sexual Medicine, 4*, e182–e189.
Roberts, T., & Waters, P. L. (2008). Self-objectification and that 'not so fresh feeling'. *Feminist Therapeutic Interventions for Healthy Female Embodiment, 27*(3–4), 5–21.
Rodrigues, S. (2012). From vaginal exception to exceptional vagina: The biopolitics of female genital cosmetic surgery. *Sexualities, 15*(7), 778–794.
Rothblum, E. D. (1994). "I'll die for the revolution but don't ask me not to diet": Feminism and the continuing stigmatization of obesity. In P. Fallon, M. A. Katzman, & S. C. Wooley (Eds.), *Feminist perspectives on eating disorders* (pp. 53–76). Guilford Press.
Rowen, T. S., Gaither, T. W., Shindel, A. W., & Breyer, B. N. (2018). Characteristics of genital dissatisfaction among a nationally representative sample of U.S. women. *Journal of Sex Medicine, 15*(5), 698–704.
Sanchez, D. T., Fetterold, J. C., & Rudman, L. A. (2012). Eroticizing inequality in the United States: The consequences and determinants of traditional gender role adherence in intimate relationships. *Journal of Sex Research, 49*(2–3), 168–183.
Sanchez, D. T., & Kiefer, A. K. (2007). Body concerns in and out of the bedroom: Implications for sexual pleasure and problems. *Archives of Sexual Behavior, 36*, 808–820.
Santelli, J. S., Kantor, L. M., Grilo, S. A., Speizer, I. S., Lindberg, L. D., Heitel, J., Schalet, A. T., Lyon, M. E., Mason-Jones, A. J., McGovern, T., Heck, C. J., Rogers, J., & Ott, M. A. (2017). Abstinence-only-until-marriage: An updated review of U.S. policies and programs and their impact. *Journal of Adolescent Health, 61*(3), 273–280.
Satinsky, S., Reece, M., Dennis, B., Sanders, S., & Bardzell, S. (2012). An assessment of body appreciation and its relationship to sexual function in women. *Body Image, 9*(1), 137–144.
Schick, V. R., Rima, B. N., & Calabrese, S. K. (2011). Evulvalution: The portrayal of women's external genitalia and physique across time and the current Barbie doll ideals. *Journal of Sex Research, 48*(1), 74–81.
Seal, D. W., & Ehrhardt, A. A. (2003). Masculinity and urban men: Perceived scripts for courtship, romantic, and sexual interactions with women. *Culture, Health & Sexuality, 5*, 295–319.
Seidman, S. (2010). *The social construction of sexuality* (2nd ed.). W. W. Norton & Company.
Silva, E., Pascoal, P. M., & Nobre, P. (2016). Beliefs about appearance, cognitive distraction and sexual functioning in men and women: A mediation model based on cognitive theory. *Journal of Sexual Medicine, 13*, 1387–1394.
Simon, W., & Gagnon, J. H. (1984). Sexual scripts. *Society, 22*, 53–60.
Smith, D. (1988). Femininity as discourse. In L. G. Roman & L. K. Christian-Smith (Eds.), *Becoming feminine: The politics of popular culture*. Falmer.

Stets, J. E. (2005). Examining emotions in identity theory. *Social Psychology Quarterly*, *68*(1), 39–56.
Tiggemann, M., & Kenyon, S. J. (1998). The hairlessness norm: The removal of body hair in women. *Sex Roles*, *39*(11), 873–885.
Tiggemann, M., & Lewis, C. (2004). Attitudes toward women's body hair: Relationship with disgust sensitivity. *Psychology of Women Quarterly*, *28*(4), 381–387.
Tiggemann, M., & Hodgson, S. (2008). The hairlessness norm extended: Reasons for and predictors of women's body hair removal at different body sites. *Sex Roles*, *59*(11–12), 889–897.
Toerien, M., & Wilkinson, S. (2003). Gender and body hair: Constructing the feminine woman. *Women's Studies International Forum*, *26*, 333–344.
Toerien, M., Wilkinson, S., & Choi, P. Y. L. (2005). Body hair removal: The mundane production of normative femininity. *Sex Roles*, *52*, 399–406.
Tolman, D. L. (2002). *Dilemmas of desire: Teenage girls talk about sexuality*. Harvard University Press.
Træen, B., Markovic, A., & Ingela L. K. (2016). Sexual satisfaction and body image: A cross-sectional study among Norwegian young adults. *Sexual and Relationship Therapy*, *31*(2), 123–137.
van den Brink, F., Vollmann, M., Smeets, M. A. M., Hessen, D. J., & Woertman, L. (2018). Relationships between body image, sexual satisfaction, and relationship quality in romantic couples. *Journal of Family Psychology*, *32*(4), 466–474.
Ward, L. M., Rosenscruggs, D., & Aguinaldo, E. R. (2022). A scripted sexuality: Media, gendered sexual scripts, and their impact on our lives. *Current Directions in Psychological Science*, *31*(4), 369–374.
Wiederman, M. W. (2005). The gendered nature of sexual scripts. *The Family Journal*, *13*(4), 496–502.
Woertman, L., & van den Brink, F. (2012). Body image and female sexual functioning and behavior: A review. *Journal of Sex Research*, *49*(2–3), 184–211.
Yean, C., Benau, E. M., Dakanalis, A., Hormes, J. M., Perone, J., & Timko, C. A. (2013). The relationship of sex and sexual orientation to self-esteem, body shape satisfaction, and eating disorder symptomatology. *Frontiers in Psychology*, *4*, 887.

CHAPTER 6

I DON'T WEAR BLACK: PROFESSIONAL MUSLIM WORKERS AND PERSONAL DRESS CODE

Salam Aboulhassan

Department of Sociology, Wayne State University, USA

ABSTRACT

Based on qualitative data from a large study exploring Muslim experiences in the workplace, this chapter explains how Muslim dress standards inform identity and are influenced by US cultural ideals about self-presentation and perceived anti-Muslim hostility. Theoretical sampling was used to find 25 men and 59 women, 32 of whom are veiled. These individuals worked at major corporations as numerical minorities or held professions where they encountered non-Muslims regularly. Informed by theories of orientalism and social identity, findings examine hegemonic representations of organizational power and describe how men could employ masculine practices to navigate anti-Muslim discourse and foster a sense of belonging at work. Within immigrant-centered workplaces, women face cultural backlash for appropriating Western styles deemed immodest. While working outside their community, women who wore hijabs emphasized their femininity through softer colors, makeup, or "unpinning" their veil to offset the visceral reaction to their hijab. Thus, adapting to workplace dress expectations is structured by intersections of gender, religion, and workplace location. This chapter illustrates how Muslim dress strategies indirectly reflect how Western standards of dress, behavior, and self-expression determine qualifications and approachability within workplace structures, marginalizing Muslims and reproducing racial and gender hierarchies.

Keywords: Muslims; workplace; hijab; identity theory; orientalism; self-expression

Racial and gender subtext often underlies organizational dress policies (Craig, 2020; Reddy-Best, 2018). Executive standards (i.e., dress code and daily conduct) reflect an embodied social hierarchy where European fashion signifies power and status, and people of color and women are excluded from leadership roles due to esthetic considerations (Banks, 2000; Dawson et al., 2019). The critically acclaimed program Mad Men – referencing the 1960s white-collar executives of New York's Madison Avenue – vividly depicts the tailored sharkskin suits, wingtip oxfords, and the clean-shaven façade that continue to typify executive material using forceful masculinity. Far removed from the 1960s workplace, studies continue to show how hegemonic masculinity legitimizes white organizational power. Furthermore, they show how employers assert control over their employees through dress codes and how workers prioritize self-presentation when entering the workforce (Acker, 1990; Connell & Messerschmidt, 2005; Cutts et al., 2015; Pratt & Rafaeli, 1997).

In addition to ethnic, racial, and religious differences, immigrants also bring a variety of dress expressions to the US labor market. Muslim Americans specifically use Islamic beards and the hijab to embody their faith and publicly assert their religious identity (Göle, 2003). These practices signify modesty, piety, and belief in God but have also been re-embraced in politically charged climates where Islamophobia is rampant (Mahmood, 2005; Ruby, 2005; Zahedi, 2011). Muslim Americans are one of the youngest faith communities in the United States.[1] Their education levels are similar to US Christian groups with 30% employed in professional positions (Gallup, 2009; Mogahed & Chouhoud, 2017). Underlying shifts in appearance among this group are theories of marginalized masculinities (Connell, 1995) and hegemonic femininities. Hegemonic femininities examine multiple sets of power relationships to question celebrated ideals of womanhood that justify elite women's power over others (Collins, 2004; Hamilton et al., 2019; Pyke & Johnson, 2003). The increasing power dynamics favoring non-Muslim workers also perpetuate inequality within Muslim groups, where those who do not embody Islamic identity through dress are partially privileged.

Using theoretical sampling (Strauss, 1987) to identify Muslims in professional positions, this chapter investigates hegemonic representations of organizational power through dress. Hegemonic power refers to the cultural ideologies, images, and representations that shape group and individual consciousness and support institutional policies (Dill & Zambrana, 2009). While workers use dress to conform to workplace culture and/or avoid anti-Muslim hostility in daily work interactions, effective adaptation is influenced by gender, religion, and workplace location. Visible signifiers (beard, hijab) are catalysts for discrimination for both groups (Goffman, 1963), but men could better navigate anti-Muslim discourse through hegemonic masculine practices. Despite marginalized identities, suits provide men with embodied expressions of masculinity, enabling them to negotiate overlapping social positions successfully (Barry & Weiner, 2019). Women face a disproportionate share of dress-related stigma. Apart from failing to meet white feminine ideals, women face community backlash for adopting Western styles considered immodest. Those who wear a veil have a greater need to take care of their appearance to counteract visceral reactions to their hijab outside their communities. To begin with, social identity theories explain how individuals use dress to differentiate competing social identities within organizations (Pratt & Rafaeli, 1997). Additionally, Muslims are stigmatized by orientalism, which is an imperialist mode of discourse that produces images of Eastern women and men in Western society. Gendered orientalism refers to the perception that Muslim women are culturally and antithetically distinct from Western women (Abu-Lughod, 2013; Love, 2017; Said, 1979).

DRESS AND SOCIAL IDENTITY

Dress choices require multiple frameworks for analysis (Kaiser, 2012). Georg Simmel argued that fashion reflects human tension, making people emulate those they admire and distinguish themselves from those they dislike. Moreover, dress and style reveal social class, aggravating class tension (Miller, 2005). To eliminate class distinctions, the lower classes imitate upper-class fashions, causing the upper class to abandon and re-invent new fashions. Thus, a cycle of imitation and differentiation is perpetuated, transforming taste into a symbol of class worship and linking fashion to capital accumulation and cultural capital (Bourdieu, 1984; Simmel, 1957). The correlation between specific tastes and intelligence, learning, and achievement has evolved over time. Cultural capital can be embodied (mannerisms, dress), objectified (works of art), institutionalized (credentials), and exchanged for economic or social gain. Rareness, effort, and monetary value determine cultural elements' prestige (Bourdieu, 1984).

Individuals also *do* gender through dress (West & Zimmerman, 1987). Adolescent girls and ethnic minority boys often undergo dramatic changes in their gender presentation as they become aware of their differential statuses (Halim et al., 2011). Schools are often criticized for maintaining white and heteronormative hegemonic values through dress codes (Reddy-Best & Choi, 2020; Rogers, 2022). Adults also draw on the defining beliefs, attitudes, and/or behaviors (including dress) of groups to enhance their self-esteem and self-concept (Tajfel & Turner, 1985). As such, the personal care and dress industries are billion-dollar industries accounting for 5% of consumer spending (Hamermesh, 2011). In examining workplace dominance and exploitation, scholars reveal that nametags, clothing, and jewelry communicate an organization's values and beliefs, with preferential treatment given to those who present in an esthetically pleasing manner (Acker, 1990; Cutts et al., 2015). Dress is inextricably intertwined with identity and spatially defined; it encodes a relationship between the body and culture, establishing a sense of place and identity (Craik, 1994). Especially relevant to immigrant groups, the body reveals personal information about the individual to the outside world (Kaiser, 2012).

DRESS, LABELING, AND ANTI-MUSLIM DISCOURSE

Labeling theories illustrate how individual styles that differ from the majority are classified as deviant. In its worst form, labeling impacts self-perception by stigmatizing and dehumanizing individuals (Becker, 1963; Goffman, 1963). The stigma attached to Black feminine expressions, along with European beauty standards, perpetuates a legacy of self-hatred for Black women (Bryant, 2013). Additionally, thousands of Americans wore black hoodies in protest of Trayvon Martin's unjust death, highlighting how criminal stereotypes often revolve around dress and how Black communities reclaim forms of dress as a means of addressing racial inequality (Matthews & Reddy-Best, 2022; Miller, 2005; Nguyen, 2015). For Muslim Americans, the mainstream media rarely portrays expressions of Islamic religious identity (hijab, beards) as embodied expressions of piety. Rather, they are filtered through a Western ideological model of Muslims as backward people with insatiable sexual desires and intellectual shortcomings (Love, 2017).

By dominating, and restructuring the orient, orientalism emphasizes the deepest images of the other within Western political, intellectual, and material civilizations. The elite practice their ideologies by studying other groups, legitimizing imperialist action abroad, and suppressing dissent at home (Aoude, 2006). Orientalism promotes the belief that Islamic and Western civilizations are fundamentally incompatible, vilifying Muslim men as violent and oppressive and Muslim women as oppressed (Abu-Lughod, 2013; Said, 1979). Writings by contemporary feminists revived orientalist imagery. Early European writers transformed Islamic harems (domestic spaces designated for women and children) into secluded spaces reserved for powerful men's sexual pleasure. As these descriptions evolved, terms such as "caged virgins" and/or "trapped flies" were used to portray Muslim women as oppressed, burdensome, and eroticized (Abu-Lughod, 2013; Cevik, 2018; Zine, 2002). More generally, gendered orientalism articulates how the veil symbolizes a despised difference in Western media depictions. In addition, Sikh men are often mistaken for Muslims due to monolithic and racist imagery depicting Muslim men as being dark, bearded, and wearing turbans. As beards are vilified as oppressive symbols, they risk anti-Muslim attacks (Dhillon, 2011). Esthetics and self-expression vary widely among Muslims. The images described above reflect Western dominance over the orient (Said, 1979) rather than a multicultural and diverse populace.

WORK IDENTITY AND DRESS

Workplaces, like other institutions, embody esthetic ideals. West and Zimmerman's (1987) "doing gender" framework is expanded upon by Acker (1990), who claims that organizational structures are not gender neutral. Gender is embedded in organizational processes (in power/status divisions, symbols and discourse, and interactions), reproducing white and masculine ideals at work. Workers also embody their personalities through speech, dress, and individual behavior (Connell, 1987). Although employers prefer individuals who present themselves in an esthetic manner, appearance-based discrimination is not illegal. Yet, in workplaces where beauty plays a critical role in job performance, a beauty premium has been observed, particularly among men (Deryugina & Shurchkov, 2015; Hamermesh, 2011; Ruffle & Shtudiner, 2015). Additionally, dress choices reflect competing social identities at work because of white and masculine esthetics that define organizational prototypes of leaders (through speech, dress, and interaction styles) (Hogg & Terry, 2000; Pratt & Rafaeli, 1997). Black men who fail to present properly are considered less valuable and lower status at work. Similarly, the association between unprofessionalism and Black women's natural hair results in a premium for those who straighten their hair (Dawson et al., 2019; Wingfield, 2013).

Last, *coercive assimilation* is a term used in antidiscrimination literature to describe Muslim women's identity performance at work, resulting from a subjective understanding of how promotion decisions favor workplace conformity (Aziz, 2014). Not only do white, masculine values dictate how minoritized groups should behave, dress, and speak, but also people who maintain dreadlocks or corn rows as hairstyles, speak Spanish, or wear veils face discrimination at work. Therefore, these groups will employ image management techniques (including appropriate expressions of dress) to symbolize in-group association (Aziz, 2014; Burke & Stets, 2009; Cutts et al., 2015; Miller, 2005; Nistor, 2017). Organizational literature defines *facades of conformity* as ways minoritized groups display their agreement with workplace culture. When work and personal values diverge, individuals conform (Hewlin, 2003). As courts continue to deem dress practices as voluntary and outside protected categories of identity, the importance people place on identity determines how discrimination incidents unfold (Aziz, 2014).

METHODS

This article is based on a qualitative study exploring how Muslims experience racialized and gendered workplaces. Between 2018 and 2020, I conducted in-depth interviews with 25 men and 59 women, 32 of whom were veiled. Participants included self-identified Arab Muslims working in Southeast Michigan. Between 22 and 56 years old, participants hailed from Lebanon, Palestine, Syria, Iraq, Jordan, and Yemen. Through theoretical sampling, Muslim workers in large corporations and professions where they regularly encounter non-Muslims were identified. Theoretical sampling is a grounded theory approach that relies on larger theories and/or emerging data to determine what data to collect, allowing the use of inclusion criteria separate from sociodemographic characteristics (Strauss, 1987). Due to a lack of data on Muslims in US workplaces, recruiting Muslims from each subgroup is a complex issue. Rather than sampling within an industry, I focused on semi-professional and professional positions (jobs requiring a college degree/ license). Purposive sampling involves identifying relevant cases that contain abundant information about the subject matter in a purposeful manner. To reach information-rich key informants in hard-to-reach populations, I tapped into my Arab and Muslim community networks. Additionally, snowball sampling, which recruits additional participants from initial participants' contacts and/or networks, is effective when dealing with hard-to-reach populations or when a researcher cannot construct a sampling frame because it does not exist or is difficult to acquire (Goodman, 2001). Interviews resulted in four major industry categories: social services (i.e., educators and healthcare workers), Science, technology, engineering, mathematics or STEM (i.e., engineers and software analysts), financial services (i.e., real estate agents and mortgage brokers), and others (i.e., utility or government workers). Each industry category was reviewed periodically to ensure all sub-groups were interviewed. Thirty-two respondents described their workplaces as embedded in Arab/Muslim immigrant communities.

INTERVIEWS AND DATA ANALYSIS

Interviews ranged between 45 and 120 minutes. Participants were assigned pseudonyms, and employers' names were omitted. Interview topics included career advancement, religious expression at work, and workplace interaction. Because Islam emphasizes modesty for Muslims, dress choices were often discussed in relation to religious expression. Participants noted that clean, professional appearances expressed modesty, leading to discussions about style, color, and grooming. Participant workplace attire was observed during 41 interviews conducted during or immediately after work hours. In the early stages of data analysis, field notes emphasize the importance of dress among Muslims (Fetterman, 2010). These notes describe color, dress shirts, ties, tie clips, jewelry, and makeup, among other esthetic considerations.

I suspended all theoretical expectations to allow emerging data to inform theory (Glaser & Strauss, 1967). Focused and open coding techniques were used to identify emerging themes (Emerson et al., 1995). Open coding enabled me to code terms, ideas, or concepts related to dress codes. These topics included the hijab, shaving beards, and style variations. Using focused coding, relationships between codes were identified, contributing to categories such as (1) assimilation through dress, (2) workplace hostility, and (3) dress and shame. Furthermore, I reexamined quotes or stories to organize them around various aspects of identity (e.g., gender, religious visibility, and type of work). Data collection and analysis combined with existing literature revealed subgroup differences and how workplace location influenced dress choices.

RESULTS

Participants discussed dress with two objectives: embodying hegemonic images of success at work and navigating anti-Muslim bias. Through self-expression, men developed their work identity and circumvented religious fundamentalism assumptions. It is mainly when men maintained full Islamic-style beards that they were subjected to workplace hostility. The experiences of women differed across abstract immigrant boundaries that distinguished workplaces where Muslims are numerical minorities from those that employ and/or serve significant Arab/Muslim populations. While this distinction creates new intersectional experiences for all Muslims, men did not emphasize self-presentation differences. Regardless of their location, workplaces can serve as central sites where men prove and negotiate their manhood (Berdahl et al., 2018). Another explanation is that ethnic communities offer men more security to express themselves (Naber, 2006). For women, immigrant workplaces reproduced cultural gender norms associated with the immigrant community. Additionally, the pressure to reproduce feminine displays increased for women who wear a veil when working outside the community. By adding color, avoiding baggy clothing, and exposing their neck, they emphasized femininity to combat discrimination caused by their hijab.

MEN AND THE SUIT

Men demonstrated a unique preference for wearing suits. As material cultural artifacts, suits are critical symbols for men confronting marginalized masculinities. Historically, Black and Latino men have worn suits in an effort to gain visibility and fight the perception that they do not conform to hegemonic masculinity (Barry & Weiner, 2019). Omar, an engineer, described wearing suits daily to communicate his awareness of how hegemonic masculine esthetics shape perceptions of success (Connell, 1995). Despite the relaxed dress policy in public school systems, Mahmoud, a principal, also preferred wearing shirts and ties daily, honoring a traditional form of masculinity (Connell & Messerschmidt, 2005). As a commercial banker in an industry known for marginalizing minoritized groups (Roth, 2004), Tarek discussed prioritizing his appearance:

> I'm really good at getting frank feedback. I always tell people "tell me things that are not HR appropriate"...The typical polished white privileged American guy was the role that I was instructed to have. I was wearing suits, but I wasn't wearing the right suits. He said, "Go and find this website right now." I played it off, but I spent 500 bucks on these golf shirts with these little whales. He said go get them tailored to fit you perfectly and make sure you shave every single day ... I'm so concerned about making the right image, to match what they saw on paper.

Tarek's white-assuming position conceals his ethnicity and religious identity, granting him access to the information he needs to succeed, "I recognized early on in my life that I could be identified as white ... I have incredible professional advantages in the workplace." Studies prove phenotype matters when comparing wages among Latino workers, with lighter-skinned men earning more (Gomez, 2000). Tarek's racial status ensured he had access to the unofficial rules of white middle-class success. The concept of *white assuming* over *white passing* better reflects how individuals understand their own experiences when discussing racialized power relations (Bueno-Hansen & Montes, 2019). Furthermore, Tarek's ability to "play off" this knowledge and his desire to match his appearance with his credentials demonstrate how cultural capital can be embodied as a cultivated style that becomes social currency (Bourdieu, 1986).

Unlike Tarek, Ahmed visibly presented as Muslim. His religious displays as a school principal in a predominantly white area garnered strong reactions from colleagues and parents alike. In addition to carrying Islamic prayer beads, Ahmed prayed openly in his office and displayed pictures of his wife and daughters (all of whom wear veils). On wearing a suit daily, Ahmed stated,

> You play the game – like code-switching ... I am part of a privileged society in certain areas, and then in certain areas I'm not. I recognize my privilege. I utilize my privilege, and I also recognize where I'm not privileged.

In bilingual communities, code-switching occurs when languages are alternated to express thoughts, emphasize membership, or convey feelings. In employment practices, code-switching can also involve soft skills such as changing accents, attitudes, and attire (Krasas, 2018). The concept of *white racial frames* illustrates how the white majority understands Latino and Black speech patterns, assuming there is linguistic disorder (Hill, 2008). Using the term, Ahmed described how he manages interpersonal tension resulting from individualistic faith expressions by dressing accordingly.

Moreover, participants used their image to counter stereotypes that link terrorism to Muslim masculinity. Haysam, an attorney, stated, "I don't go to an airport with a full beard, because I don't want the *look*" to provide context when describing his fashion choices:

> I always wear a suit. I always try to look my best because I know how people perceive you the first time they see you. I feel like there's already a layer of discrimination. I can take that layer off by looking presentable, smelling good. I think I've become a very good attorney because of my communication skills. I would always try to make somebody feel good as I'm talking to them, to normalize myself before we would even [discuss] the case.

Haysam's desire to present a non-threatening appearance and Ahmed's use of code-switching are similar to how Black men shave their beards, keep their desks clean, and whistle tunes to counteract stereotypes regarding their threatening character (Dawson et al., 2019; Wingfield, 2013). Among Black professionals, code-switching is a survival technique that dismantles barriers between white and Black colleagues, increasing networking and promotional opportunities (Santiago et al., 2021). Furthermore, due to increased discrimination after 9/11, English proficiency is especially important for Arab Americans (Ajrouch & Jamal, 2007). Haysam addressed both beauty ideals surrounding grooming and communication skills in light of images linking Arabic-speaking Muslim men to terror. The juxtaposition of Haysam's image with the violent caricature of bearded terrorists hijacking airplanes illustrates the significance of the beard among Muslim men.

Following 9/11, writings on American masculinity emphasized the clean-shaven appearance of the authentic American man (Ferry, 2017). In this study, 16 men were clean-shaven, 4 maintained short corporate-style beards no longer than 2 inches long, and 5 maintained faded or short-boxed beards between 3 and 6 inches long (Lawson, 2021). Western perceptions of Islamic practices as signs of extremism and radicalization influence beard maintenance (including their removal) among men (Abbas, 2019; Naderi, 2018). According to Malik, an engineer, beards are no longer understood through piety frameworks (Abbas, 2019) when he described an encounter with other Muslim men, "When [they] saw me growing a beard, it's like what's your problem? Like I had become religiously conservative." Other men believed US culture has embraced beards as a masculine esthetic (Lawson, 2021) noting that it was a part of the general culture or that it was fashionable to maintain a beard. Generally, men attributed their clean-shaven appearances to esthetic preferences and work identities, illustrating how a beard represents unruly, untamed masculinity, whereas a clean-shaven appearance indicates conformity at work (Harding, 2002).

Beards were considered primary Muslim markers, regardless of preferences. Rashad, a nurse in a hospital that employs and serves Arabs and Muslims, emphasized the importance of workplace location in allowing him to maintain a full beard, "My beard, I love my beard. It trumps anyone's opinion ... Now people who work outside of the community – I still have 30 percent of my coworkers who are minorities, Arabs. The patients, same thing." Haysam reiterated this sentiment, "In this community, it's not an issue... I would not want to go to Oakland County or Macomb County."[2] Hadi, a program manager working outside the boundaries of the immigrant enclave, described the supervisor's reaction to his beard:

> They didn't want me to keep my beard. They thought it wasn't professional – they thought it was very distracting and they thought it was a "terrorist look." I said, no, this is my beard, it's part of me. I'm not taking that off …. They try to write you up, not approve overtime [or] vacation. This is part of my identity. I'm not going to break my standards, and what I believe in just because you don't like it.

Hadi's beard bears religious significance, exacerbating his conflict with his supervisor. Beards aren't commanded in the Qur'an. Muslim men often wear beards to emulate the Prophet and symbolize devotion (Ball & Haque, 2003). Hadi ultimately requested a transfer, noting subtle mistreatment (write-ups and denying time-off requests) after refusing to shave. Haysam and Rashad's descriptions of working within immigration boundaries frame the discussion of women's experiences.

WOMEN

Dress played a crucial role in women's professional identity, helping them exude professionalism and establish their positions. Sexist and racist assumptions associated with hegemonic forms of femininity and masculinity presented unique challenges to women. Furthermore, workplace location influenced how women's dress affected their relationships at work. Employers in immigrant-dense neighborhoods provide employment opportunities for community members and protect workers from out-group workplace discrimination (Hellerstein et al., 2011; Magee et al., 2007). They include real estate, mortgage, and law offices, as well as schools and hospitals situated within ethnic enclaves. These work sites also reproduce gender norms specific to their immigrant communities, consequential for women.

Immigrant Workplaces

Women in immigrant workplaces discussed being chastised for immodest dress when conforming to US feminine fashions. Celine, a school administrator who described her clothing choices as form-fitting, poised, and confident, stated:

> There was a lot of, this very western looking woman is dressing inappropriately .... My principal told me, you're very smart and very pretty, but I think you need to go buy new clothes .... There was always a complaint about how I dressed. She's too sexy. She's too sexy. It shut me down. It pulled me away from people. It made me hate women.

In *Walker* v. *IRS*, a Black plaintiff claims she was treated unfairly by her Black manager because she had lighter skin. The case was dismissed for lack of evidence, but it marked the first time the courts distinguished colorism from racism (McCray, 2012). Celine's dilemma is a direct result of her cultural dress expression rather than her phenotype. Cultural re-authenticity contextualizes the consequences associated with Arab American women violating normative gender expectations within Arab culture (Naber, 2006). Her narrative demonstrated the institutionalization of gender expectations within immigrant workplaces, penalizing those who embody US forms of feminine beauty and exacerbating tensions among minority women. As Celine indicated,

> I had to overcompensate. Muslim hijabi women working in the schools, I think I unconsciously had to let them know that I was a good Muslim to be accepted by them ... I would bring up God, I'm not a sinner. I'm like you even though I'm dressed like this.

To address the tension, Celine noted a change in self-perception and behavior. Recreating US expressions of professionalism also meant challenging gender expectations within immigrant communities, where cultural retention is women's primary responsibility (Naber, 2006).

For Naima, a manager who wears a veil, modesty issues also divided people of different national origins: "The Yemeni community asks, are you too Americanized? From the Arab non-Yemeni community, they're always surprised I'm well put together as a Yemini woman. That's not the expectation." Along with criticism for abandoning modesty requirements, Naima described inaccurate assumptions about Yemeni American conservatism. Interaction patterns between Arab ethnic groups in Detroit are structured around these assumptions, with women's behavior and bodies dividing the groups. Ayatt, a school administrator who wears a veil, elaborated, "Yemini women in this community don't necessarily dress the way I might ... They assume that I'm Lebanese. The tone shifts when they realize that I'm Yemeni ... they look me up and down." Mormon women also describe community scrutiny for ignoring traditional gender norms when deciding to work (Leamaster & Einwohner, 2018). Symbols of American cultural identity are stigmatized in immigrant workplaces, as evidenced by Naima, Ayatt, and Celine, and women are reprimanded for performing immodest behaviors while also compromising their religious identities (Casey, 2018).

Outside the Community

Muslim women disrupted hegemonic expectations associated with their positions when they stepped outside their immigrant communities for work. Batool's dress choices are influenced by images of the Rambo litigator (Pierce, 1996), whose aggression in court is a hallmark of successful lawyers:

> Close your eyes and think about what TV taught you about attorneys, they all look like the guy from "Law and Order," with salt and pepper, full head of hair, and a perfect suit. They [client] want to walk in with that guy ... When they're standing next to me, they're like, are you going to be a bull dog in there or are you going to stay quiet? ... To earn respect, I have to be perfect. I have to dress perfectly, I have to look perfect, I have to articulate every sentence succinctly.

Compared with other Black professional women, Black women lawyers are less likely to style their hair naturally due to perceptions of their aggressiveness (Karl et al., 2022). Alternatively, Batool illustrated how Arab and Muslim women are pressured to perfect their image because of sexist assumptions regarding their quiet and soft dispositions and litigation skills. Her experience echoed Haysam's, who previously linked dress to communication. Both described wardrobe choices as part of broader identity projects intended to portray successful US integration. Overlaps in experiences have enabled minority men to empathize with and support minority women who face unique challenges at work (Wingfield, 2013). Unfortunately, Muslims often lack access to other Muslim professionals in their fields who can offer support when problems arise at work.

Veiled women exemplify the consequences of failing to meet hegemonic feminine standards. Eighteen women who veiled were numerical minorities at their workplaces. Four others held positions that required them to travel beyond their ethnic communities in order to perform their duties (i.e., real estate agents). There has been research demonstrating workplace discrimination against hijab-wearing women (Aslam, 2011; Koura, 2018). While women faced a range of hostile reactions to their hijab, they primarily used clothing to dispel assumptions of conservatism. They observed that other Muslims (both men and women who do not veil) have an easier time maintaining their appearances since they are not concerned with fitting the hijab into hegemonic notions of beauty, femininity, and professionalism. This section describes several veiled strategies, such as wearing fitted rather than baggy clothes, wearing bright colors, and showing their necks and/or hair.

Veiled Strategies

This group of women preferred structured and contoured styles. They reflected on their dress choices by revisiting awkward encounters where Muslim women are stereotyped. To explain her dress choices as a tax analyst, Fay recounted an incident with older white men she described as corporate clients:

> Very on point with the way I presented myself. Very careful with how I spoke. I upped the A-game when it came to English. Obviously, it's my first language. But I wanted to make sure that it was perfect...They were intrigued. One was rude. They asked, "Are you allowed to walk into society by yourself?" [Laughs] "But you're so well-dressed, and you're dressed modern." I was wearing a suit. They wanted me in a full blown 'abaya.

While Fay offered another account of how Muslims link dress and English fluency, she emphasized how organizational cultures have adopted and reproduced inaccurate perceptions of her hijab as a symbol of oppression and backwardness, as evidenced by the assumption that her movements were restricted and the surprise reaction to her modern appearance.

Fay also addressed the 'abaya. 'Abayas are part of conservative veiling practices. The garments tend to be black, loose, and have large sleeves. Women wear these garments as a generalized form of religious dress in some regions of the Arab world (Al-Qasimi, 2010). Women who veiled in this study did so in its most common expression, covering their hair and neck. None reported wearing 'abayas. Amani, a real estate agent, used this term to describe the opposite of professionalism among Muslim women, "Not like those 'abayas some women wear. I won't wear that ever. I don't like them. But it also has to do with dressing the part – the American part – in suits." Thus, 'abayas are symbols of religious conservatism, sloppiness, and unprofessionalism. Amani's statement also reflected the emergence of a hijab-fashion subculture among career-driven Muslim women who strive to emulate Western middle-class women (Nistor, 2017). Yet, in Muslim countries like Saudi Arabia where 'abayas are mandatory, working women are more positive about the 'abaya's fashionable qualities and its ability to differentiate women at work according to their personalities or roles (DeCoursey, 2017). Linda, an automotive engineer, described how these demands conflicted with her desire for modesty:

> I want to wear [shirts] to my knees, but I'm scared because that makes me seem more conservative. I wore it a couple of times. No one has made comments. It's an internal thing. I feel like people are not going to accept it, or people are going to think I'm very conservative …. It comes from the notion of, you're oppressed, or someone is forcing you to wear it, and "Why don't you dress like us? Why don't you look like us?"

Having to recreate Eurocentric styles to find employment also makes Black women feel inauthentic and causes identity loss (Dawson et al., 2019). Online communities have emerged, such as surviving hijab, providing Muslim women the opportunity to express their feelings about the hijab, including their experiences at work (Pahwa, 2021).

Another strategy involves choosing bright colors over black. Color carries meaning and is context-specific. It impacts individual thoughts, feelings, and actions. For example, red can be perceived negatively when worn by an opponent or when no context clues are provided while blue and green are positively linked to performance and task engagement (Elliot & Maier, 2014). Historically, Muslims used black (i.e., clothing and flags/banners) to symbolize political opposition and protest. However, no Qur'anic injunction requires Muslims to wear specific colors. Depending on the circumstances, the Prophet of Islam wore colored turbans. Furthermore, in some traditions, Muslims are even discouraged from dressing in black (Takim, 2018). Women associated colors with fields, skin tones, personal preferences, and expressions of beauty. Lisa, a hospital pharmacist, stated,

> I'll buy trendy, colorful ones. I wear some make-up because I feel like I'll be like a plain Jane if I'm wearing a scarf and [no] eyeliner or something for my features to stand out. I probably do it to overcompensate but I still want to look pretty, I still want to look presentable.

Using color and makeup, Lisa countered the stereotype that women who wear a veil are pale, unfeminine, and outside hegemonic images of beauty. Color, according to Amani, counteracted the perception of conservatism that is often associated with Muslim women in the mainstream media:

> I don't wear black ever. The media, they always show women in black shawls. I will wear black clothes, but I'll wear a really nice colorful scarf ... Very colorful ... I don't want to say I'm ashamed. It's more comfort. I just keep getting that feeling of constantly getting stared at. I know people are thinking, who is she? What's she doing here?

A "daughter of terrorists" metaphor has been used to explain Arab Muslim women as extensions of violent Arab and Muslim men (Naber, 2008). To transform the esthetic black symbol of oppression into a more positive symbol of professionalism, those in black suits wore hijabs with color and patterns.

The last strategy involved unpinning the veil. A few described it as wearing a turban, showing some hair, or unpinning their hijab to expose their neck. In such situations, context was critical (e.g., real estate agents when conducting showings outside of their communities). Hana, a supply chain manager, explained why she draped her veil rather than pinning it,

> I'd be noticed less if I wear it this way as opposed to if I wore it more wrapped up .... It's not that it's a bad thing but it's like a super religious Muslim coming in. I suppose if you wear it looser, they're more like willing to come up to you and not stay away.

Identity theories explain how individuals *try on* identities when securing their position within groups (Parmentier et al., 2013). *Covering* explains how individuals modify their behaviors to ease the intrusiveness of a stigmatized symbol or trait (Dhillon, 2011; Goffman, 1963). As opposed to unpinning her veil, Jehan, a teacher, explained how showing her hair can facilitate workplace relationships with non-Muslim women:

> I showed them without it. They were interested. I was teaching them what it's about and that I'm just like everybody else. I have hair under this – because they didn't understand. Nobody understood ... I would invite them over too to eat all the time. I was trying to build all these relationships. It took some time.

It has been established that hair serves as a crucial marker of distinction between men and women, as well as among women. It is a crucial metric of beauty, femininity, and conformity to gender expectations (Weitz, 2001). Jehan's decision to reveal her hair is understood to be a signal of conformity and femininity, earning her a premium in professional relationships. In addition, exposing her hair in order to facilitate others' understanding of her hijab is another example of othering, in which members of a majority group perceive Islamic practices as strange. Overall, women unpinned their veils to foster meaningful relationships and dismantle assumptions about conservatism, as Hana explained in her statement about being noticed less and Jehan explains in her strategy of revealing her hair.

The preceding narratives demonstrate how the hijab expresses affiliation or differentiation between groups (Nistor, 2017). Dress strategies were crucial during interviewing and the first few months of employment, confirming research suggesting that outgoing graduate students are very concerned with their appearance, linking success to appearance at the beginning of their careers (Cutts et al., 2015). Some women said their individual styles returned after some time. Laura, a software engineer, stated:

At some point somebody told me, you know you're allowed to wear jeans, right? [Laughs] So I started wearing whatever I want. I know I don't dress like everyone here and I don't feel pressured to. I don't wear turbans, hats to make it look like I'm not wearing a headscarf. At this point, whether you're wearing jeans, a dress, or you're completely modest, if you're wearing a hijab, that immediately sets you apart.

Linda's biggest challenge was getting comfortable, feeling accepted, and accepting her veil would always be visible.

CONCLUSION

Muslim professionals' occupational experiences are scarcely studied. This chapter addressed how racial, ethnic, religious, and gender identities intersect to create complex organizational patterns (Acker, 1990; Berdahl et al., 2018; Connell, 1987; Martin, 2004; Wingfield, 2013), resulting in the stigmatization and subordination of sub-groups of US Muslims. First, hegemonic masculine/feminine discourses marginalize Muslim workers and perpetuate racial and gender hierarchies at work. Narratives explain how Western standards of dress, behavior, and self-expression evoke professionalism. Second, a socially constructed Muslim terrorist trope is amplified by cultural symbols such as the hijab and the Islamic beard (Gotanda, 2011; Karlsen & Nazroo, 2015) and portrays Muslims as aggressive and violent. Dressing in suits daily helped men establish in-group membership and dispelled stereotypes concerning aggressive behavior. This is in line with research articulating how minority men are partially advantaged at work given their gender (Wingfield, 2013). Even as stigmatized symbols, beards were also considered acceptable expressions of US masculinity. In addition to mediating anti-Muslim prejudice, the fact that most men preferred clean-shaven appearances and did not discuss beards as crucial to their Muslim identities reflected the shift in rituals in diaspora, requiring an integrated study of how Muslims reestablish religious practices in new settings (Nasir, 2016).

While some minority women alter their appearance/demeanor at work to minimize their femininity due to exaggerated hyper-feminine stereotypes (Kwon & Adams, 2018), veiled Muslim women use their wardrobes to make themselves more feminine and approachable. By wearing soft colors, makeup, and unpinning their veils, they revealed the privileges associated with their investment in femininity (Bahraini, 2021; Collins, 2004; Hamilton et al., 2019). Women also used 'abayas to distinguish between conservative – code for unprofessional – Muslims and more progressive, professional Muslims. 'Abayas were associated with conservatism, which perpetuates a stereotype of Muslim women who veil and prevents women like Linda from wearing long shirts. Racist ideologies also privilege Black professionals with lighter skin tones and/or straight hair. One study found that Black women criticize candidates with Afrocentric hairstyles, forcing them to adopt Eurocentric styles to prove competency (Dawson et al., 2019). While Muslims may encounter colorism based on their phenotype (Bahraini, 2021), they also confront sub-group discrimination based on their embodied religious identities. Workplace location also exacerbates dress code issues. Celine's story showed how Arabs and Muslims work to preserve their ethnic and religious identities, how gender influences ethnic boundary-making, and how immigrants' workplaces become places where boundaries are drawn, contested, and reimagined (Ajrouch, 2004; Naber, 2006). Immigrant workplaces promote in-group stigma that pressures women to conform to cultural expectations while stigmatizing American values, cultural expressions, and those with specific national identities (Casey, 2018; Goffman, 1963; Göle, 2003; Ryan, 2011).

Narratives generally illustrated an unwelcoming workplace where differences are devalued and despised. As they leave work, US Muslims loosen their ties and shed the weight of their appearance, their code-switching, and their desire to fit in. They shed a façade of professionalism based on concealing religious differences and creating a comfortable working environment. In a seemingly secular society, workplaces are asked to consider ways religious groups may express their faith at work. Affirmative action was the primary policy initiative aimed at increasing underrepresented groups in US workplaces. In 2023, the US Supreme Court ruled that race-conscious admissions policies violate the constitution and effectively ended affirmative action programs at universities and colleges. In her dissent, Justice Sotomayor claimed that the decision further entrenched racial inequality within institutions of higher learning (Totenberg, 2023). This landmark decision will have a profound effect on society at large – including the workplace. This decision could potentially worsen the situation for Muslim workers who lack mentors and role models to guide them in workplace environments. The ruling does not mean employers must abandon initiatives to diversify their workforce, but leaders must prioritize supporting their employees in expressing their personal identities if they are to foster an inclusive workplace culture (Welbourne et al., 2017).

LIMITATIONS AND FUTURE RESEARCH

This study focuses on how Muslims construct meanings of gender, religious identity, and work as they secure professional positions in US workplaces rather than developing generalizable findings. Muslim and Arab immigrants across the US differ in their upbringing, class background, and discrimination experiences. National, sectarian, and cultural differences may exacerbate localized experiences. Thus, narratives are not representative of the larger Muslim and Arab populations.[3] As such, this research opens the possibility for future studies. First, studies investigating how Muslim or Arab immigrants dress within their immigrant communities are lacking. It is imperative that future research addresses the tension between Celine and other Muslim women in her workplace, resulting from her dress choices. In addition, future research could examine how hegemonic ideologies affect the appearance of queer presenting Arab and Muslim men in immigrant-centered workplaces. Additionally, studies should explore how various intersections of gender, race, ethnicity, and/or immigration status have contributed to dress stigmas among Muslim and Arab populations in the United States.

NOTES

1. Gallup's Center for Muslim Studies reported that 36% of Muslim Americans were between ages 18 and 29 by the 21st century. Comparatively, 17% of Catholics, 9% of Protestants, 16% of Jews, and 18% of the general US population fell into this age bracket.

2. About 75% and 79% of Oakland and Macomb residents identify as white. The US Census counts residents of Middle Eastern origin as white, but foreign-born residents represent only 13% and 12% of these counties (US Census Bureau, 2021).

3. The metropolitan Detroit area has the second largest Arab population in the United States. Over 40% of this group were Muslims at the turn of the century. This region also has a majority Shi'a Muslim population (DAAS), a minority sect within Islam.

REFERENCES

Abbas, M. (2019). 'I grew a beard and my dad flipped out!' Co-option of British Muslim parents in countering 'extremism' within their families in Bradford and Leeds. *Journal of Ethnic and Migration Studies, 45*(9), 1458–1476.

Abu-Lughod, L. (2013). *Do Muslim women need saving?* Harvard University Press.

Acker, J. (1990). Hierarchies, jobs, bodies: A theory of gendered organizations. *Gender & Society, 4*(2), 139–158.

Ajrouch, K. J. (2004). Gender, race, and symbolic boundaries: Contested spaces of identity among Arab American adolescents. *Sociological Perspectives, 47*(4), 371–391.

Ajrouch, K. J., & Jamal, A. (2007). Assimilating to a White identity: The case of Arab Americans. *The International Migration Review, 41*(4), 860–879.

Al-Qasimi, N. (2010). Immodest modesty: Accommodating dissent and the 'abaya-as-fashion in the Arab Gulf States. *Journal of Middle East Women's Studies, 6*(1), 46–74.

Aoude, I. (2006). Arab Americans and ethnic studies. *Journal of Asian American Studies, 9*(2), 141–155.

Aslam, S. (2011). Hijab in the workplace: Why Title VII does not adequate protect employees from discrimination on the basis of religious dress and appearance. *UMKC Law Review, 80*(1), 221.

Aziz, S. F. (2014). Coercive assimilationism: The perils of Muslim women's identity performance in the workplace. *Michigan Journal of Race and Law, 20*(1), 1–65.

Bahraini, A. (2021). The more ethnic the face, the more important the race: A closer look at colorism and employment opportunities among Middle Eastern women. *Humanity & Society, 45*(4), 617–637.

Ball, C., & Haque, A. (2003). Diversity in religious practice: Implications of Islamic values in the public workplace. *Public Personnel Management, 32*(3), 315–330.

Banks, I. (2000). *Hair matters: Beauty, power, and Black women's consciousness.* New York University Press.

Barry, B., & Weiner, N. (2019). Suited for success? Suits, status, and hybrid masculinity. *Men and Masculinities, 22*(2), 151–176.

Becker, H. S. (1963). *Outsider: Studies in the sociology of deviance.* Free Press.

Berdahl, J. L., Cooper, M., Glick, P., Livingston, R. W., & Williams, J. C. (2018). Work as a masculinity contest. *Journal of Social Issues, 74*(3), 422–448.

Bourdieu, P. (1984). *Distinction: A social critique of the judgement of taste.* Routledge.

Bourdieu, P. (1986). The forms of capital. In J. Richardson (Ed.), *Handbook of theory and research for the sociology of education* (pp. 241–258). Greenwood.

Bryant, S. L. (2013). The beauty ideal: The effects of European standards of beauty on Black women. *Columbia Social Work Review, 11*(1), 80–91.

Bueno-Hansen, P., & Montes, A. (2019). White passing? No! Seeing myself in my own light. *Latino Studies, 17*(4), 522–531.

Burke, P. J., & Stets, J. E. (2009). *Identity theory.* Oxford University Press.

Casey, P. M. (2018). Stigmatized identities: Too Muslim to be American, too American to be Muslim. *Symbolic Interaction, 41*(1), 100–119.

Cevik, G. (2018). Boudoirs and harems: The seductive power of Sophas. *Journal of Interior Design, 43*(3), 25–41.

Collins, P. H. (2004). *Black sexual politics: African Americans, gender, and the new racism.* Routledge.

Connell, R. W. (1987). *Gender and power: Society, the person and sexual politics*. Stanford University Press.
Connell, R. W. (1995). *Masculinities*. University of California Press.
Connell, R. W., & Messerschmidt, J. W. (2005). Hegemonic masculinity: Rethinking the concept. *Gender & Society*, 19(6), 829–859.
Craig, V. (2020). Does my sassiness upset you? An analysis challenging workplace and school regulation of hair and its connection to racial discrimination. *Howard Law Journal*, 64(1), 239–266.
Craik, J. (1994). *The face of fashion*. Routledge.
Cutts, B., Hooley, T., & Yates, J. (2015). Graduate dress code: How undergraduates are planning to use hair, clothes, and make-up to smooth their transition to the workplace. *Industry and Higher Education*, 29(4), 271–282.
Dawson, G. A., Karl, K. A., & Peluchette, J. V. (2019). Hair matters: Toward understanding natural black hair bias in the workplace. *Journal of Leadership & Organizational Studies*, 26(3), 389–401.
DeCoursey, C. A. (2017). Attitudes of professional Muslim women in Saudi Arabia regarding wearing the abaya. *Asian Culture and History*, 9(2), 16.
Deryugina, T., & Shurchkov, O. (2015). Now you see it, now you don't: The vanishing beauty premium. *Journal of Economic Behavior & Organization*, 116, 331–345.
Dhillon, K. P. (2011). Covering turbans and beards: Title VII's role in legitimizing religious discrimination against Sikhs. *Southern California Interdisciplinary Law Journal*, 21(1), 215.
Dill, B. T., & Zambrana, R. E. (2009). Critical thinking about inequality: An emerging lens. In C. R. McCann & S. King (Eds.), *Feminist theory reader: Local and global perspectives* (pp. 176–186). Taylor & Francis Group.
Elliot, A. J., & Maier, M. A. (2014). Color psychology: Effects of perceiving color on psychological functioning in humans. *Annual Review of Psychology*, 65(1), 95–120.
Emerson, R., Fretz, R., & Shaw, L. (1995). *Writing ethnographic fieldnotes*. University of Chicago Press.
Ferry, P. (2017). The beard, masculinity, and otherness in the contemporary American novel. *Journal of American Studies*, 51(1), 163–182.
Fetterman, D. M. (2010). *Ethnography: Step-by-step* (3rd ed.). Sage.
Gallup. (2009). *Muslim Americans: A national portrait – An in-depth analysis of America's most diverse religious community*. Gallup Press.
Glaser, B. G., & Strauss, A. L. (1967). *The discovery of grounded theory: Strategies for qualitative research*. Aldine.
Goffman, E. (1963). *Stigma: Notes on the management of spoiled identity*. Touchstone.
Göle, N. (2003). The voluntary adoption of Islamic stigma symbols. *Social Research: An International Quarterly*, 70(3), 809–828.
Gomez, C. (2000). The continual significance of skin color: An exploratory study of Latinos in the Northeast. *Hispanic Journal of Behavioral Sciences*, 22(1), 94–103.
Goodman, L. A. (2001). Comment: On respondent-driven sampling and snowball sampling in hard-to-reach populations and snowball sampling not in hard-to-reach populations. *Sociological Methodology*, 41(1), 347–353.
Gotanda, N. (2011). The racialization of Islam in American law. *The Annals of the American Academy of Political and Social Science*, 637, 184–195.
Halim, M. L., Ruble, D. N., & Amodio, D. M. (2011). From pink frilly dresses to 'one of the boys': A social cognitive analysis of gender identity development and gender bias. *Social and Personality Psychology Compass*, 5(11), 933–949.
Hamermesh, D. S. (2011). *Beauty pays*. Princeton University Press.
Hamilton, L. T., Armstrong, E. A., Seeley, J. L., & Armstrong, E. M. (2019). Hegemonic femininities and intersectional domination. *Sociological Theory*, 37(4), 315–341.
Harding, N. (2002). On the manager's body as an aesthetics of control. *Tamara: Journal of Critical Postmodern Organization Science*, 2(1), 63–76.
Hellerstein, J. K., McInerney, M., & Neumark, D. (2011). Neighbors and coworkers: The importance of residential labor market networks. *Journal of Labor Economics*, 29, 659–695.
Hewlin, P. F. (2003). And the award for best actor goes to …: Facades of conformity in organizational settings. *Academy of Management Review*, 28(4), 633–642.

Hill, J. H. (2008). *The everyday language of white racism*. John Wiley and Sons.
Hogg, M. A., & Terry, D. I. (2000). Social identity and self-categorization processes in organizational contexts. *The Academy of Management Review, 25*(1), 121–140.
Kaiser, S. B. (2012). *Fashion and cultural studies*. Berg.
Karl, K., Peluchette, J. V., & Dawson, G. (2022). Why so much ado about a hairdo? Examining how the hair choices of Black women vary by occupation. *Journal of Business Diversity, 22*(1), 10–22.
Karlsen, S., & Nazroo, J. Y. (2015). Ethnic and religious differences in the attitudes of people towards being British. *The Sociological Review, 63*, 759–781.
Koura, F. (2018). Navigating Islam: The hijab and the American workplace. *Societies, 8*(4), 125.
Krasas, J. (2018). The work of code switching. *Religion & Theology, 25*(3–4), 190–207.
Kwon, E., & Adams, T. L. (2018). Choosing a specialty: Intersections of gender and race among Asian and White women medical students in Ontario. *Canadian Ethnic Studies, 50*(3), 49–68.
Lawson, M. (2021, December 28). *Re: The 22 best beard styles for 2022*. https://www.beardbrand.com/blogs/urbanbeardsman/beard-styles
Leamaster, R. J., & Einwohner, R. L. (2018). "I'm not your stereotypical mormon girl": Mormon women's gendered resistance. *Review of Religious Research, 60*(2), 161–181.
Love, E. (2017). *Islamophobia and racism in America*. New York University Press.
Magee, W., Fong, E., & Wilkes, R. (2007). Neighbourhood ethnic concentration and discrimination. *Journal of Social Policy, 37*, 37–61.
Mahmood, S. (2005). *Politics of piety: The Islamic revival and the feminist subject*. Princeton University Press.
Martin, P. (2004). Gender as social institution. *Social Forces, 82*, 1249–1273.
Matthews, D. L., & Reddy-Best, K. L. (2022). Negotiations of women's Black and activist identity through dress on the college campus, 2013–2019. *Clothing and Textiles Research Journal, 40*(2), 91–106.
McCray, T. (2012). Coloring inside the lines: Finding a solution for workplace colorism claims. *Law and Inequality: Journal of Theory and Practice, 30*(1), 149–178.
Miller, J. I. (2005). Fashion and democratic relationships. *Polity, 37*(1), 3–23.
Mogahed, D., & Chouhoud, Y. (2017). *American Muslim poll 2017: Muslims at the crossroads*. https://www.ispu.org/wp-content/uploads/2017/06/AMP-2017_Full-Report.pdf
Naber, N. (2006). Arab American femininities: Beyond Arab virgin/American(ized) whore. *Feminist Studies, 32*(1), 87–111.
Naber, N. (2008). Look, Mohammed the terrorist is coming! In A. Jamal & N. Naber (Eds.), *Race and Arab Americans before and after 9/11. From invisible citizens to visible subjects* (pp. 276–304). Syracuse University Press.
Naderi, P. S. D. (2018). Non-threatening Muslim men: Stigma management and religious observance in America. *Qualitative Sociology, 41*(1), 41–62.
Nasir, M. A. (2016). Islam in diaspora. Sharia law, piety, and brotherhood at al-Farooq Mosque, Atlanta. *Journal of Islamic Studies, 54*(1), 59–93.
Nguyen, M. T. (2015). The hoodie as sign, screen, expectation, and force. *Journal of Women in Culture and Society, 40*(4), 791–816.
Nistor, L. (2017). Hijab(istas) – as fashion phenomenon. A review. *Social Analysis, 7*, 59–67.
Pahwa, S. (2021). Styling strength: Pious fashion and fitness on surviving hijab. *Journal of Middle East Women's Studies, 17*(1), 96–116.
Parmentier, M., Fischer, E., & Reuber, A. R. (2013). Positioning person brands in established organizational fields. *Journal of the Academy of Marketing Science, 41*(3), 373–387.
Pierce, J. L. (1996). *Gender trials: Emotional lives in contemporary law firms*. University of California Press.
Pratt, M. G., & Rafaeli, A. (1997). Organizational dress as a symbol of multilayered social identities. *The Academy of Management Journal, 40*(4), 862–898.
Pyke, K. D., & Johnson, D. L. (2003). Asian American women and racialized femininities: 'Doing' gender across cultural worlds. *Gender & Society, 17*(1), 33–53.
Reddy-Best, K. L. (2018). LGBTQ women, appearance negotiations, and workplace dress codes. *Journal of Homosexuality, 65*(5), 615–639.

Reddy-Best, K. L., & Choi, E. (2020). Male hair cannot extend below plane of the shoulder and "no cross dressing": Critical queer analysis of high school dress codes in the United States. *Journal of Homosexuality*, *67*(9), 1290–1340.

Rogers, C. (2022). Don't touch my hair. How hegemony operate through dress codes to reproduce whiteness in schools. *Du Bois Review*, *19*(1), 175–191.

Roth, L. M. (2004). The social psychology of tokenism: Status and homophily processes on Wall Street. *Sociological Perspectives*, *47*(2), 189.

Ruby, T. F. (2005). Listening to the voices of hijab. *Women's Studies International Forum*, *29*, 54–66.

Ruffle, B. J., & Shtudiner, Z. (2015). Are good-looking people more employable? *Management Science*, *61*(8), 1760–1776.

Ryan, L. (2011). Muslim women negotiating collective stigmatization: 'We're just normal people'. *Sociology*, *45*(6), 1–16.

Said, E. (1979). *Orientalism*. Vintage Books.

Santiago, R., Nwokoma, N., & Crentsil, J. (2021). Investigating the implications of code switching and assimilating at work for African American professionals. *Journal of Business Diversity*, *21*(4), 72–81.

Simmel, G. (1957). Fashion. *American Journal of Sociology*, *62*(6), 541–558.

Strauss, A. L. (1987). *Qualitative analysis for social scientists*. Cambridge University Press.

Takim, L. (2018). Black or white: The turbanization of Shi'i Islam. *The Muslim World (Hartford)*, *108*(3), 548–563.

Tajfel, H., & Turner, J. C. (1985). The social identity theory of intergroup behavior. In S. Worchel & W. G. Austin (Eds.), *Psychology of intergroup relations* (pp. 7–24). Nelson-Hall.

Totenberg, N. (2023). *Supreme Court guts affirmative action, effectively ending race-conscious admissions*. NPR. https://www.npr.org/2023/06/29/1181138066/affirmative-action-supreme-court-decision

US Census Bureau. (2021). *Quick facts*. https://www.census.gov/quickfacts/fact/table/US/PST045221

Weitz, R. (2001). Women and their hair: Seeking power through resistance and accommodation. *Gender & Society*, *15*(5), 667–686.

Welbourne, T. M., Rolf, S., & Schlachter, S. (2017). The case for employee resource groups: A Review and social identity theory-based research agenda. *Personnel Review*, *46*(8), 1816–1834.

West, C., & Zimmerman, D. H. (1987). Doing gender. *Gender & Society*, *1*(2), 125–151.

Wingfield, A. H. (2013). *No more invisible man: Race and gender in men's work*. Temple University Press.

Zahedi, A. (2011). Muslim American women in the post-11 September era. *International Feminist Journal of Politics*, *13*(2), 183–203.

Zine, J. (2002). Muslim women and the politics or representation. *The American Journal of Islamic Social Sciences*, *19*(4), 1–22.

CHAPTER 7

MILLENNIAL AGENCY AND LIBERATION WITHIN BLACK AMERICAN BEAUTY STANDARDS

Jaleesa Reed

Department of Human Centered Design, Cornell University, USA

ABSTRACT

This qualitative study investigated the relationship between beauty standards and identity in the United States from the perspective of 20 self-identified millennial Black women. During semi-structured virtual interviews, participants defined Black, American, and millennial beauty standards distinctly. American beauty was associated with Eurocentrism and mainstream media representation. Interpretations of a millennial beauty standard were aligned with perceptions of the generation as tolerant and politically conscious. Black American beauty standards embraced the range of hair textures and skin tones present in the African diaspora. While participants were cognizant of the different beauty ideals present, their interaction with beauty standards was ambivalent. Interviewees found beauty knowledge accessible through social media. However, they remain confined to a restrictive beauty standard due to workplace expectations around professionalism. Participants negotiated where and when to express their intracultural beauty ideals but participated in the beauty industry through processes of learning how to care for their hair in its natural state. Even though they have autonomy and flexibility in expressing their cultural styles, personal and professional repercussions are *still plausible. Future studies can expand on these findings by exploring perceptions of American beauty standards from a different generation, region, or identity.*

Keywords: Millennials; Black American; hair; beauty standards; agency

Tensions between Black American and White American beauty standards originated in chattel slavery when African people were brought to the United States for the purpose of forced labor (Davis-Bundrage et al., 2018). During slavery, hair styling played a pivotal role in communal life. Because slave masters disregarded African hair, as "tufted, matted" and "wooly" (Gates, 1957, as cited in Johnson & Bankhead, 2014), they paid less attention to training Black people's hair to match Euro-American esthetics. Instead, straight facial features such as thin noses and lips, light skin tones, and straight hair were prized in the beauty hierarchy. Though a level of control was used to remove meaning and pleasure from participating in beauty rituals, it did not erase the memory of creative possibilities available to enslaved people through self-fashioning.

Hair styled in elaborate designs can reflect clan affiliation, status, age, and religion (Byrd & Tharps, 2014). Reusing simple tools, such as wool carding combs for hair styling, helped enslaved peoples create versatile hairstyles that challenged conventional American esthetics. These styles relied on hair appearing wild and unkempt, which gave the impression, to outsiders, that enslaved people cared little about their hair and made no attempts to manage it. However, examining printed advertisements created to capture runaway slaves suggests that hair styling was one of the few avenues where enslaved people were allowed to exercise creative agency (White & White, 1995). Eighteenth-century WANTED posters depict a range of hairstyles for runaway slaves from "long and bushy" to "combed and parted neatly," demonstrating the connection between African hairstyling traditions and enslaved people in the United States (White & White, 1995).

While enduring repeated attempts to defeminize the Black female body throughout American history, Black women continued actively cultivating and embracing their own esthetic (Hobson, 2005). By the 19th century, hair cropping, the practice of cutting long hair and shaving heads, was a common punishment for enslaved women. Used frequently as a means to control female slaves and their partners, hair cropping remained an effective punishment in Caribbean prisons decades after slavery ended in the West Indies (Allain, 2020). For Black Caribbean women, the threat of cutting their hair often compelled them toward obedience faster than flogging. Colonial officials took advantage of the relationship Black Caribbean women had with their hair and recognized that forcefully removing it was a useful tactic in controlling their behavior. For the women, styling their hair was a source of joy and pride, which they invested time and labor into despite attempts to convince them that their hair was not worth the investment (Allain, 2020).

In the United States, hair cropping was usually carried out by plantation mistresses, who interpreted an enslaved woman's long, black, and silky hair as "circumstantial proof that husbands, brothers, or sons had been illicitly visiting the slave quarters" or that they would be tempted to do so soon (White & White, 1995, p. 65). Furthermore, in cities like New Orleans, numerous "fancy-girl" marketplaces existed exclusively to auction enslaved women selected for their beauty, skin color, and grace (Sterling, 1984). Women from these markets were typically sold to brothels or wealthy businessmen. In the latter case, enslaved women were greeted by White mistresses who understood the level of desire connected to their long hair and proceeded to remove it upon arrival (Byrd & Tharps, 2014). Within the Judeo-Christian plantation system, long hair was seen as a defining feature of "respectable womanhood" (Greensword, 2022). Preventing enslaved women from growing their hair effectively separated them from a core element of their African heritage, consequently excluding them from achieving American femininity as well.

In this sense, Black American women have been negotiating the relationship between their beauty and others attempts to control it throughout generations, stemming as far back as the 17th century (Weathers, 1991). While a Black American beauty standard may include Eurocentric esthetics on the surface, millennial Black women are aware that mainstream American and global ideals of beauty are rooted in preferences around Eurocentric hair texture, skin tone, and femininity. This chapter investigates millennial Black women's perceptions of beauty standards in the United States and how their relationships to beauty are potential sites for survival, agency, and liberation.

BLACK BEAUTY IN THE AFRICAN DIASPORA

Throughout this chapter, references to Eurocentric and White American beauty standards are used interchangeably to refer to dominant beauty ideals reflecting a hierarchy of facial and bodily features from Northern and Western Europe. As social constructs, beauty and race rely on biological characteristics such as hair texture, skin tone, and body shape or size as reference categories. In the case of beauty, characteristics like hair texture and skin tone carry meanings that are often reduced to expressions of race.

Definitions of Black beauty continue to evolve. In the 1980s, *Ebony* magazine highlighted Black beauty's inability to be defined decisively because it is always evolving in relation to Blackness (Bennett, 1980). Black beauty is a "matter of doing," a performance rather than strictly the combination of characteristics that one is born with (Tate, 2007). These definitions account for esthetic variation within Black communities but do not draw attention to the changing meanings based on place. *Ebony* defines Black beauty in relation to standards in the United States, while Tate's (2007) research adds perspectives from Black women in the United Kingdom and Jamaica. In the United States, race is constructed around a Black–White binary with other races and ethnicities falling along the spectrum

(Omi & Winant, 2014). These definitions rely on race as a reference point while acknowledging that constructions of beauty change.

In the Dominican Republic, to be White, Black, or "Mixed" has different meanings even though hair texture and skin tone remain the primary measures of these racial classifications. Candelario (2000) argues that a Dominican American esthetic is made visible through the Black and White binary. By studying Dominican beauty salons in the United States, Candelario (2000) highlights how Dominican American women resist being aligned too closely with Blackness by changing their hair from a state described as "bad hair that is relaxed" through the use of "roller sets, relaxers, and doobies (hair wraps)" (Candelario, 2000, p. 139). Refining the curl was a part of the process of maintaining a Dominican racial identity. As one participant stated: "Black women are confusing, but the hair lets you know" (Candelario, 2000, p. 151).

These natural or braided hairstyles are distinctly Black in the United States but convey different meanings elsewhere. Black American college students' conceptions of race changed when studying abroad in the Dominican Republic. There, wearing their hair in short natural afros or cornrows associated them with a different nationality. In the United States, their features placed them within the Black American category. In the Dominican Republic, these features were attributed to a Haitian nationality (Simmons, 2008). Even though hairstyles changed others' perceptions of their nationality, their racial identity still relied on skin color. In the Dominican Republic and Cuba, race is designated by referencing hair textures and skin tones which are malleable. This contrasts with the one-drop rule in the United States, where one Black ancestor in a family lineage typically designates the descendent as Black (Sweet, 2022). In the beauty salon and when studying abroad, attempts to define the boundaries of beauty standards reveal the slippery nature of race. With these rigid American conceptions of Blackness and Whiteness in place, Candelario (2000) demonstrates that there is no liberation in the subversion of Whiteness or Blackness through beauty because the racial categories, and their reliance on phenotype, remain intact within US borders. Accordingly, dominant beauty standards lean toward the majority population in a country, whether by number or ideology. However, the interconnectedness of race and beauty changes once diasporic differences are accounted for.

What constitutes a Black standard of beauty, if there is no universal agreement on the boundaries of Blackness? Definitions of beauty are restricted to time and place, but the African diaspora transcends both. Thanks to the duration of the Transatlantic slave trade and the stops in various countries made along the route, time, and place provide opportune points for connecting beauty and race throughout the diaspora. Hair texture and skin tone are weighted differently within each country as evidenced in studies conducted throughout the African diaspora from studying Dominicans in the United States (Candelario, 2000) and the Dominican Republic (Simmons, 2008) to Afro-Cubans in Cuba (Mbilishaka et al., 2020). In this study, to be Black is to have ancestry that originates in Africa, comprising multiple African ethnicities, indigenous to the continent of Africa, and in the international African community (McKittrick & Woods, 2007). Despite the influence and connection to the African diaspora, interpretations of

Blackness and beauty in this chapter reflect the lived experiences of millennial Black women within the United States.

THEORETICAL FRAMEWORK

Beauty culture and standards are interpreted using a Black Feminist theoretical approach which centers the perspectives of millennial Black women. Data collection and analysis were guided by Black Feminist Theory (Hill Collins, 1990). Black beauty standards appear to be identifiable due to visibility of hair and skin. Yet, these characteristics are mistakenly overemphasized when differentiating beauty ideals from one group to another.

Beauty's legibility and relationship to identity make the body a "viable subject" (Tate, 2007). Essentializing Blackness and beauty with hair texture and skin tone does not allow room for difference or the range apparent in Black beauty. Attempting to define beauty as a continuum that embraces differences reveals that beauty exists at the intersection of politics, esthetics, and identification (Tate, 2007). If Black beauty is performative, and based on societal constructions of beauty and race, then there is also the possibility that Black beauty can be performed differently. The ways that personal style is used to convey power and authority can mask the "power of appearance" (Clutario, 2023) or obstruct the relationship between presentation, public pageantry, and power. Fashion's capacity to include and exclude is inherent to its nature (Simmel, 1957). All fashion becomes inclusive at some point despite its origin in exclusivity. Beauty works similarly because beauty standards encourage exclusivity. Nonetheless, beauty is generally seen as universal and obtainable by all.

METHODS

Data were collected by the author from a study exploring millennial Black women's relationship to beauty retail spaces in the United States. Semi-structured interviews were conducted through Zoom with 20 millennial Black women in February and March of 2021. Participants were primarily recruited through Instagram using a purposeful random sampling approach. An IRB-approved flyer was shared on the author's public Instagram account, directing potential interviewees to complete a screening survey created on Google Forms. The author also invited others to share the Instagram post and flyer which aided in reaching participants outside of the author's region and network. Prior to the interview, the consent form was shared with potential participants through email along with a Zoom link. Signing on to Zoom at the interview time signified informed consent on the interviewee's behalf.

The study's interview guide was divided into five sections: perceptions of beauty, experiences in mainstream beauty retailing, generational differences in buying beauty products, experiences at beauty supply stores, and envisioning new beauty retail spaces. Participants are referred to by their chosen pseudonyms as often as possible to distinguish their individual contributions to the data.

SAMPLE

Participants were born between 1981 and 1996, which represents millennials at the upper and lower range of the generation. Eighteen of the 20 participants identified as monoracial, as in both parents were of the same race. Individuals further described their racial identity as African-American (9), Black-American (5), Black (4), Afro-Creole (1), and Afro-Caribbean (1). In terms of class, seven participants described themselves as lower middle class, while nine considered themselves members of the middle class. The remaining four were members of the upper middle class (2) and working class (2). Details of participants' age and location are displayed in Table 7.1.

FINDINGS

Participants' definitions of American beauty, Black beauty, and millennial beauty were analyzed and compared. Participants characterized beauty standards according to physical features, mainstream acceptance, and media representation. Through their extensive investment of time and money into skin, body, and hair care, the women in this study adhered to Eurocentric beauty standards while also promoting and participating in Black standards of beauty. Despite their familiarity with the beauty industry and knowledge around expectations, they also lacked interest in conforming to American beauty standards. Instead, from the workplace to their local communities, millennial Black women negotiate when and where they can fully express their style.

Table 7.1. Location and Birth Year of Participants.

Name	Birth Year	Location During Interview
Angelique	1988	Hartford, CT
B. Wells	1989	Atlanta, GA
Jesse	1991	Florida
Cooper	1993	Washington, DC
Taylor	1993	Athens, GA
Morgan	1994	Gaffney, SC
Mavis	1994	Chicago, IL
Nicole	1986	St. Louis, MO
Garcelle	1987	New York City, NY
Michelle	1987	New Jersey
Natasha	1989	Miami, FL
Tiana	1989	Duluth, GA
Dionne	1990	Raleigh, NC
Heather	1990	Athens, GA
Jones	1990	San Diego, CA
Kennedy	1992	Marietta, GA
Kora	1981	Washington, DC
Marie	1996	Ann Arbor, MI
Diamond	1994	Atlanta, GA
Sunshine	1994	Athens, GA

MILLENNIAL PERCEPTIONS OF AMERICAN BEAUTY

Millennials have a shared experience of living during the United States' engagement with the Iraq War (2003–2011) and the War in Afghanistan (2001–2021). As a generation, they also witnessed polarizing social and political changes such as the legalization of same-sex marriage, the impact of climate change, and the increase of gun violence in the United States. Their view of American beauty is informed by these lived experiences; millennial Black women's perceptions of American beauty are situated within their intersectional identities. As a generation, they have shared experiences, but their identities as Black women affect their individual interpretations of American beauty. As a result, participants viewed the American beauty standard as heavily associated with Whiteness, representation in mainstream media, and negativity. Natasha, for example, described the American standard as "very White," and full of "judgment" and "critique" while Sunshine and Mavis framed American beauty colloquially as "trash."

Characteristics such as being White, thin, and blonde were mentioned as markers of American beauty, but they are the least likely to be associated with Black American women. When describing the differences between a millennial, American, and Black standard of beauty, participants did not include themselves in descriptions of American beauty. Yet, most of them self-identified as Black American or African American. Only five out of the 20 participants identified their race as Black only. In their descriptions of American beauty, millennial Black women observe the parts, name the whole, and inadvertently exclude themselves from this standard even though they qualify as American. Participants were cognizant of what American beauty is while acknowledging their exclusion from it, partly because they did not see themselves represented within it.

Morgan, 34, from South Carolina, described how the American beauty standard has changed "to embrace the Kardashian shape" compared to her childhood when she pictured Paris Hilton, who is White, thin, and usually blonde, as the ideal representative of American beauty. Kim Kardashian, a celebrity notorious for her repeated appropriation of Black culture and style, was mentioned by multiple participants as the American representative of beauty. In subtle ways, participants noted that the Kardashian shape, which is considered curvy, was a commodity. Mavis, for example, explained that the American beauty standard was "lost" because "White girls don't want to be White anymore." She indicated that, in some ways, beauty standards have expanded to embrace realistic body sizes and shapes, while also restricting them to a very specific public expression. Cooper also alluded to this notion when she stated that "anti-Blackness exists in everything" especially in relation to acceptance of facial features and body sizes: "Lip fillers, big hips, big butts, are in now. But still, when Black women do certain things – while they may be okay for the Kylie Jenner's of the world to do it, Black women can't do it necessarily still." Mavis and Cooper's observations suggest that the American beauty standard was shifting in line with the features that mainstream media outlets now prized, but they also noted that these features were only acceptable on White bodies.

Black beauty culture is in style, and this is not limited to body size. If mere representation was the goal, Black American features may be interpreted as accepted through their visibility in mainstream media. However, participants were careful to distinguish between surface-level representation and actual inclusion and acceptance. Angelique, 35, from Connecticut, summed up the state of American beauty by noting that "being a Black girl is really in right now." Dionne, 33, from North Carolina, expressed a similar sentiment when she stated, "my lips are in," in reference to the size of her lips and the current beauty trend of overlining lips with lipliner or using lip injections to make them appear lifted and full. These features were once sources of ridicule in minstrel shows in the United States and Canada, where white actors (usually) covered their faces with black paint or burned cork and overemphasized their lips and noses to imitate Blackness and entertain audiences (Thompson, 2023). Today, as Dionne pointed out, people pay to alter their facial features through cosmetic surgery. Because some of these procedures are reversible, many can experience them without the added burden of misrepresentation.

When participants assert ownership over their facial features, they inadvertently reinforce the assumption that facial features are biological indicators of race. Thus, they identify a Black beauty standard but do not fully subvert the norms. In reference to Black beauty standards, Garcelle stated "Black people are not a monolith ... people think stereotypical things, especially [about] Black women with the black lips and the big butts. And everybody doesn't have that. I know so many people who don't." Garcelle recognizes the range of beauty that exists within the Black American community but also experiences the industry's lack of care while modeling for a Target skincare beauty campaign:

> I was realizing, while I was doing this shoot, the things that weren't, I guess, geared towards Black beauty. It was just like they thought it was general. [...] The sunscreen was so white and chalky. [...] The hair person couldn't really do my hair, and the makeup person, I hated the way she did my eyebrows. And there was no people of color on set.

The issue of hair stylists and makeup artists lacking experience with textured hair and darker skin tones has been an ongoing problem for the fashion industry (Duan, 2017; Shoaib, 2023). Garcelle's experience extends these issues from the runway and fashion magazines to commercial beauty campaigns. For a commercial shoot, it is reasonable to expect at least one person to be knowledgeable about textured hair, especially when the brand seeks to represent diversity. Access to that representation also includes providing the necessary resources to sustain model success. Garcelle's experience reinforces the industry's tendency to assume that Black models are valuable for their "exotic" appeal (Cheddie, 2002) and should be content with what is available, even when it is not suited to their needs.

Generally, the American beauty standard was perceived as White by participants, and its relationship to Black beauty was considered superficial at best. While some participants saw their features as assets in popular culture, others were critical of the type of Black female beauty that was accepted in the media. Marie, 27, from Michigan, named actress Tika Sumpter as an accepted version of Black American beauty but then qualified by stating "she's more the American beauty type, she's just darker toned." Even though Sumpter's skin tone is darker than the readily accepted light or medium tones, her facial features and body size are more aligned with the American beauty ideal, as participants described it. True integration of a Black American beauty standard where Black features are appreciated rather than appropriated requires nuanced representation. Interviewees were aware that full social acceptance of Black beauty does not exist despite the increased presence of Black women in commercial media. In this study, participants possessed the political consciousness to interrogate media representation, and some were invested in representing alternative versions of Black beauty, but most lacked the power to fully divest from the association with stereotypes.

Using Judith Butler's framework of performative reiteration, Black people who resist the need to perform according to dominant esthetics valued in Black culture are engaged in the process of liberating Black consciousness. Even within Black anti-racist esthetics, normalized racializing standards are also reproduced and codified. True liberation from beauty standards requires one to redefine their understandings of Eurocentric beauty standards *and* to release the need to pursue any forms of beauty standards (Tate, 2007). Liberation through beauty is possible if individuals subvert appearance norms through disidentification. Ascribing to a Black beauty standard can be restrictive, but also a possibility for changing relationships to beauty (Tate, 2007; Tate & Fink, 2019). Agency, therefore, is a requirement for liberation from and through beauty standards.

A MATTER OF SURVIVAL: BEAUTY AT WORK

A Brief History of Hair-based Discrimination

Black hair and how it should be styled for professional settings has been a legal point of contention throughout American history. In 1786, the Tignon Law was enacted in New Orleans; it sought to distinguish enslaved women from free women by requiring them to wear headscarves and wraps to hide their hair. Enslaved women did cover their hair, but they also accessorized and personalized the wraps, turning a policy meant to suppress them into an additional outlet for creative expression. No legal cases were documented (Gould, 1997), but the law served its purpose in utilizing apparel and appearance to stratify society.

Controlling how Black people wear their hair continues to be a legal affair. In 1981, Renee Rogers, a Black American flight attendant, sued American Airlines for a policy that did not allow cornrows (a braided hairstyle) in the workplace, claiming that it disproportionately and negatively affected Black women due to their hair texture, African-American heritage, and the style's prevalence among Black people (*Rogers* vs *American Airlines, Inc.*, 1981). Ultimately, Rogers lost the case. The judge ruled that cornrows were not an expression of African-American heritage because Bo Derek, a White actress who wore a similar braided hairstyle in the movie 10, "introduced" the braids into mainstream culture (Donahoo & Smith, 2022). Even though Derek was associated with the style temporarily, the distinction was clear. On one body, the braids were merely a style choice, and on another, they were grounds for termination.

Less than a decade later in 1987, Cheryl Tatum, a Black restaurant cashier, was fired from her job at a Hyatt hotel after refusing to change her hairstyle, which was described as "tight braids swept into a pageboy silhouette" (Shipp, 1987). Tatum was not the only Black female employee reprimanded but she was the only one who refused to change her hairstyle. Others, like Sydney M. Boone, a Black telephone operator, who worked at a different Hyatt site, wore a wig over her braids when she was notified of the company policy (Shipp, 1987). In these cases, adherence to a corporate-approved image for employees allowed discrimination to continue as these policies disproportionately affected and targeted Black people. Similar hair-related cases have been filed as recently as 2021. Black women are 1.5 times more likely than other women in the United States to be sent home from work due to their hairstyle (JOY Collective & Dove, 2019). Within their identity group, Black women with straighter hair are also less likely to experience microaggressions in the workplace compared to Black women with coily or textured hair (JOY Collective & Dove, 2023). These cases suggest that Black women are experiencing hair discrimination at higher rates than their White colleagues, leading to social and economic impacts on their lives.

In response to these patterns, the CROWN Act (Creating a Respectful and Open World for Natural Hair) was created to legally prohibit race-based hair discrimination. Introduced in 2019, by the CROWN Coalition, National Urban League, Color of Change, and the Western Center on Law & Poverty, the Act aims to remove hair discrimination as an obstacle for employment and educational opportunities. Such discrimination is race-based because it restricts the presence of natural hair styles typically worn by people of African descent – such as cornrows, locs, braids, or afros – from workplaces and schools through policies like dress codes and coded standards of professionalism (Legal Defense Fund, 2022). To date, the CROWN Act has been adopted in 20 states, with similar legislation also enacted at the municipal level (CROWN Coalition, 2023). The existence of the CROWN Act demonstrates that narratives of "good" and "bad" hair are not just esthetic performance but also carry legal consequences.

Authenticity in the Workplace

Though the millennial Black women in this study differentiated between Black and White American beauty, they felt habitually confined to an American beauty standard due to workplace expectations. Angelique, a multiracial millennial, was aware of how she presented herself as a young professional. She examined her work appearance and behavior by asking herself questions such as:

> Am I coming off too aggressive? Am I using my hands too much? Is my hair looking professional? Can I wear braids? Can I wear my hoop earrings to work or is that going to look too urban for them?

Especially in meetings with senior management, it was critical to present herself as "capable, even though [she] may not look how somebody feels like [she] should look."

While most women are constantly made aware of their appearance in work settings, Diamond, from Chicago, described an experience where her beauty was used as a prerequisite for a prospective job. While applying to work at a restaurant, she reviewed the job responsibilities and noticed that pictures of applicants were required:

> The job announcement was like [send a] resume [and] two pics. Send pictures? Like what does that have to do with the job? I've never had to send a picture, and it turned me off so bad [...] I don't want to be anywhere, where my looks are a factor. Or the thought of me being sexualized [...] I just feel like it's shady. I have nice pictures, you know, I ain't got a problem sending in the picture. It's just like, do I want to work for someone that's asking for a picture to be in a restaurant? [...] Nowadays, it's like the beauty is trumping your actual credentials.

Angelique and Diamond describe two separate instances where their appearance was a measurement of their proficiency in the workplace. As a data coordinator, Angelique worried about her style choices and mannerisms undermining her capabilities. Diamond also worried that her looks were more valuable than her credentials during the application process although she earned a graduate degree. In Diamond's case, working at the restaurant was an additional income source to her main job as a public health analyst. Because she did not need the job, she had the ability to opt out of the application process and refuse to send in her pictures with a resume but that is generally not the case for others seeking employment.

Participants also discussed the tension between being beautiful enough for a professional role and the invisible work of considering how their style choices may affect how others view Black women as a group. This concern was not unique to study participants. In higher education (Townsend, 2021) and other workplaces (Dawson et al., 2019), Black women feel pressured to conform to Eurocentric standards by negotiating their hair styles and mannerisms. In line with this, participants made style choices that balanced their identity and the pressure to conform with their career goals. Even though Angelique was concerned about how others perceived her, she also found her style to be a source of strength:

> I don't even want to water myself down, so there has been times where I walked into a meeting with somebody who is in a pretty high position of power and I may have my braids in, my hoop earrings on, and I may be wearing my red lipstick, and talking with my hands, but it's important for me to show that on that platform, I can still be myself.

Failing to ascribe to the workplace dress code can have real consequences: several legal cases have demonstrated how Black hairstyles are associated with negative stereotypes leading to personal and professional disadvantages (Banks, 2021; Onwuachi-Willig, 2010). Participants, like Angelique and Diamond, were aware that choosing to follow a Black beauty standard in a White space can result in the loss of a job and a source of financial support for their family.

Millennial Black women participate in the beauty industrial complex as a form of creative expression; choosing their hairstyle or makeup is a daily negotiation process (Reed & Medvedev, 2019). Historically, Black women have had limited political or economic power in the United States, and supporting a family can mean choosing between seemingly ordinary decisions about their hairstyle in order to remain employed (Okazawa-Rey et al., 1987). Due to the potential loss of a career opportunity, millennial Black women cannot afford to ignore mainstream beauty standards. They share concerns with previous generations of Black women who expressed their heritage in the workplace with far less social flexibility. Instead, millennials balance their career goals with cultural style choices in the workplace.

ENTRIES TO AGENCY: A (MILLENNIAL) BLACK AMERICAN BEAUTY STANDARD

Eighteen out of the 20 women interviewed felt that the Black American community recognized a different version of the American beauty standard. Kora, 42, from Chicago, described Black beauty as "challenging the stereotypes of White Anglo-Saxon beauty effortlessly." Tiana, 34, from Georgia, described it as a "variation of different things [...] instead of just one image in comparison to American beauty." Others described Black beauty as "raw," "heterogeneous," "rebellious," "multifaceted," and existing on a "spectrum" and "continuum." In their eyes, a Black beauty standard recognized the variety of hair textures, body sizes, and skin tones that existed within the African diaspora and found them all acceptable to some degree. However, environments, exposure to diverse representation, and digital media influenced the extent to which they related to a Black American beauty standard.

Sites of Influence

A Black American beauty standard is individual and contextual; environments can influence interpretations of Blackness and beauty (Gadson & Lewis, 2022; Walker Gautier, 2021). Location, including where participants lived and went to school, influenced their perceptions of Black American beauty. Sixty-five percent of them were raised in predominantly Black or Brown neighborhoods and, because of this, viewed Black beauty ideals as the baseline. The women who grew up in predominantly White neighborhoods discussed Black beauty through its proximity to Whiteness and were reluctant to consider a Black esthetic as an alternative to an American beauty standard. These participants were frequently exposed to White representations of femininity and beauty as the dominant form. When asked to define Black beauty, Jesse replied that the question made her feel "hesitant" and "caught off guard" because she was "not used to hearing those words together." Beauty was seen as the "total opposite" of Blackness because the immediate image in Jesse's mind was a "White, blonde girl that's living her best life on TV." Marie also described the Black beauty standard as trying to be "independent of American beauty" even though they "end up doing the same thing." In Marie's view, a Black beauty standard does not liberate. Instead, it represses Black Americans because straighter hair textures and lighter skin tones are still privileged above other characteristics. Heather, from Mississippi, also framed American and Black American beauty standards as "not quite the same, but not completely different" in terms of associating "lighter skin" and "looser curls" with acceptance and attraction. In comparison, Kennedy had to "grow to love beauty" because she associated the industry with Whiteness: "nine times out of ten, when I think about it, I mean as an industry, it's White. It's something that I never felt was attainable. [It] felt like it wasn't for me."

City demographics are not an absolute predictor of one's relationship to beauty standards. Cooper, who also grew up in a predominantly White neighborhood, viewed Black American beauty separately due to family influence. Cooper "always associated [her] version of beauty [with] other Black women." Her parents were "vocal about the fact that [...] the world may not think this, but this is what beauty is [...] to be brown skinned and have dark skin." Cooper shared an upbringing similar to Natasha, who also traced her beauty ideals to her formative years. Natasha was born in the United States, but her parents immigrated from Haiti to Florida prior to her birth. For her, Black beauty was the only beauty standard that she knew. Once she enrolled at a Predominantly White Institution (PWI) for college, she was able to "articulate the differences" between her beauty standard and others. Namely, she noticed how she "didn't grow up with the issue of colorism" and had no issues with liking her "big nose, full lips, or hips" because the women around her also looked like her. Confronting these differences at a PWI encouraged her to embrace her features rather than reject them. Exposure and proximity to a community where Black features were the default allowed Natasha and Cooper to remain confident in their identification with a Black American beauty standard. Without the constant reinforcement of Black as beautiful in their early lives, participants could not see the viability of a Black American beauty standard. Jesse points this out with her admission that "Black" and "beauty" do not seem to align. Instead, pejorative representations of Blackness color Jesse's ability to imagine a beauty standard where Black women are also seen as "living [their] best life."

Flawed Representations

Outside of the makeup of their respective cities, diverse media portrayals of Black womanhood provide behavior and style references for Black girls, adolescents, and young women. Black celebrities like Cicely Tyson and Nina Simone were noted as women who confidently wore their natural hair and embraced their Blackness in photoshoots and films. Taylor, who described celebrities and influencers as "not my deal," described Cicely Tyson's beauty in terms of how she carried herself, how "she walked with clear purpose and intention," and how "she communicated with people." Notably, Tyson was also the first Black woman to wear her hair in an afro while starring in a recurring role on the TV show "Eastside/Westside" in the 1960s (Alleyne, 2021). For Taylor, Cicely Tyson provided an ideal example of Black American beauty in terms of grace and style. In comparison, Kora from Washington, DC pictured "big hair, pronounced features, dark, smooth skin, and high cheekbones" as markers of Black beauty, and she associated these characteristics with Black American jazz icon Nina Simone.

Celebrities, such as Beyoncé, Halle Berry, Kerry Washington, Viola Davis, Lupita Nyong'o, and Zendaya, were identified as representations of a Black American beauty standard. These examples represent a diverse group in terms of age, skin tone, and hair texture. In the case of print media, the majority of Black women in magazine advertisements have medium skin tones, regardless of the magazine's target audience (Mitchell, 2020). While interviewees believed that a millennial standard of beauty existed, they could not identify one representative that captured their definition of millennial beauty. As Morgan from South Carolina aptly stated, millennials lack an "it girl," or an individual that captures the distinct identities embraced within millennial culture. Yet, even among the celebrities named, none fall squarely within the millennial range of birth years. Three of them are in Generation X, two are on the cusp of Generation X and Y, and Zendaya was born during the cut-off year between Millennials and Gen Z. While these examples could be considered early or late millennials, none of them could fully represent millennial experiences.

Millennials are often depicted as more liberal than Generation X (1965–1980) in the media, but there is still a considerable amount of conservative representation among them (Twenge, 2023). In 2020, 4 out of every 10 millennials identified with the Republican party. Despite this, participants connected the lack of a millennial representative to a generational view of beauty politics. According to Tiana, millennials "embrace different standards of beauty" because they are "socially progressive." Michelle also described the "new beauty standard" as one where millennials were accepting of gender, sexuality, and racial differences. Heather defined millennial beauty standards as "broader and more inclusive," especially regarding body positivity. Heather felt that millennials recognize that "being fat does not just magically take away all desirability" and reclaiming the word fat was evidence of millennials accepting themselves and an expansive definition of beauty.

Participant observations of these changing beauty ideals are supported by diverse media representation and marketing campaigns for indie beauty brands. Beauty brands in this category are typically cause-oriented direct to consumer companies that appeal to consumers interested in organic or "clean" ingredients (Gupta, 2021). The surge in indie beauty brands and their seemingly inclusive marketing practices suggests that millennial values are taking hold of the beauty market to an extent. In some sense, participants bought into the notion that beauty brands were accurately representing their generation's societal outlook because marketing campaigns resonated with their social and esthetic sensibilities. In actuality, marketing representation and products are better examples of how millennials buy into the beauty industry rather than how they are represented within it.

Millennial Beauty Standards in Digital Communities

Millennials and successive generations view American beauty trends through an expansive lens due to their exposure to global beauty ideals. In Black American beauty culture, YouTube played an extensive role in building new digital communities where people with similar hair textures can, together, learn new ways of maintaining their hair (Ellington, 2015; Neil & Mbilishaka, 2019). From millennials to Generation Z (born between 1997 and 2012), today's Black American beauty esthetic integrates knowledge gained from watching beauty influencers like Jackie Aina, and exposure to celebrity skincare and cosmetic brands, such as Rihanna's Fenty Beauty. While millennial Black women benefit from this new level of access to seeing their physical features popularized online, outsiders who were not privy to the ways that these styles emerged, or their historical relevance are now able to view, admire, and ultimately adopt Black beauty trends without consequence.

YouTube was used to learn hair, beauty, and skincare techniques but a small segment of participants were also invested in the lifestyles of content creators. Influencers, such as Jaclyn Hill (Jaclyn Cosmetics), Tati Westbrook (Tati Beauty), and Cashmere Nicole (Beauty Bakerie), were mentioned in a friendly manner. Eventually, when these influencers pursued their own cosmetic lines, participants also purchased these products as an extension of their trust in the recommendations. Beauty influencers could entice them to buy new products, but the resulting product usage was limited. Nicole declared that most millennials reserved makeup for special occasions rather than everyday errands because a full made-up look required considerable time and effort. Accordingly, B. Wells described the millennial relationship to cosmetics as "necessary and optional" because millennials could adapt to mainstream beauty standards on their own terms.

Some participants also described a process of unlearning beauty conditioning and relearning the value of their features. Sunshine cut her processed hair off as a gesture of restarting the relationship with her hair in high school. During her teen years, she found this journey influential in helping her find herself and redefine her connection to beauty. Mavis, who referred to herself as a "recovering colorist," recounted realizing that "all Black people are recovering from something" and for her, that something was colorism. After watching an episode of *The Grapevine*, a panel style discussion show geared toward Black millennials on YouTube, Mavis realized that she was "technically one of the darkest out of [her] friend group" and found herself dating people with lighter skin tones than hers, and code switching among different groups of Black people. She eventually sat down and faced herself in starting her "self-love journey":

> I had to tell myself, like, "look in the mirror, and you're going to sit here and look in this mirror for 45 minutes." And I like cried and all of that, I didn't want to look in there, but it was like I had to really look in the mirror. Even when it came to my hair texture, [when] I started my locs, I was looking at other people whose textures never looked like mine and getting frustrated that my hair don't look like theirs. Because, sis, she's 3B! you're 4B, okay?!

Mavis describes how she learned to appreciate her beauty as it was instead of in comparison to a White American beauty standard. She also alludes to gaining new insight when she differentiates a 3B curl type from 4B. These designations are based on a hair typing system created by Andre Walker, a hair stylist for Oprah Winfrey (Hill et al., 2018). 3B and 4B curls have similar spacing between each curl, but type 4 refers to tightly coiled curls and type 3 refers to a curl between wavy (type 2) and coiled (type 4). Mavis considered herself beautiful but recognized that her hair and skin tone were not measuring up to an ideal beauty. Digital media, including the show that pushed her to reflect, exposes millennials to multiple interpretations of Black beauty. Without YouTube access, Mavis may not have realized that there was nothing inherently wrong with her hair; she just needed different products and styles suited for her hair needs.

Social media has significantly aided the spread of hair education for millennial Black women (Childs, 2022). Exchanges between content creators and viewers provide personalized hair advice and access to a knowledgeable hair community. These platforms also showcase the rich variety of hair types, textures, and styles within the Black American beauty ideal. This exposure assists with dismantling historically negative perceptions of Black hair as unmanageable and, instead, provides free advice to people interested in embracing their natural hair.

For millennial Black women, Black American entertainers influenced how strongly they identified with an intracultural beauty standard. Though they recognize that alternative beauty standards may exist, they do not consider themselves free to interact with these standards all the time. Choosing when to participate in Black or White American beauty standards does not overrule the fact that they must participate in one or the other to be accepted in either community. While a White American beauty standard may be tolerated in Black communities, the Black beauty standard is not equally validated in White spaces. In this sense, if a Black person chooses to fully identify and participate in an intracultural standard, they willingly accept the potential consequences that may come with failing to meet societal expectations around appearance.

PATHWAYS TO LIBERATION

Compared to Generation X and Generation Z, millennial Black women have divergent perceptions of ideal beauty. Their relationship with beauty was self-assured, with a desire to stand out or "make sure that your look is the only look in a space." In contrast, beauty for their mothers' generation was seen as "natural," "organic," and "minimalist with makeup." Morgan's mother, who was born in the 1970s, viewed millennials as "very low effort" because they chose to wear oversized t-shirts and multiple accessories instead of assembling a statement outfit. Other participants' mothers shared this view. Diamond's mother described beauty standards in her youth:

> Your hair mattered, your gold hoops mattered, the gold bangles to match your hoops mattered. But makeup wasn't [...] a thing that you had to have together when going out ... it was [focused on] making sure that you had your hair laid, the latest outfit, and nice shoes.

Aside from viewing millennials as lacking effort in their attire choices, Black mothers from Generation X also supported a personalized beauty that was manageable and presentable. For example, Angelique's mother had a "very specific idea of what it means to be beautiful and feminine," which involved directing her to wear makeup and lose weight, among other things. To be presentable, Taylor's mother paid to have her daughter's hair straightened with a hot comb or flat iron every two weeks throughout her childhood. Despite the significant expense, her mother viewed the time saved in managing Taylor's hair during the week as a worthy opportunity cost. Angelique's and Taylor's parents resolved to manage their respective child's appearance through their body shape and hair style in ways that brought them closer to Eurocentric beauty standards. Angelique's mother expected her to be thinner, while Taylor's mother made a tradeoff between the effort required to upkeep her daughter's hair and her style's proximity to the American beauty ideal. Choosing between a Eurocentric or Black beauty standard reinforces the existing binary of acceptable physical traits. Given the structural conditions that exist for Black Americans, beauty standards offer a space for resistance but not revolution as the views of participants' parents demonstrate. Millennial Black women continue to reframe the conversation around beauty by embracing their intracultural standards and boldly expressing it in new spaces. Yet, while their beauty politics are progressive, their participation in the beauty industrial complex is not.

Within the group, the millennial beauty standard was characterized as "laidback" with the freedom to "do the things that we want to do [and] look how we want to look." However freeing the external expression of beauty may seem, the labor behind it remains largely invisible. Considerable work is required to turn "laidback" into an acceptable style. Accordingly, participants reported spending about 30–45 minutes prepping their hair, skin, or body daily. For extended hair and body care routines, an additional two hours once or twice a week was included. Michelle, a retail director in New York City, recalled spending three to five hours once a week washing and prepping her hair for work in addition to her daily routines. Based on the 8–10 hours spent weekly, Michelle requested "special accommodations for Black women" from her company's Human Resources department. The department dismissed her request, stating that "we all have to make choices." For Black women, hairstyle choices for professional spaces are laden with cultural meaning and likely to be misinterpreted. Protective styles, such as cornrows, twists, or locs, would reduce the time investment on Michelle's part. Yet, these styles are often deemed unprofessional as evidenced by the cases of hair discrimination and the necessity of the CROWN Act. Despite sharing similar concerns around professionalism at work with previous generations, the type of work and expectations bound to those spaces still affect the degree to which millennial Black women can pursue a "comfortable" or "laidback" look.

The process of becoming beautiful is rarely as effortless and harmless as beauty companies would like consumers to believe. Drawing attention to the labor inherent in Black women's self-fashioning highlights the actual beautification process that takes place when individuals try to emulate media meant to represent ideal beauty standards for the masses. The esthetic labor required to uphold this image is often deemed insignificant, making the actual time, effort, and money needed for upkeep invisible. This process, which includes fashioning skin, hair, make-up, and apparel, also extends to managing one's voice, emotions, and body language to portray an acceptable version of Black femininity (Elias et al., 2017). Beauty and achievement are portrayed as worthy pursuits for young

Black women, making the choice of adhering to beauty standards an attractive one. As a result, the reception of the final look becomes more important than the agency that women can exhibit when they can manage their beauty on their own terms.

Participants felt that beauty management could be an act of self-care but mostly viewed it as a requirement in society. In comparison, Generation Z and Alpha prioritize their beauty routines as a matter of self-care (Krieger, 2023). Both groups are motivated by an underlying investment in appearing beautiful, to oneself or others, keeping the beauty industrial complex profitable. Liberation requires a conscious relationship with beauty where distinction does not reinforce cultural importance. Instead, embracing the multiplicity of beauty, globally, paves the way to deconstructing beauty as a matter of political economy.

LIMITATIONS AND FURTHER RESEARCH

Findings were informed by 20 self-identified millennial Black women located in the United States. These demographic limitations provide an in-depth look at one case of Black American beauty but also nuanced interpretations of Blackness, place, and beauty attuned to generational differences. Participants were recruited through purposeful random sampling, but the majority resided in the Southeast region of the United States. Studies can also include women from other regions to compare place-based perspectives of beauty. Perceptions and relationships to a White American beauty standard may differ for Black women in different regions of the United States due to their lived experiences in those areas. Future studies could also interview Black women from other generations for comparison.

Interpretations of Blackness and its relation to American beauty standards are also connected to individual positionality within the African diaspora. Most of the women in this study considered themselves to be African American, but others also identified as Black, biracial, Afro-Creole, and Afro-Caribbean. Therefore, these findings are bound more by nationality and generation than a monolithic interpretation of Black identity. Future research could place further limitations around what it means to be a Black American or focus on comparing one diasporic identity across nations to further identify the characteristics of a shared, diasporic beauty standard.

CONCLUSION

During slavery, there were deliberate actions taken to minimize Black women's beauty, and still, today, Black women's freedom to fully express their esthetic is limited to specific times and places. The separation of personal and public space, throughout slavery, Reconstruction, Jim Crow, and the Civil Rights Movement provided the means for an alternative beauty standard to evolve throughout the years. African beauty culture was purposefully disconnected from enslaved peoples, leading them to create Black American beauty standards alongside White

American beauty ideals. The inclusive and exclusive nature of fashion also extends to beauty. Though American beauty standards are represented as racial opposites, they share a historical and national affiliation.

Histories of beauty tend to represent Black women's beauty in opposition to White women's within the United States (Marwick, 1998). But the American beauty ideal shifted during participants' lives, and these changes are reflected in the incorporation of Black women's beauty ideals into mainstream media. Participants connected their beauty perceptions to media representation and products used to manage their appearance. Through their participation in the beauty industrial complex, study participants connected a millennial beauty standard to American expectations. Viewing beauty participation as progressive conflicts with the act of purchasing beauty products, reinforcing the notion that pursuing an ideal beauty is a worthy use of time.

Policies and work dress codes hinder Black women from expressing their full selves in the workplace. Broadening acceptance of other types of beauty in professional and public environments frees people from molding their appearance and behavior into a socially accepted form. Beauty, then, has been used to control Black women, excluding them and other women of color from a standard that feels immovable in its certainty: To be American and beautiful is to be "White," "thin," "blonde," and "blue-eyed" – a standard that the majority of White Americans do not meet.

The freedom to express one's cultural beauty standard is repressed when it is characterized as unsuitable for the workplace, causing participants to engage in beauty ideals for personal and professional gain. Though they moved in, out, and through White and Black American beauty standards, they favored an intracultural beauty standard. When participants chose their cultural standard, they exited the comparison process with Eurocentrism. In essence, they traded one standard that is out of their reach for a community-based standard with its own set of hierarchies. This refutes the idea that a Eurocentric beauty is the only standard worth measuring up to.

While the measurements of American beauty change, its basis in Whiteness does not (McMillan Cottom, 2019). As capital, beauty must be stratified, divisive, and advantageous for some. Still, there is a difference between beauty for sale and beauty for assessment. Participants recognized the centrality of Whiteness in an American beauty standard and then chose to embrace the alternative as an outlet for identity expression. By highlighting a diasporic view of beauty, participants signified their knowledge of the beauty spectrum present in Black expression. Recognizing this range affected internal and external perceptions of their identity, leading some to learn new ways of seeing. Navigating how others' perceptions may impact their professional, fiscal, and physical livelihood was a clear reason to participate in and pay attention to American beauty standards.

What would it mean to be liberated from beauty standards? Liberation from beauty regimes would be for all. Claiming a path that uplifts cultural beauty standards rather than Eurocentrism is a pathway to potential liberation. Yet, advantages associated with assimilation along with social constraints around expression make this path difficult to pursue. By (re)defining American, millennial, and Black ideals of beauty, participants identified alternative ways to build and frame beauty knowledge. This is a first step toward beauty as liberation. Black women's ability to liberate themselves from beauty standards depends on their freedom to operationalize the agency needed to separate one's self-identity from the beauty management process. Millennial Black women in this study see the possibility of beauty when it is separated from Whiteness. As "alternative" beauty ideals emerge and coexist, notions of beauty move past being dismissed as an individual matter, social construct, or sign of inner virtue (Tate, 2007). Decentering Whiteness in the designation of what is and is not beautiful also leaves room for conceptualizing beauty outside of commodification. In this space of possibility, cultural beauty standards can be refashioned as valuable markers of difference rather than a commodity.

REFERENCES

Allain, J. M. (2020). "They are quiet women now": Hair cropping, British imperial governance, and the gendered body in the archive. *Slavery & Abolition*, *41*(4), 772–794. https://doi.org/10.1080/0144039X.2020.1749489

Alleyne, A. (2021, January 29). *Cicely Tyson was an early champion of Black beauty*. CNN. https://www.cnn.com/style/article/cicely-tyson-black-beauty-legacy/index.html

Banks, P. A. (2021). Hair rules: Race, gender, and stigmatization in schools. *Journal of Law and Social Change*, *25*(1), 1–9. https://doi.org/10.2139/ssrn.3798082

Bennett, L., Jr. (1980, November). What is Black beauty? Appraisal of the grandeur of Black womanhood provides new and startling answers. *Ebony Magazine*, *36*(1), 159–161.

Byrd, A. D., & Tharps, L. L. (2014). *Hair story: Untangling the roots of Black hair in America* (revised ed.). St. Martin's Griffin.

Candelario, G. (2000). Hair racing: Dominican beauty culture and identity production. *Meridians*, *1*(1), 128–156. https://doi.org/10.1215/15366936-1.1.128

Cheddie, J. (2002). The politics of the first: The emergence of the Black model in the Civil Rights Era. *Fashion Theory*, *6*(1), 61–82.

Childs, K. M. (2022). "The shade of it all": How Black women use Instagram and YouTube to contest colorism in the beauty industry. *Social Media + Society* (April–June) 1–15. https://doi.org/10.1177/20563051221107634

Clutario, G. A. (2023). *Beauty regimes: A history of power and modern empire in the Philippines, 1898–1941*. Duke University Press.

CROWN Coalition. (2023). *About*. The Official CROWN Act. https://www.thecrownact.com/about

Davis-Bundrage, M., Medvedev, K., & Hunt-Hurst, P. (2018). Impact of Black women's hair politics on bodily health. In S. Barak-Brandes & A. Kama (Eds.), *Feminist interrogations of women's head hair: Crown of glory and shame* (1st ed., pp. 159–175). Routledge. https://doi.org/10.4324/9780429505430

Dawson, G. A., Karl, K. A., & Peluchette, J. V. (2019). Hair matters: Toward understanding natural Black hair bias in the workplace. *Journal of Leadership & Organizational Studies*, *26*(3), 389–401.

Donahoo, S., & Smith, A. D. (2022). Controlling the crown: Legal efforts to professionalize Black hair. *Race and Justice*, *12*(1), 182–203. https://doi.org/10.1177/2153368719888264

Duan, N. S. (2017). Black women's bodies and Blackface in fashion magazines. *Critical Studies in Fashion & Beauty*, *8*(1), 65–98. https://doi.org/10.1386/csfb.8.1.65_1

Elias, A., Gill, R., & Scharff, C. (2017). Aesthetic labour: Beauty politics in neoliberalism. In A. S. Elias, R. Gill, & C. Scharff (Eds.), *Aesthetic labour: Rethinking beauty politics in neoliberalism* (pp. 3–49). Palgrave Macmillan UK. https://doi.org/10.1057/978-1-137-47765-1_1

Ellington, T. N. (2015). Social networking sites: A support system for African-American women wearing natural hair. *International Journal of Fashion Design, Technology and Education*, *8*(1), 21–29. https://doi.org/10.1080/17543266.2014.974589

Gadson, C. A., & Lewis, J. A. (2022). Devalued, overdisciplined, and stereotyped: An exploration of gendered racial microaggressions among Black adolescent girls. *Journal of Counseling Psychology*, *69*(1), 14–26. https://doi.org/10.1037/cou0000571

Gould, V. M. (1997). "A chaos of iniquity and discord": Slave and free women of color in the Spanish ports of New Orleans, Mobile, and Pensacola. In C. Clinton & M. Gillespie (Eds.), *The devil's lane* (pp. 232–246). Oxford University Press. https://doi.org/10.1093/acprof:oso/9780195112436.001.0001

Greensword, S. N.-K. (2022). Historicizing Black hair politics: A framework for contextualizing race politics. *Sociology Compass*, *16*(8). https://doi.org/10.1111/soc4.13015

Gupta, P. (2021, March 4). *The quiet, quick rise of indie beauty brands*. Forbes. https://www.forbes.com/sites/columbiabusinessschool/2021/03/04/the-quiet-quick-rise-of-indie-beauty-brands/

Hill, K., Adesola, A., Prajjwhal, D., Washington, G., & Legand, I. B. (2018, November 8). *Towards creation of a curl pattern recognition system*. IP, Computer Vision, and Pattern Recognition.

Hill Collins, P. (1990). *Black feminist thought knowledge, consciousness, and the politics of empowerment*. Routledge.

Hobson, J. (2005). *Venus in the dark: Blackness and beauty in popular culture*. Routledge.

Johnson, T. A., & Bankhead, T. (2014). Hair it is: Examining the experiences of Black women with natural hair. *Open Journal of Social Sciences*, *2*(1), 86–100. https://doi.org/10.4236/jss.2014.21010

JOY Collective & Dove. (2019). The CROWN research study: Creating a respectful and open workplace for natural hair [Corporate Research Study]. https://static1.squarespace.com/static/5edc69fd622c36173f56651f/t/5edeaa2fe5ddef345e087361/1591650865168/Dove_research_brochure2020_FINAL3.pdf

JOY Collective & Dove. (2023). *CROWN 2023 workplace research study*. https://static1.squarespace.com/static/5edc69fd622c36173f56651f/t/63ebfc0b10498b76e985c45b/1676409868811/DOVE_2023_study_infographic_FINAL-02.png

Krieger, L. (2023, August 10). *The rise of the baby beauty fanatics*. ELLE. https://www.elle.com/beauty/makeup-skin-care/a44639827/the-rise-of-the-baby-beauty-junkies/

Legal Defense Fund. (2022). *Natural hair discrimination FAQ*. Legal Defense Fund. Retrieved November 6, 2022, from https://www.naacpldf.org/natural-hair-discrimination/

Mbilishaka, A., Ray, M., Hall, J., & Wilson, I.-P. (2020). 'No toques mi pelo' (don't touch my hair): Decoding Afro-Cuban identity politics through hair. *African and Black Diaspora: An International Journal*, *13*(1), 114–126. https://doi.org/10.1080/17528631.2019.1639298

K. McKittrick & C. Woods (Eds.) (2007). *Black geographies and the politics of place*. Between the Lines.

McMillan Cottom, T. (2019). In the name of beauty. In *Thick and other essays* (pp. 33–72). The New Press.

Mitchell, T. A. (Ed.) (2020). Critical race theory (CRT) and colourism: A manifestation of whitewashing in marketing communications? *Journal of Marketing Management*, *36*(13–14), 1366–1389. https://doi.org/10.1080/0267257X.2020.1794934

Neil, L., & Mbilishaka, A. (2019). "Hey Curlfriends!": Hair care and self-care messaging on YouTube by Black women natural hair vloggers. *Journal of Black Studies*, *50*(2), 156–177. https://doi.org/10.1177/0021934718819411

Okazawa-Rey, M., Robinson, T., & Ward, J. V. (1987). Black women and the politics of skin color and hair. *Women & Therapy*, *6*(1–2), 89–102. https://doi.org/10.1300/J015V06N01_07

Omi, M., & Winant, H. (2014). *Racial formation in the United States* (3rd ed.). Routledge.

Onwuachi-Willig, A. (2010). Another hair piece: Exploring new strands of analysis under Title VII. *Georgetown Law Journal*, *98*, 55.

Reed, J., & Medvedev, K. (2019). The beauty divide: Black millennial women seek agency with Makeup Art Cosmetics (MAC). In A. Lynch & K. Medvedev (Eds.), *Fashion, agency, and empowerment: Performing agency, following script* (1st ed., pp. 11–28). Bloomsbury. https://doi.org/10.5040/9781350058293

Rogers vs *American Airlines, Inc.*, 527 F. Supp. 229 (S.D.N.Y. 1981), No. 81 Civ. 4474 (U.S. District Court for the Southern District of New York December 1, 1981). https://law.justia.com/cases/federal/district-courts/FSupp/527/229/2369655/

Shipp, E. R. (1987, September 23). Braided hair style at issue in protests over dress codes. *The New York Times*, 1.

Shoaib, M. (2023, March 13). *Why fashion month is failing Black models with textured hair*. Vogue Business. https://www.voguebusiness.com/beauty/why-fashion-month-is-failing-black-models-with-textured-hair
Simmons, K. E. (2008). Navigating the racial terrain: Blackness and mixedness in the United States and the Dominican Republic. *Transforming Anthropology, 16*(2), 95–111. https://doi.org/10.1111/j.1548-7466.2008.00019.x
D. Sterling, (Ed.) (1984). *We are your sisters: Black women in the nineteenth century*. Norton & Company.
Sweet, F. (2022). One drop rule. In *Encyclopedia of Arkansas*. https://encyclopediaofarkansas.net/entries/one-drop-rule-5365/
Tate, S. (2007). Black beauty: Shade, hair and anti-racist aesthetics. *Ethnic and Racial Studies, 30*(2), 300–319. https://doi.org/10.1080/01419870601143992
Tate, S. A., & Fink, K. (2019). Skin colour politics and the White beauty standard. In C. Liebelt, S. Böllinger, & U. Vierke (Eds.), *Beauty and the norm* (pp. 283–297). Springer International Publishing. https://doi.org/10.1007/978-3-319-91174-8_12
Thompson, C. (2023). Casting Blackface in Canada: Unmasking the history of 'White and Black' minstrel shows. *Canadian Theatre Review, 193*, 16–20. https://doi.org/10.3138/ctr.193.004
Townsend, C. V. (2021). Identity politics: Why African American women are missing in administrative leadership in public higher education. *Educational Management Administration & Leadership, 49*(4), 584–600. https://doi.org/10.1177/1741143220935455
Twenge, J. M. (Ed.) (2023). Millennials (born 1980–1994). In *Generations: The real differences between Gen Z, Millennials, Gen X, Boomers, and Silents – And what they mean for America's future* (pp. 163–243). Atria Books.
Walker Gautier, S. (2021). Black beauty: Womanist consciousness as a protective factor in Black women's body image satisfaction. *Journal of Black Psychology, 47*(8), 631–656. https://doi.org/10.1177/00957984211034960
Weathers, N. R. (1991). Braided sculptures and smokin' combs: African-American women's hair culture. *Sage, 8*(1), 58–61.
White, S., & White, G. (1995). Slave hair and African American culture in the eighteenth and nineteenth centuries. *The Journal of Southern History, 61*(1), 45. https://doi.org/10.2307/2211360

CHAPTER 8

BALLET IS [WHITE] WOMAN: ANTI-BLACK STANDARDS OF BEAUTY WITHIN BALLET

Sekani L. Robinson

Sociology Department, California State Polytechnic University, USA

ABSTRACT

The ballet industry has long been criticized for using excessively thin and exclusively Anglo-looking ballerinas. The statement that they fit the "look" or comments such as this in the 2015 New York Daily Post*: "A lot of people feel ballerinas should all be the same color" (Keivom, 2015) have been used to exclude Black and Brown ballerinas. This chapter describes the relationship between race, gender, and beauty within the ballet industry. It describes the challenges that Black women experience and the anti-Blackness that takes place within ballet due to Eurocentric beauty standards. Through a focus on the emphasis on hair texture, flesh-tone tights, and pointe shoes, and on the racist history of America and ballet, this chapter demonstrates how ballet continues to discriminate against and marginalize Black women.*

Keywords: Race; embodiment; culture; occupational spaces; beauty; esthetic

I started ballet when I was two years old and trained until I graduated from high school. I even took a few classes in undergrad. Though I trained in ballet for years, and I had the typical love/hate relationship for ballet – as many other ballet dancers would echo, I always knew that ballet was not a space for a Black girl like me. I didn't analyze it much, but I just knew that becoming a professional ballet dancer was not really an option for me. But I enjoyed it. So, I kept with it. While I knew that there were very few Black ballerinas, I admittedly believed that ballet was a White woman's space and that Black dancers occupied modern and hip-hop spaces. Little did I know how systemic and stigmatized this belief was. I share this anecdote because it is the origins of my understanding behind race and ballet and, more broadly, understanding how Black people navigate and negotiate their Blackness when in spaces that have historically excluded Black individuals.

As I began my journey of understanding being a Black dancer in an exclusively White space, I came across Thomas F. DeFrantz and his scholarship around Black social dances. DeFrantz describes Black social dances and Black dancers through the lens of Du Bois' 1903 theory of *double consciousness*. Du Bois conveys *double consciousness* as, "Two-ness, -an American, a negro; two souls, two thoughts, two unreconciled strivings ... in one dark body, whose dogged strength alone keeps it from being torn asunder" suggesting a doubling of desire of being Black and existing in an American (White) space (Du Bois, 1986, p. 8). This duality is enacted as black dancers navigate the dance world and occupy dance forms in which they are not reflected in.

In conjunction with DeFrantz, many Black scholars have analyzed Black people in "white spaces" – such as professional workplaces (Wingfield, 2015; Wingfield & Alston, 2014; Wingfield & Chavez, 2020; Wingfield & Wingfield, 2014), ordinary, everyday spaces (Anderson, 2021), art spaces (Banks, 2020), to understand how they navigate these spaces designed to exclude them. Ballet, specifically, has maintained this exclusive space in overt and covert ways, and throughout this paper, I examine how these forms of exclusion take place. In this chapter, I engage with scholars such as Patricia Hill Collins, Adia Harvey Wingfield, Thomas F. DeFrantz, and Elijah Anderson, and more to explore how the ballet industry employs a racialized esthetic that excludes Black women and how the Black women that *do* make it into this professional industry navigate this anti-Black space. I address: *what can we learn from looking at the historical exclusion of Black women from ballet? What does that tell us about gender and race?*

BALLET IS WOMAN

Before diving into the Black women's experiences, I first address where the statement "Ballet is woman" stems from and it's within American ballet's history. "Ballet is woman" was famously stated by Russian choreographer and one of the alleged founders of American ballet, George Balanchine. When making this statement, Balanchine may have not specified what kind of woman, but his descriptions and feelings toward the *ideal* ballerina have been described many times in detail. He described that ideal ballerina as supernatural, by being extremely thin, having very low to no body fat, long, lean, with long legs, a short torso, and a small head (Gottschild, 1996; Mitchell, 1987) to the point of looking prepubescent, mythical, and overall unattainable – which is similar to dominant Western standards of beauty and attractiveness (Mears, 2011). Balanchine also believed that a ballerina's skin should be the color of a "freshly peeled apple" (Picart, 2012, p. 691). This cannoned the standard of the ideal ballerina *look* that is still praised today.

Lynn Garafola (1985) focuses on ballet from the 19th century. She contextualized the shift and focus around men, in ballet, to women, in ballet, and how that created an evolution of the ideal ballerina. Garafola (1985) argues:

> More than any other era in the history of ballet, the nineteenth century belongs to the ballerina. She haunts its lithographs and paintings, an ethereal creature touched with the charm of another age. Yet, even when she turned into the fast, leggy ballerina of modern times, her ideology survived ... it has yet to rid its aesthetic of yesterday's cult of the eternal feminine. (p. 35)

This ideal body image is depicted in the work of Edgar Degas (1834–1917), who is famous for pastel and charcoal drawings, paintings, and sculptures of dancers; during the most iconic era of ballet history, that is, the Romantic era of ballet (Laurens, 2017) includes over 1,500 pieces solely of White, thin women in bell-shaped tutus. This hegemonic balletic look demonstrates how aesthetics are subjective and align with society's Eurocentric ideologies of beauty. Following Balanchine, in 1975, a director of a major ballet company stated:

> The carriage of the Black dancer is not classic. It's the position of the spine. The litany of bodily excesses and deficiencies lay at the ready to exclude the Black body from miscegenation within the White body or corps de ballet: critics rhetorically constructed and essentialized the black dancer as possessing a too-stocky bone structure, protruding buttocks, and feet that were too flat and too large. (Gaiser, 2006, p. 272)

In May 2014, another executive director told *Pointe Magazine*, "I've heard from the mouths of dance professionals that Black dancers categorically cannot become ballet dancers because they don't have the right body" (Carmen, 2014). Since its inception, Black people's bodies have been racialized as not fitting the required *look* for ballet and face forms of esthetic discrimination that they ultimately cannot fulfill. Throughout this chapter, I describe the challenges that Black women experience and the anti-Blackness that takes place, within ballet, due to Eurocentric ideals of beauty standards. I focus on race, gender, beauty, and embodiment as it describes how Black women navigate a space that discriminates Blackness and the range of Black beauty features.

THE *LOOK*

Given some historical context of the ideal ballet body, I now address how the ballerina *look* is being classified, understood, and contextualized. Scholar Ashley Mears (2011) clarifies the term *look* as a fixed set of physical attributes. This *look* is a form of bodily capital (Wacquant, 2004) in which like models, ballet dancers sell this exceptionally difficult and unrealistic standard to the directors, choreographers, ballet masters and mistresses, and audiences. Mears states that a look is a type of commodity in which the products that steam from the cultural economy are inscribed with high levels of esthetic or semiotic content (Currid,

2007; Entwistle, 2002) in a conscious attempt to generate desire among consumers (Mears, 2011). These *looks* provide social status, social mobility, privilege, and identity over and above their utility to function as a commodity (Mears, 2011). Given that professional ballet is an occupation, their *look* is a form of esthetic labor, and for Black women, they are enduring a racialized form of esthetic labor in that they are trying to attain an image that is not inclusive to them. This racialized esthetic labor will be explored more through the controlling of Black bodies.

"THE BLACK SWAN": CONTROLLING THE BLACK BODY

Patriarchal ideologies surrounding Black women's bodies are powerfully shaped by what Patricia Hill Collins (1990) refers to as "controlling images"– cultural images of a subordinate group developed by a dominant group that work to justify oppression.

Controlling images of Black femininity influence the roles available to Black women in ballet. As McCarthy-Brown (2011) writes, "the stereotyped African American woman does not fit into the ideal ballet feminine aesthetic. African American women are, therefore, used to emphasize their extreme opposite: 'ultra-feminine' white women" (p. 393; see also Atencio & Wright, 2009). Forms of racialized sexualization in ballet shape both perceptions and experiences of Black women in ballet requiring them to be objectified through the "white male gaze" (Genné, 2005, p. 50; McCarthy-Brown, 2011). For instance, in McCarthy-Brown's interview with the artistic director for Oakland Ballet, she discovered a Black ballerina had been cast in a role of servitude (the maid) before the director even saw her dance. Controlling images help encourage experiences like the typecasting of Black ballerinas as servants that echoes one idea of controlling images that are ascribed to Black women (2011).

As an occupation, ballet demands embodied performance. Ballet dancers' bodies are observed, evaluated, criticized, touched, and manipulated. The dancer's body is not a *natural* one but is socially produced through discipline and requires significant investments of cultural, economic, and social capital to produce. Analyzing ballet dancers as employees and understanding ballet *as work* offer an important site to explore issues that have been raised in research on other forms of labor, like sex work: contemporary definitions of beauty and desirability, the objectification of the body, and the racialized hyper-sexualization of Black women's bodies (e.g., Brooks et al., 2003; Montemurro, 2001; Murphy, 2003). I show how Black women simultaneously negotiate racialized forms of gendered labor and gendered forms of racial labor and impression management.

Bodily objectification is a feature of postindustrial consumer culture (e.g., Bordo, 1993; Pope et al., 2000). As is true in other occupations, ballet dancers learn to monitor, regulate, and manage their bodies, as bodily capital within their occupation (e.g., Kang, 2010; Mears, 2011; Mears & Finlay, 2005). Feminist scholars Bartky (1998, p. 1527) and Gimlin (2002) examine how women discipline and alter their bodies to conform to patriarchal ideals of beauty and to appease gender roles through gendered cultural performance. This notion can also be applied to ballet dancers who conform to a standard of beauty requiring controlling their weight, body shape, and hair to attempt to embody a particular look.

Black women's bodies are constantly sexualized and depicted as deviant sexual beings. Women such as Josephine Baker and Sarah "Saartjie" Baartman were highlighted and paraded as sexual objects, and this has affected Black women's ability to be seen as pure and feminine, which influences marginalization and discrimination for Black women in occupations such as modeling and ballet. Scholarship demonstrates and explains the sexualization of Black women and continuous discrimination of Black women's bodies.

Brenda Dixon Gottschild (2003) conceptualizes the black body in dance through Afrocentric theory, which redefines and confronts the marginalization of hegemonic, racist beauty standards toward Black women and provides agency through collective consciousness (Asante, 1998; Patton, 2006). Afrocentric theory also shapes racial stigmas of a Black dancer's body. Gottschild addresses racial identities and racial embodiment by deconstructing historical context within the racial stigmas that are attached to specific parts of the body, e.g., feet, butt, skin/hair which all embody the Afrocentric theory. She points to Afrocentric features as being minstrelized (stereotypical expressions) into the "coon construct" and used as a constant reminder as to why Black people do not have the right body type for ballet. However, explaining how "the coon body and spirit were also cool" (p. 286) as well as introducing the concept of enculturated somatophobia all challenges these stigmas.

Throughout this chapter, I contextualize how the racial stigmas associated with Black ballet dancers are both overt and covert and how Black ballet dancers navigate and negotiate their existence within this historically White space.

METHODOLOGY: INTERVIEWING THE CAST

The experiences of Black women in classical ballet have been neglected and undertheorized in the sociological literature on work and occupational inequalities, discrimination, culture, embodiment, and emotions. This research demonstrates how the intersections of race, gender, and class shape looks and aesthetics within the service economy.

Positionality, Reflexivity, and Accessing Elite Populations

While conducting this research, I realized how important my positionality was in both gaining access and collecting stories from my participants. As a Black woman, who has practiced ballet and who now works within the ballet industry, I did not have much trouble gaining access to the dancers. I was also able to connect with my participants and generate trust that provided a privileged insight into our shared professional experiences. Our shared experiences allow for a fundamental element of an Afrocentric standpoint (Okanlawon, 1972) in which "Black people share a common experience of oppression" (Okanlawon, 1972, p. 94).

My positions provided me access to dancers and allowed me to engage in conversations that would have been difficult for those outside of the industry. It allowed me to reflect more on my own experience and relationship with ballet, as I shared a little in the introduction, and see the patterns that Black women experience due to White supremacy and whiteness within the ballet institution.

Participants

This study is based on 53 semi-structured interviews of Black women and men within ballet. I conducted *20* in-depth interviews of Black women who were/are employed by major US-based ballet companies, *8* in-depth interviews of Black men who were/are employed by major US-based ballet companies, and *25* in-depth interviews of Black women who have not danced professionally but have trained intensely for a minimum of 5 years. Twenty interviews are a substantial proportion of the total population of professional Black women in ballet today and throughout time. Black women make up less than 5% of the ballet companies today; fewer than 1 in 20 ballerinas dancing professionally are Black women.

Participants were recruited throughout the United States, typically in major metropolitan cities including Los Angeles, California, Salt Lake City, Utah, Houston, Texas, Boston, Massachusetts, Washington, DC, and New York City in which many of the participants reside. The participants were between 18 and 85 years old and represented generations of current and former ballet enthusiasts in the US ballet industry. For the dancers, I asked questions about their occupational trajectory, bodily management, and overall experience of being a Black ballet dancer. For participants that did not make it professionally, I asked about their dance background, how/why it ended, bodily management, and overall experience being a Black dancer. The surveys included both interviewees and additional people who were interested in doing the survey but not interested in being interviewed. The surveys provided information about childhood exposure to ballet, financial resources, family support, and the roles that they had been offered and performed. For this chapter, I opted to use pseudonyms when referring to my participants.

I employed several methods to recruit dancers. I used my position as a Black former dancer, relied upon my networks with former dancers, and as an employee of a major ballet company to gain access to dancers and administrators. I studied the major ballet company's websites and social media, that is, Instagram and Twitter, to identify and locate current Black dancers. I contacted them through direct messaging or through email and confirmed their interest in completing a survey and possibly an interview. During data collection, many dancers were in the middle performance season and were not available for interviews.

Once I completed the interviews, I coded them using Excel, looking for emergent themes, which provided more of a grounded theory approach. This led me to focus on specific themes such as how Black women face stereotypes and discrimination symbolically and overtly within the creative industry of ballet. I examined how creative fields, particularly ballet, create exclusive racialized and classed spaces that constrain career attainment for Black people and ultimately reiterate the exclusive culture within creative spaces. My findings reveal how Black women challenge the monolithic ideologies behind Black people in ballet by sharing a variety of ways in which they maintain and or gain the cultural capital needed to enter the space of ballet; I then share the constraints they face such as discrimination and marginalization following by the racial fatigue and constant exclusion, through particular roles, in which they face in ballet.

These interviews help expose how ballet is a microcosm of racism and discrimination which reflects US society more generally. Here, I examine how esthetic workers, in this case, Black women in ballet, are required to attain a hegemonic ideal look that is based on Eurocentric ideals of beauty which affects the dancers *both* physically *and* emotionally.

THE BLACK DANCING BODY

Ballerinas are not just required to have a particular look/appearance, but they are also required to dance with a particular musicality and emotion. This is what makes a ballet dancer good for a particular company. However, the look/appearance plays a major role in first getting the dancer into the door and keeping the dancer in the company. My participant, Jenae, briefly describes the balletic look and how she views her own body in comparison to the ideal balletic look. She states,

> I'm expected to look, you know. Kind of like prepubescent, you know, in a way we're not like other people, but that was just how we were, and I fit that look until college, where I struggled to maintain that look, and so I struggled with seeing myself every single day, like in the mirror more so than when I was in high school because my body was consistently changing. I wanted to look a certain type of way. And that affected, how teachers would talk to me. I remember I was at a point where I was really rushing around in my life, I didn't really have a whole lot of time to eat and take care of myself. And I was kind of doing a whole bunch of things that I could have easily eliminated things to make more time to take care of myself. But I didn't. And I remember I was really thin to the point where I felt like I was at my skinniest and it wasn't necessarily healthy either. And people would ask me, "Are you okay?" "What's going on?" And I had a teacher who came up to me during class and she was like, "You look great. But I just want to make sure that you're okay, that you're taking care of yourself." Which like, partially to me, was good of her to ask. But then it also made me like, so conscious of, like, whoa, people can notice that my body's changing and then the rest of the class I got more compliments than I have ever had before, you know, so it's a little bit mind boggling to go through. But then later that year and into the pandemic, I learned to embrace some things that I've kind of been affected by due to ballet and how I look.

Janae is explaining the gendered esthetic labor that *all* women in ballet have to maintain. As Mears states, this is what the consumers want, and given that the body is the commodity, the dancer is required to produce this look and is not necessarily protected from the health risks of maintaining/achieving this body.

Similarly, to Janae, Amiyah describes a point in her career where she felt that she needed to lose more weight because she was not being chosen for principal roles even though she felt she was talented enough. She states,

> It was disheartening to me because every ballet that came up, any new ballet, I was never given the first prima ballerina roles. I was never even told to understudy that role. I was given the second ballerina role but to me, I should have gotten the first. With my talent, I should

have been ... that bothered me, and I felt like maybe I don't look good enough. So I went down the street, from the building and there was a store, run by a Muslim, and in the front of the store, it had a book that says, *How to Eat to Live*, so I don't know why but I bought the book and I started following the book and lost 10 pounds in about a week or something like that (laughs) and so all of a sudden, I was getting attention but it also got to the point where the choreographer started worrying about me. He said, "you know, you have to eat" (laughs) and I said, "I'm eating" (laughs) and so it was an obvious difference and the more I danced I got better, felt better, and got roles.

Both Jenae and Amiyah discuss how they lost weight and the way people reacted toward their weight loss. They described being perceived in a more approving and encouraging way despite how they actually felt and how the way they even lost the weight. I even remember having my own body evaluated both as a dancer but also while working with the ballet company during their summer intensive as a counselor. When I would be in the studios, I could see the teachers examining my body and took me back to my days as a dancer.

It is also worth noting how both of their teachers checked in on them to make sure that they were okay even though they still were praising their weight loss and not actually knowing the cause or process of the weight loss. This is only one aspect in which ballet dancers try to fit into the ballet esthetic. While I explained the balletic *look* in general and how my participants understand and navigate this esthetic labor, I now explore how it is not only gendered but also racialized.

White hegemony has historically exploited Black people and their bodies for athletic advantages. Ballet still holds to traditional rigid white ideologies of beauty in which they overtly and covertly try and maintain. Ballet has not been very accessible to Black people; therefore, there is very little documentation in ballet history concerning Black people's involvement in ballet. However, there is a history in which Black people have been involved since the inception of American ballet. As Golden (2018) states, "Ballet historically constructs beauty as slender, dainty 'white' beauty, black ballerinas were forced to dance as troupes of African primitivism rather than alongside white ballerinas in traditional costumes with traditional choreography" (p. 5).

Consequently, Black women in ballet face forms of racialized and gendered esthetic requirements that they ultimately cannot fulfill or blatantly do not complement them esthetically and respectfully. Amiyah is a dancer that challenged these stigmas throughout her career to be a professional ballerina. However, her journey was not easy. Amiyah describes her experience of being a Black woman trying to navigate the ballet institution and the discrimination that she faced and how it did not fit into the ideal ballerina esthetic of George Balanchine. She states,

I think I had been at the school for two years and I've seen all my classmates getting into the company and all of a sudden, you know, what was going on here. You know, I don't want to spend two years of my life here or three, four years of my life here. And Mr. Balanchine is not going to take me to the company. So, I asked the director, Diana Adams, at that time, I said to her can you ask Mr. Balanchine what is his plan for me? She went and she came back to me, and she said that after talking with him, she said, well, he said that he loves your feet, you know, but he was not ready to take a Black girl into the company right now because that would break the color line. And he was not ready to do that at the time. So, she told me, and she said she started crying and she said, don't give up, don't give up, don't stop.

Despite her artistic director – a Black male, being admitted, as a dancer, into the company, prior to Amiyah, Balanchine was not ready for a Black woman. This is when we see the intersections of both race and gender. Black feminist in the 1980s and 1990s address this intersection as a unique form of both racial and gendered disadvantage and how centering Black women's experiences are necessary for understanding the various ways in which social, economic, and political institutions shape Black women's lives (Collins, 2002; Crenshaw, 1989) and also displays in how Black women are excluded within many conversations within race and gender. Discourse around Black people and their bodies have been racialized as monolithic and through stereotypes and racialized myths, they create ideologies in which Black people's bodies do not fit the required look for ballet. However, Camyron addresses how she does have the right look and challenges the monolithic stigma attached to Black people's bodies. She states,

I think for me sometimes I find it hard when people ask me, what my story is, [because] I'm like I honestly had a wonderful time training because I have the ballet body. But if you ask someone else, they're like, I had a hard time. But I think, like, it's just so difficult to be just placed in this one mold of, like, how it's supposed to be [because of being a Black dancer].

Camyron shares a unique perspective in that she is addressing the monolithic ideology that Black dancers are placed in, and it is important to address how this monolithic ideology/stereotype creates discrimination for a whole race – this relates to Collins deconstruction around controlling images and how they are stigmas that are created to marginalize Black women. Not only does Camyron share that she does have the ideal ballet body type, for ballet, but she also shares that she has enjoyed her experience in ballet and did not have a traumatic experience. This creates a greater dynamic in understanding the Black experience in ballet. It is not that *all* Black people have the same body type, it is that *all* Black dancers are being perceived that way and so they are experiencing similar discourses and stigmas, despite fitting the stereotype, which displays and contributes to the racism within this space. Noni states,

Yeah, so I'm like really tall, really thin and have long limbs. So, I guess I do conform to the typical ballet body. But, you know, I'm still black, so I have like a little bit of curves, a little bit. But yeah, I think I do conform to the typical ballet body. And I didn't really realize that is rooted in whiteness, so it's like, you know, a lot of ballet dancers are white and that's a type of body that they have. But, you know, black people, our bodies are really, really different. They come in different shapes, sizes, and things like that.

Noni also addresses having the ideal body type but acknowledges how that does not matter because she is Black and understands the racial exclusivity that is associated with body type and esthetic look within ballet. It also calls to question the standard of Black beauty. Black women cannot just fit the general standards they have to be exceptionally beautiful, White, or have Eurocentric features in order to be considered.

BALLET WITH A FRENCH TWIST: HAIR POLITICS AND CULTURAL AESTHETICS

Hair was always the emphasized topic while interviewing my Black women participants. Every time I brought up the topic of hair, every Black woman had reaction; as Banks (2000) states, "Black women share a collective consciousness about their hair, through it is articulated in a variety of ways" (p. 21). Hair, particularly for Black women, is multidimensional. It embodies an array of complexities that accompany political and social identities and issues and is an indicator of anti-Blackness within beauty industries while also being a marker of race, ethnicity, embodiment, and beauty (DeLongoria, 2018).

Hair is a concept of beauty and because ballet still embodies hegemonic Eurocentric ideals of beauty, the concept of beauty holds a significant place when addressing women in ballet. The beauty ideals that are implemented within this predominately white institution included hair. Therefore, the Black women, in my study, navigated and negotiated ways to occupy the space and manage their hair. Cita shares,

> My hair was a worry (laughs). Especially when I got to New York City Ballet because Balanchine loved when we did pieces with our hair out and that was my biggest nightmare. Because I did not have the same hair.

Cita addresses how her hair texture created a barrier for her to *fit* in and *fit* the esthetic requirement. She also shared how that made her feel emotionally. Amiyah also shares how she had to navigate and style her hair to *fit* the esthetic requirement. She states,

> What they call the classical bun is parted in the middle. And it comes down and it has to cover your ears and then it goes back and forth (gesturing how the bun goes) and so on. That's how we did our buns. So, when I decided, okay, I'm going natural. I'm going to wear an afro – which I did outside of class, but in class, you know, I had to pull it back. But how do I do the classical bun with an afro. I ended up putting hair over my ears. So just brushing my hair down and putting the extra hair like a bun. (Gesturing the process) sort of like your hair like that and pulling it under. That's how I did that. He didn't say anything, as long as I had a classical look, then nobody said anything.

Amiyah was a little different from Cita in that she just describes how she did the best she could with her hair and as long as no one questioned it, it was accepted. However, it is still similar to Cita in that they are acknowledging that their hair does not fit the required look and that they had to both navigate a way to make it fit that look while also negotiating how they had to manipulate their hair to achieve this goal. Jenae also shares how she has to navigate ways to style her hair so that it could fit the ideal look. She states,

> I feel like the whole reason why I used to straighten my hair as a kid, what it's for ballet, because that was the way that it would be able to get in the bun and it would be easy to do and like, I wouldn't have to worry about it. And then it was another step of assimilation. It would be one less thing that, you know, I would stand out with. I would fit in a little bit better.

Jenae addresses how she navigates her hair in order to assimilate and not stand out as much. This conversation touches on both Anderson's (2021) work on Black people having to navigate the white space as a condition of existence and Wingfield

(2015) in which Black women are "reclaiming their time" (p. 349) by rendering workplaces that are essentially unwelcoming toward Blackness and Black women more comfortable. Given that ballet stresses uniformity, Black women find ways to achieve the required hairstyles in order to stay within the ballet institution and demonstrate that they are more than qualified to be in the space. Hair is part of the costume, a costume that created among whiteness.

Aside from the ballet bun, the French twist is the other hairstyle most associated and required within ballet. Abby discusses some challenges with attaining this specific hairstyle required and how she both navigates this challenge and negotiates how much aesthetics labor she wants to give in order to achieve this look. While acknowledging the different experiences that everyone has when discussing hair, Gabi shares her experience,

> It's pretty easy for me to make a bun. I will say that French twists are definitely the hardest thing. Just to keep it contained and that's when I feel like straight hair would be a little easier like I need like 500 pins for French twists because my hair is all over the place but for the most part, I would say that it's pretty easy for me to get it in like a classical hairstyle.

Dani also shares her hair experience and how diverse Black people's hair can be. She states,

> I think I had more of a hair issue. I remember one time I had this one director, and he did not say this out of malice, but he wanted to be sure that my hair could do the desired French twist look and I said yes my hair can do that, but it may look a little differently but know that my hair texture can do it and I have had other ballerinas in the room that never saw 4C hair [tightly coiled/curled hair that makes an afro] blown out or saw it shrink and then saw it in twist. They've never seen the variety and diversity of what 4C hair can do so I spent a lot of time educating ballerinas in there, who were not of color, what Black hair actually is because the other Black person in there, her hair was relaxed. So, they were not sure what the natural hair was like or have never seen 4C hair and how I would come in with it one day being 2 inches long and then after blowing it out and it's 6 inches long. So, educating them on that and that's the biggest issue I had, and it wasn't an issue it was a moment of education.

Dani and Abby explain the complexities of Black women's hair and how everyone does not have the same experience, but hair is an important conversation because it is a symbolic indicator that their hair is not the desired esthetic within the ballet space and so they must navigate ways to manipulate their hair to achieve the required look. Capri shares a similar experience: "When I was younger, I would always put my hair in a bun and straightening my hair all the time and it ruined my hair like it got so dry."

This is significant because Capri addresses how she had to manipulate her hair to achieve the required look and she describes how some of the hairstyles required for the ideal ballet look damages Black women's hair. The constant manipulation and tension on their hair, to achieve this balletic look, is not good for a lot of Black women's hair, and these racialized consequences are not considered and acknowledged.

Whiteness and White supremacy continues to create a complicated history for Black[1] women and their hair. It was not until 2019 that the Crown Act[1] was created to "Create a Respectful and Open World for Natural [Black] Hair" – and end hair discrimination after constant incidents of hair discrimination in schools, the military/army, and occupational spaces (thecrownact.com, 2019). The balletic esthetic is not inclusive to Black women and their hair texture; therefore, Black women are continuously navigating ways to achieve this esthetic, even if it meant sacrificing the health of their hair to fit into balletic beauty standard.

THE BALLETIC LINE: MANAGING MARGINALIZATION, DISCRIMINATION AND CONTROLLING IMAGES

In 1988, Peggy McIntosh identified one facet of white privilege as the ability to "choose blemish cover or bandages in 'flesh' color and have them more or less match my [white] skin" (p. 21). Many of my interviewees identified their experiences of rejection as dancers, including not being able to find proper clothing, such as tights, pointe shoes, and leotards that matched their skin tone. Each invested labor into altering clothing they could find to conform to the (white) dress code and making it work for their (Black) bodies. Black women in ballet must spend time and money experimenting with dye and makeup to match their skin tone in order to fit esthetic ideals produced, in part, to exclude their bodies.

Costumes and makeup in ballet are mundane elements of the trade. But, as McIntosh (1988) points out, white privilege operates through the mundane; mundane experiences pile up and work to justify patterned and structural forms of rejection and discrimination. For instance, pointe shoes were created in the 1820s, and it was not until 2017 that a few companies started to make pointe shoes and tights for darker skinned women. Pointe shoes, leotards, and tights reflect the racialized symbolic image of "the ballerina."

Many forms of exclusion such as attempting to find "flesh colored" tights, leotards, and pointe shoes or being required to use lighter make up, as Janet Collins (Lewin & Collins, 2011) and Raven Wilkinson (Dougherty, 2006) were to look more European create structural and symbolic forms of discrimination that impact Black women. Amiyah shared with me the story of how she unknowingly became the influence behind flesh-tone tights. She shares how she would wear flesh-tone tights over her pink tights because she wanted to look slimmer. She stated,

> I started with the brown tights because it was much easier for me. It just looked so much better. I like the look of it. I did so and I kept on doing that because you could wear whatever you wanted over your tights. So, to me, the brown tights made me look thinner and it just seemed like a whole throwing of the line, you know, so I thought nothing of it until Yvette told me, you know, that started with you.

Once her artistic director saw her wearing flesh tights, he then decided to have everyone within the company wear flesh-tone tights. This became an act of declaration over the art form in which it defined classicism and racial exclusion that transformed through the *ballet pink* standard.

In the early 1800s, the Paris Opera Ballet sought to create and have dancers wear pink tights and shoes because bare legs were too risqué for Parisians to view. The concept of *ballet pink* complimented the all-White company's skin tone and from then on it has always been required and many people associate this blush shade of pink as *ballet pink*. However, Amiyah decided to navigate a way to wear tights that she felt complimented her body and her *balletic lines* better – she just wanted to look thinner and longer, that is, trying to *fit* the esthetic requirement. This racialized declaration transcended through the 1990s when Liliana became the first Black principal dancer at a major ballet company in the Southwest.

Liliana and Sage both advocated for flesh-tone tights that complemented their skin tone within their companies. In fact, in 2018, Sage made a statement, via Instagram, that she would no longer perform on stage wearing pink tights and would wear brown tights that complimented her skin tone. During the Black Lives Matter protest in 2020, I witnessed petitions for skin-tone tights to be the standard in ballet companies and ballet attire companies are now creating ballet tights as well as pointe shoes that compliment an array of skin complexions. These symbolic interactions, through balletic attire, demonstrate racial exclusion and how Black women navigate the space. Tina shares how her experience was no different when she was required to wear a certain shade of makeup that did not complement her skin tone. Laughing, she stated, "The teachers didn't understand that with my skin tone, I couldn't wear the red lipstick that my friend Sally is wearing. And I don't know I guess in that sense I did feel a certain isolation."

Dancers described having different outfits and makeup because what worked for other (White) dancers did not work for them. Cita, a former dancer in a major company, explained,

> When I was dancing Cocoa in *The Nutcracker*, the costume [was] pink. So, I asked them to change the color, but they just removed the tights, and I would wear it bare skinned, and I would put a big rhinestone on my naval (laughs) … I would just use my pancake [pad used to apply makeup] that I used for my face on my shoes …. That was difficult because all the elastic bands [in costumes] were pink. Which I never really did anything about it when I first joined. I didn't think much of it but as I got more involved in my roles and being an artist, as opposed to a student, I started looking back at myself and started striving for perfection so I started pancaking [covering with skin tone makeup] my straps and stuff like that so I could look like everyone else even though I wasn't the same color. It was more so about the colors matching their skin tones and it just looked like the bodies; you didn't see the straps so, I eventually learned how to do that [camouflage the straps] for my skin tone but no one helped me with it. You just sort of do those things on your own.

Jenae also shares her experience of discovering flesh-tone tights and how similarly to overs; it accentuates her balletic lines which is the main purpose of ballet and the balletic look:

> I didn't realize that you could change the color of your pointes. And once I found that out, I never wore pink shoes ever again because I just I don't know. They always say that like pointe shoes and tights should be like an extension of your legs. But the reason why I feel so disconnected and far away from it is because, they never matched my skin color. And sometimes, it wouldn't bother me until I got a little older where I was realizing, this is kind of weird. Like, I would rather, have my, barefoot in a shoe that's matching with my skin color. That made me feel more confident in my own skin, in my own dancing, instead I felt like I was playing a role, which was fine sometimes. But when I really wanted to feel comfortable and I really wanted to feel like an individual in my dancing, I did enjoy having my pointe shoes match my skin color.

Many of my interviewees identified their experiences of exclusion and having to navigate the "white space" by the obstacles they faced when looking for proper clothing that complimented their skin tone. Therefore, not only was this a constant reminder they are unable to find flesh-tone attire within a ballet attire store, but they are also reminded of the additional invested labor they have to endure by altering the clothing buy in order to conform to the (white) dress code in order to make it work for their (Black) bodies and pronounce their existence. This labor came with an additional cost, involving time, energy, additional financial burdens, and emotional costs associated with confronting the question of why these required tools of the trade were not made with their bodies in mind. Pointe shoes alone range between $80 and $130 depending on the style and brand, and then there are other fees such as leotards, ballet skirts, tights, classes, summer intensives, and miscellaneous fees.

Black dancers experience symbolic forms of discrimination through the esthetic requirements in ballet as an industry and workplace. And while they work toward navigating ways to maintain an esthetic that satisfies those requirements and works for them too, this process creates additional labor that comes with attendant emotional and financial burdens. It depicts what Du Bois describes through double consciousness – this twoness and trying to negotiate and navigate these identities and having to view oneself through the eyes of others in order to *fit* this *look* that is not inclusive to them.

CONTROLLING IMAGES

Many of the Black ballerinas in this study were intimately aware of controlling images and were mindful of how they presented themselves to avoid being stereotyped. *The Nutcracker* was an emotionally charged topic for every participant. The performance offers a powerful example of the racialized and gendered roles specifically for Black and Asian dancers. Indeed, there have been numerous news articles about the racial depictions within *The Nutcracker* (e.g., Crabb, 2019; Fieldstadt, 2019; Fisher, 2018). Within this study alone, Aaliyah was a part of the 60 percent of the Black women I interviewed who were specifically assigned the role of the Arabian princess. In the ballet, the Arabian princess is portrayed as exotic and erotic wearing a bralette and the only dancer baring midriff, while also requiring her to move her body in sensual ways around the male dancer with whom she is partnered.

Consistent with Collins (2002) historicization of the Black jezebel, the critic's racist comment ("... up there looking just like Lil'Kim") discursively compares Aaliyah's role to a video vixen. This illustrates one instance of how controlling images operate to discursively cast Black women as overly "exotic" or "sexualized." Since the music industry is still controlled by White elites – less likely to value and be knowledgeable of the diversity and complexity among Black women – Black women are routinely homogenized to look like "Black prostitutes" and "jezebels" (Collins, 2002). Aaliyah understood the critic's comment to be reflective of controlling images which, for Aaliyah, was exactly what she has worked so hard to challenge through the images shown in her non-profit organization. She continues to state,

Society has to be ready as a whole too because artistic directors and staff are only one part but people who spend money to come to the ballet have to be mentally prepared so that when they come to see *The Nutcracker*, they don't assume that I am wearing a Lil' Kim Blonde, wig and are educated and aware that it is a veil, and we *all* wear it and just because you see a Black woman on stage, in an Arabian costume that *everybody* wears, you don't immediately go to Lil' Kim.

While the Aaliyah and I discussed stereotypes, another current dancer, Daphne, discussed her understanding of how employers, in ballet, incorporate Black women in ways that remarginalize them: "They don't want to see a Black ballerina in a bun, or a tutu or the tights, or the pointe shoe. They don't want you to look like that traditional image. They want you looking very contemporary as possible."

A retired (principal) dancer echoed what the previous dancers had argued when describing challenges that Black women negotiate as ballerinas:

> When I was supposed to do La Sylphide, they were like, "Oh, she won't be soft. I mean yeah, she can jump but she can't be soft." It's just like when you have a soft dancer that needs to do something like the black swan, like the white swan and the black swan has two personalities – one is soft and one is harder or sexier but it's the same ballet dancer with the same body, it's just a personality shift so I call bullshit on that .... Just like the whole idea of the Black personality –you know like what's seen on TV, the media or wherever ... like what people may think or just pure ignorance that there is vulnerability and there is softness and there is strength and there are all these many things we can be.

The women in this study resisted being pushed out of ballet and were constantly working toward challenging controlling images by showing how multidimensional Black women can be. They all mentioned, however, how it is up to society to be open to receiving them in a multidimensional light. McCarthy-Brown (2011) has argued that this common experience of typecasting Black women in roles that reiterate controlling images of Black women works to protect racial hierarchies embedded in ballet. Black women in ballet disrupt stereotypes and controlling images by challenging the myths that have historically worked to justify their exclusion and so casting them in roles or describing them in ways that reiterate controlling images works to (re)maintain racial hierarchies they challenge just by existing in ballet.

CONCLUSION

My unsettling feeling of not belonging in ballet, growing up, was not inaccurate but more so intentional. The lack of inclusion and Black representation within ballet was intentional, the stigmas around Black people and ballet were intentional, and throughout my time, I was constantly trying to navigate and negotiate my existence in the space as many of my participant did. The concepts of beauty and embodiment are a catalyst for more discrimination and marginalization. The narrow ideologies of beauty and body image are embedded in many occupations and create greater inequalities for women who are not upper-middle-class white, slender, and heterosexual. As Mears states, "the implicit frame of beauty is so narrowly molded around whiteness that any deviation from a White bourgeois body is viewed as problematic" (Mears, 2011, p. 38). Esthetic labor and reproductive labor continuously favor women who more closely fit the idea of hegemonic femininity in which complicates the unidimensional scholarship of gender and work that came before the 1990s. Scholars such as Kimberlé Crenshaw, Dorothy Roberts, Patricia Hill Collins, bell hooks, Angela Davis, and others have been of great influence in developing and solidifying intersectionality and calling attention to the multidimensions of women's experiences by calling attention to the marginalization of nonwhite women and their bodies in society, particularly work.

As we can see, "Ballet is Woman" is directed toward a very specific woman. Throughout the 20th century, the intended *woman* is described as a thin, almost prepubescent, white, middle-class heterosexual woman, and through symbolic and direct interactions, Black women understand that they are not the intended woman and that ballet is not an inclusive space for them, but they are "reclaiming their time" within this space. Black women have navigated a racialized and gendered way of attaining the esthetic requirements while producing a particular emotional labor to appear grateful and a "good" employee within this cultural space.

Black women are faced with a double consciousness of being Black within the space while constantly having to view themselves through the lens of someone else – someone white. Throughout this chapter, I show how Black women are reclaiming their time within a historically white space as well as how they are solidifying their existence within a space that has historically excluded them. The intersections of race and gender are important to acknowledge within this space because Black women are not only being challenged through their gender – as I describe the history of the ballet look, but also how their race creates an additional form or esthetic labor because they are given esthetic requirements that favor white women. As Black women continue to reclaim their time and solidify their existence within these white spaces, we can begin to hopefully challenge and change these racialized esthetic requirements to provide a more inclusive space.

NOTE

1. The Crown Act is not yet acknowledged in every state within the United States.

REFERENCES

Anderson, E. (2021). *Black in White space: The enduring impact of color in everyday life*. The University of Chicago Press.

Asante, M. K. (1998). *Afrocentricity*. Africa World Press.

Atencio, M., & Wright, J. (2009). Ballet it's too whitey: Discursive hierarchies of high school dance spaces and the constitution of embodied feminine subjectivities. *Gender and Education 21*(1), 31–46.

Banks, I. (2000). *Hair matters: Beauty, power, and black women's consciousness*. NYU Press.

Banks, P. A. (2020). *Diversity and philanthropy at African American museums: Black renaissance*. Routledge/Taylor & Francis Group.

Bartky, S. L. (1998). Skin deep: Femininity as a disciplinary regime. In B.-A. Bar On & A. Ferguson (Eds.), *Daring to be good: Essays in feminist ethico-politics*. Routledge.

Bordo, S. (1993). *Unbearable weight: Feminism, western culture, and the body*. University of California Press.
Brooks, B., Jarman, J., & Blackburn, R. M. (2003). Occupational gender segregation in Canada, 1981–1996: Overall, vertical and horizontal segregation. *Canadian Review of Sociology*, 40(2), 197–213.
Carmen, J. (2014). Behind Ballet's diversity problem. Pointe Magazine. https://pointemagazine.com/behind-ballets-diversity-problem/
Collins, P. H. (1990). Black feminist thought in the matrix of domination. *Black Feminist Thought: Knowledge, Consciousness, and the Politics of Empowerment*, 138, 221–238.
Collins, P. H. (2002). *Black feminist thought*. Routledge.
Crabb, M. (2019). Misty Copeland is right: Blackface and Yellowface have no place on ballet stages. *The Star*. Retrieved from https://www.thestar.com/entertainment/stage/opinion/2019/12/21/misty-copeland-isright-blackface-and-yellowface-have-no-place-on-ballet-stages.html?rf
Crenshaw, K. (1989). *Demarginalizing the Intersection of Race and Sex: A Black Feminist Critique of Antidiscrimination Doctrine* (pp. 139–168). University of Chicago Legal Forum.
Currid, E. (2007). *The Warhol economy: How fashion, art, and music drive New York City*. Princeton University Press.
DeLongoria, M. (2018). Misogynoir: * Black hair, identity politics, and multiple black realities. *Africology: The Journal of Pan African Studies*, 12(8), 39–49.
Dougherty, O. (2006). *Stillness broken*. https://youtu.be/iTrHN69ByTs?si=q9qUbz6HQGCknv0m
Du Bois, W. E. B. (1986). *The Souls of Black Folk*. Buccaneer Books, Inc.
Entwistle, J. (2002). The esthetic economy: The production of value in the field of fashion modelling. *Journal of Consumer Culture*, 2, 317–339.
Fieldstadt, E. (2019). *Misty Copeland Calls out Russia's Bolshoi Ballet for Blackface. They Refuse to Stop*. NBC News. Retrieved from https://www.nbcnews.com/news/us-news/misty-copeland-calls-out-russia-s-bolshoi-ballet-blackface-they-n1104206
Fisher, J. (2018). Op-Ed: 'Yellowface' in 'The Nutcracker' isn't a benign ballet tradition, it's racist stereotyping. *Los Angeles Times*. Retrieved September 3, 2020, from https://www.latimes.com/opinion/op-ed/la-oe-fisher-nutcracker-chinese-dance-revisionism-20181211-story.html.
Gaiser, C. (2006). Caught dancing: Hybridity, stability, and subversion in dance theatre of Harlem's Creole "Giselle". *Theatre Journal*, 58, 269–289.
Garafola, L. (1985). The travesty dancer in nineteenth-century ballet. *Dance research Journal* 17(2), 35–40.
Genné, B. (2005). Glorifying the American woman: Josephine Baker and George Balanchine. *Discourses in Dance*, 3(1), 31–57.
Gimlin, D. (2002). 1. The hair salon: Social class, power, and ideal beauty. In *Body work: Beauty and self-image in American culture* (pp. 16–49). University of California Press.
Golden, E. D. (2018). From Tropes to Troupes: Misty Copeland and the Hyper-Whiteness of Ballet. The Cupola: Scholarship at Gettsburg College. Student Publications. 700.
Gottschild, B. D. (1996). *Digging the Africanist presence in American performance dance and other context*. Greenwood Publishing Group, Inc.
Gottschild, B. D. (2003). Black White Dance Dancers. *The Black Dancing Body: A Geography From Coon to Cool* (pp. 12–40).
Kang, M. (2010). *The managed hand: Race, gender, and the body in beauty service work*. University of California Press.
Keivom, J. (2015). Searching for the next "Misty": Why black ballerinas are in such short supply. *NY Daily News*. Retrieved from https://www.nydailynews.com/new-york/finding-misty-black-ballerinas-rare-article-1.2288544
Laurens, C. (2017). *Little dancer aged fourteen*. Other Press.
Lewin, Y. T., & Collins, J. (2011). *Night's dancer: The life of Janet Collins*. Wesleyan University Press.
McCarthy-Brown, N. (2011). Dancing in the margins: Experiences of African American ballerinas. *Journal of African American Studies*, 15(3), 385–408.
McIntosh, P. (1988). White privilege: Unpacking the invisible knapsack. In P. Rothenberg (Ed.), *Race, class, and gender in the United States: An integrated study* (pp. 20–31). Worth Publishers.
Mears, A. (2011). *Pricing beauty: The making of a fashion model*. University of California Press.

Mears, A., & Finlay, W. (2005). Not just a paper doll: How models manage bodily capital and why they perform emotional labor. *Journal of Contemporary Ethnography, 34*(3), 317–343.

Mitchell, A. C. (1987). *An analysis and definition of the artistic director's role in a small ballet company* [PhD dissertation, University of California].

Montemurro, B. (2001). Strippers and screamers: The emergence of social control in a noninstitutionalized setting. *Journal of Contemporary Ethnography, 30*(3), 275–304.

Murphy, R. (2003). Fertility and distorted sex ratios in a rural Chinese county: Culture, state, and policy. *Population and Development Review, 29*(4), 595–626.

Okanlawon, A. (1972). Africianism – A synthesis of the African world-view. *Black World, 21*(9), 40–97.

Patton, T. O. (2006). Hey girl, am I more than my hair? African American women and their struggles with beauty, body image, and hair. *NWSA Journal, 18*, 24–51.

Picart, C. J. S. (2012). A tango between copyright and choreography: Whiteness as status property in Balanchine's ballets, Fuller's serpentine dance and graham's modern dances. *Cardozo JL & Gender, 18*, 685–725.

Pope, H. G., Phillips, K. A., & Olivardia, R. (2000). *The Adonis complex: The secret crisis of male body obsession*. Simon and Schuster.

The Official CROWN Act. https://www.thecrownact.com

Wacquant, L. J. D. (2004). *Body & soul: Notebooks of an apprentice boxer*. Oxford University Press.

Wingfield, A. H. (2015). Being Black – but not too Black – in the workplace. *The Atlantic*. https://www.theatlantic.com/business/archive/2015/10/being-black-work/409990/

Wingfield, A. H., & Alston, R. S. (2014). Maintaining hierarchies in predominantly White organizations: A theory of racial tasks. *American Behavioral Scientist, 58*(2), 274–287.

Wingfield, A. H., & Chavez, K. (2020). Getting in, getting hired, getting sideways looks: Organizational hierarchy and perceptions of racial discrimination. *American Sociological Review, 85*(1), 31–57. https://doi.org/10.1177/0003122419894335

Wingfield, A. H., & Wingfield, J. H. (2014). When visibility hurts and helps: How intersections of race and gender shape Black professional men's experiences with tokenization. *Cultural Diversity and Ethnic Minority Psychology, 20*(4), 483.

CHAPTER 9

CONSUMING BEAUTY, CONSTRUCTING BLACKNESS: A CONSTRUCTIVIST GROUNDED THEORY ANALYSIS OF RACIALIZED GENDERED EMBODIMENT PRACTICES THROUGH SHAMPOO PRODUCT DESCRIPTIONS

Shameika D. Daye

University of Central Florida, USA

ABSTRACT

The racialized gendered body in consumer culture invokes the construction of identities and representation of beauty through embodiment practices. As companies hone in on consumer racial marker distinctions to enhance uniqueness as otherness for profit, an analysis of hair products marketed for Black hair textures provides an opportunity to analyze how products use these at the intersection of race, gender, and beauty. This study uses constructivist grounded theory to analyze the product names and long descriptions for 124 shampoos marketed for Black hair textures on the websites of two major retailers to answer the following questions: What message does the discourse of shampoo product descriptions marketed to Black hair textures communicate about beauty? What message does the discourse of shampoo product descriptions marketed to Black hair textures communicate about Blackness? How does this discourse define the embodiment of Black beauty through hair? The results reveal that the racialized gendered body in consumer culture invokes the construction of identities and representations of beauty through embodiment practices. Through advertisements and product descriptions, beauty companies create ideal images of the lived experiences achieved through consuming beauty products. By constructing visual interpretations of racial signifiers through text, marketing strategies encourage the consumption of otherness, creating a racialized space for Blackness consumption. Combining the five senses with the descriptions of shampoo products marketed for Black hair textures helps us see how beauty embodiment practices reinforce racialized and gendered practices to subjugate the Black body.

Keywords: Black beauty; Black hair; consumption; consumerism; embodiment; shampoo

The natural hair movement in the early 2000s revived interest in the Black hair market. As the celebration of Black hair textures as a symbol of Black identity and pride ushered in, along with it came an increase in Black hair product consumption. The consumption of shampoo products for Black hair textures normalizes Black hair as an embodied identity beauty practice that dismisses hegemonic narratives that work to maintain racial embodiment discrimination (Ndichu & Upadhyaya, 2019; Tafari-Ama, 2016). Embracing Black as beautiful challenges the valuation system in the current beauty regime that reinforces how race and gender are read on the body, encouraging the creation of new approaches to beauty (Craig, 2006; Havlin & Báez, 2018; Rocha et al., 2016; Tate, 2009). The consumption of Black hair products pushes against the normative perceptions of Eurocentric beauty and claims the inclusion of the Black body in beauty's definition. Since neither representations of Blackness nor beauty are monolithic, claiming Black beauty risks classifying and essentializing the body as racial and feminine, which may reinforce social order hierarchies within the Black beauty ideal (Black & Sharma, 2001; Tate, 2007).

The commodification of beauty holds beauty as a symbol of status and worth. Beauty work adopted as standard practice contributes to the beauty industry's rewards for capitalizing on femininity consumption for profit. Participation in beauty practices socializes women to embody femininity as an object consciously aware of how its perceived appearance is the subject of the gaze of others (Fair et al., 2018; Glapka, 2018; Mason, 2018). As the Black female body is intersectional, Black women do race and gender as they do beauty (Butler, 2006; Kwan & Trautner, 2009; Sims et al., 2020; Tate, 2007; Thompson, 2009b). Black hair product consumption practices that enhance racial signifiers encourage agency of the body as a self-aware subject (Kwan & Trautner, 2009; Mason, 2018; Vandenberg, 2018). Although hair is a site on the body where ideas of feminine representation are evaluated daily for all women (Weitz, 2001), for Black women, hair is also a site where Blackness is continuously contested. As Black hair textures are viewed as both a positive and negative representation of difference (Brown, 2018; Mercer, 1994), Black women who consume products made specifically for Black hair engage in a collective project rearticulating Black beauty through hair stylization and consumption practices (Craig, 2006).

Black consumers spend approximately 473 million dollars on hair care yearly (Holmes, 2020). As companies hone in on consumer racial marker distinctions to enhance uniqueness as otherness for profit, an analysis of Black hair shampoo products provides an opportunity to analyze how product descriptions use discourse to communicate beauty and Blackness at the intersection of race, gender, and beauty. Using Charmaz's (2014) constructivist grounded theory, this study analyzes the product names and long descriptions for shampoos marketed for Black hair textures on the websites of two major retailers to answer the following questions: What message does the discourse of shampoo product descriptions marketed to Black hair textures communicate about beauty? What message does the discourse of shampoo product descriptions marketed to Black hair textures communicate about Blackness? How does this discourse define the embodiment of Black beauty through hair? The results reveal that the racialized gendered body in consumer culture invokes the construction of identities and representations of beauty through embodiment practices. Through advertisements and product descriptions, beauty companies create ideal images of the lived experiences achieved through consuming beauty products.

REVIEW OF RELATED LITERATURE
Marketing Black Hair Consumption

Marketing beauty products to Black women in the United States began with the growth of the Black middle class in the early 20th century (Banks, 2021; Byrd & Tharps, [2001] 2014). During this time, companies were marketing products to Black women seeking to lighten their skin and straighten their hair to conform to white beauty standards (Byrd & Tharps, [2001] 2014; Giddings, 2006). Marketing practices shifted in the late 1960s; the post-civil rights era saw an increase in cultural markers consumption, including products made distinctly for wearing Black hair types in their "natural" state (Taylor, 2016). Marketing specific products to particular ethnic groups has continued to the present day, as evidenced in the $2.51 billion Black hair care industry (Holmes, 2020). Previous studies about Black hair product consumers and consumption have found that the Black women who purchase and use these products face a tension between the celebration of Black hair, on the one hand, and the use of power and discourses that uphold a dominant beauty standard in opposition to Black hair textures, on the other hand (Ndichu & Upadhyaya, 2019; Rocha et al., 2016). A postfeminist study on Black hair consumption found that Black women consumers see their hair consumption practices as a site of defiance against the racial inscription of Blackness where they can redefine Blackness and Black beauty on their terms

(Glapka, 2018). The present study extends this research by focusing on shampoo product descriptions explaining how the racialized gendered body in consumer culture invokes the construction of identities and representation of beauty through embodiment practices.

Racial Embodiment and Black Beauty

Research on racial embodiment suggests that the body is read as racial through visual perceptions of markers that indicate the classification of the materialized body (Alcoff, 1999; Glapka, 2018; Taylor, 1999). Black hair textures have been used to signify and subjugate Blackness on the body since the transatlantic slave trade (Byrd & Tharps, [2001] 2014; Collins, [2000] 2009; Patton, 2006; Thompson, 2009a). However, during the Black Power movement of the 1960s, wearing "the natural" as a Black hair stylization practice became a source of agency and racial pride where the afro became a symbol of valor that signaled one's commitment to Black authenticity (Alcoff, 1999; Byrd & Tharps, [2001] 2014; Craig, 2006; Tate, 2007). The Black anti-racist tradition, which values doing Black beauty through normalizing the racialized body as the Black beauty standard, creates its own exclusions as it overlooks the inclusion of Black women who do not reflect Afro-centric features (e.g., dark-skin or coiled hair) (Brown, 2018; Tate, 2007). Despite including self-defined beauty representations, Black beauty uses dominant beauty regime ideals to measure, evaluate, discipline, and judge beauty (Bordo, 2003; Brown, 2018; Craig, 2006; Tate, 2009). As a result, beauty consumption practices facilitate reading a body's achievement of race and beauty (Glapka, 2018; Rocha et al., 2016; Sims et al., 2020). What is Black and beautiful holds political and cultural meaning in the Black community. Black beauty rejects using white beauty as the standard which subordinates other forms of beauty while also setting standards for what representations of Black hair textures are visually consumed and constructed as beautiful (Tafari-Ama, 2016; Tate, 2007; Weitz, 2001).

Beauty Images and Standards

In the book *Black is Beautiful: A Philosophy of Black Aesthetics*, Taylor (2016, p. 115) states that "Body beauty judgements are not just about what we say when presented with representations of certain bodies; they are also related to the conditions of entry into all manner of social institutions and practices...." As Black bodies are evaluated on external racial signifiers like hair and skin color, ideal images encourage the subjugation of these sarkaesthetics.[1] Since hair, unlike skin, can be manipulated and transformed, judgments challenge hair that has not conformed to the dominant standard:

> Because the appearance of hair and some of its characteristics are capable of change, the choice by Blacks either to make no change or to do so in ways that do not reflect the characteristics and appearance of the hair of whites, represents an assertion of the self that is in direct conflict with the assumptions that underlie the existing social order. (Caldwell, 1991, p. 384)

The social order enforces dominant ideological beauty standards set forth by images in consumer culture. As the "ideal" images through beauty industry advertisements promote the commodification of bodies (Featherstone, 1982), advertisements use marketing strategies to encourage women to "… create an individual look through consumption of mass produced products" (Black & Sharma, 2001, p. 109). Despite the hope for a future where hair care products would focus more on hair texture than race (Byrd & Tharps, [2001] 2014), the continued use of the Black/white binary standards in the beauty industry promotes the white supremacist dominant beauty standard. This standard encourages the continued use of objectifying Black bodies through controlling images as product descriptions use these images to perpetuate anti-Black esthetic practices in their marketing (Collins, [2000] 2009; Tate, 2007). The pressures Black women face to conform to dominant beauty standards and combat negative controlling images impact Black beauty and Black beauty practices, including how Black women style and care for their hair (Patton, 2006; Tate, 2007; Thompson, 2009b). Since the invention of the hot comb by Madam C.J. Walker in 1905 and the chemical straightener by George E. Johnson in 1954, products to maintain and conform Black hair textures for visual consumption to mimic racially white hair textures have been a profitable pursuit (Byrd & Tharps, [2001] 2014; Thompson, 2009a). Several scholars have studied how the consumption of these products has contributed to shame, inauthenticity, low self-esteem, devaluing of the self, and the persistence of self-definitions for Black women (Collins, [2000] 2009; Patton, 2006; Tate, 2007; Taylor, 2016; Thompson, 2009a). However, consumption research has yet to explore how marketing strategies used on product labels to maintain Black hair textures contribute to promoting an "ideal" image that subjugates bodies to beauty evaluations.

METHODS
Data

Data on shampoo product descriptions were collected from the websites of two major US distributors, Target.com and Wal-Mart.com, in the Fall of 2020. Filters were used to identify the products marketed for Black hair textures. On the Target.com website, the texturized hair type was used. Locs, coily, and relaxed hair types were used at The Curl Shop on the Walmart.com website. Once collected, the products were added to a spreadsheet and placed alphabetically to identify duplicates. A total of 13 duplicate products were found, and their descriptions were put together for analysis to prevent double coding. After this was complete, a total of 124 unique products were identified, and product descriptions were extracted for analysis.

Analytical Strategy

Descriptions were analyzed using Charmaz's (2014) constructivist grounded theory and conducted using NVivo qualitative data analysis software. Grounded theory methods were used as they are best suited for understanding phenomena where little is known, such as the embodiment of Black beauty through analyzing hair care products. An initial line-by-line coding analysis was conducted using *in vivo* coding of a preliminary convenience sample of 41 product descriptions to capture the language, emotions, and meanings attached to the different terms and phrases used within the product descriptions. Some ideas that emerged in this phase of the research include good versus bad hair cues given through descriptions (e.g., "dry, dull, brittle," and "luxurious, elongated locks"), ease of the process of removing impurities (e.g., "now you can wash tender scalps daily without fuss"), promises of restoration and beauty through the use of these products (e.g., "The appearance of the hair and its health alone are some huge benefits this oil issues because of its rejuvenating technology"), and promises for product to provide some mystical like results (e.g., "miracle," "inspired," "crafted," and "formulated").

Focused coding was then conducted to compare, organize, and sensitize initial codes into concepts (e.g., adding, cleansing, crafted, natural, providing, and moisture). Finally, axial coding was conducted to identify the developing categories' properties and dimensions to determine the variations within each category (Strauss & Corbin, 1998). Three preliminary categories emerged from this analysis: *esthetic hair formation*, *making hair well*, and *distinctively made*. The properties of *making hair well* in the initial analysis were healing and health. *Esthetic hair formation's* properties were sustain and regulate. Sustain's dimensions include defining and maintaining hair beauty standards (good/bad, right/wrong), while regulate's dimensions explain how these standards are to be governed (control, tame). The dimensions for healing answered the question of how hair was being made well (cure, treat), and health responded to the question of what hair was well (hydrated, strong). Finally, *distinctively made's* properties were ingredients and process. The dimensions of ingredients aim to explain the range of different ingredients that should and should not be used to care for Black hair's unique texture (aloe, no parabens) and the processes used to develop these distinct products (crafted, blended).

Theoretical Coding

After identifying the three categories, coding the complete data set was done to test each category's properties and dimensions, and a core theme emerged: racialized gendered embodiment practices. Once identified, the core theme was used to conduct theoretical coding to test the fit and worth of each category to the emerging theory (Glaser & Strauss, 1967). The theoretical coding process revealed that these descriptions use words to engage the five senses to embody racialized gendered beauty practices to the consumers who use these products. Coding with this theoretical sensitivity in mind at this analysis stage illuminated how *esthetic hair formation* used words that paint what the consumer sees, *making hair well* focused on words to make the consumer feel, and *distinctively made* applied words the consumer hears, tastes, and smells. These shampoo product descriptions construct identities and representations of beauty through embodiment practices that racialize and gender the body in consumer culture. The outcome of these efforts is the creation of ideal images used to persuade consumers of the results they can achieve through beauty product consumption.

Properties and Dimensions

Once the central theme and the emerging theory were identified, the properties and dimensions of each of the categories were revisited to interrogate how they arise in the data and to what extent they contribute to the category and emerging theory (Strauss & Corbin, 1998).

Esthetic Hair Formation

Esthetic hair formation's properties are desirable and undesirable. Desirable provides the consumer with specific images of beautiful hair, while undesirable tells the consumer what beautiful hair is not. The dimensions provide the scale and use words to control the boundaries of hair's achievement or failure to reach established beauty standards. Dimensions for undesirable provide us with various terms used to describe Black hair textures (natural, coily, curly) and combine these with a series of degraded hair features (parched, frizzy, flat) to frame Black hair as distasteful.

On the other hand, desirable's dimensions include what desirable hair should look like (shiny, soft, controlled). These dimensions influence what consumers see as hair qualities that should be revered and celebrated as beautiful and those that should be reprimanded and criticized.

Making Hair Well

Next, the properties of *making hair well* are emotional protection and tactile restoration. Emotional protection helps us understand how words conjure up an emotional feeling of hair being unsafe, in danger, and in need of protection. This property's dimensions include various aspects of healing (cure, repair, treat), defending hair (fight, defend), and hair's fragile state (weak, brittle, damaged). Tactile restoration speaks to how the hair should feel once restored to wellness. Dimensions related to tactile restoration include what one should feel when they touch restored hair (strong, smooth, nourished, hydrated).

Distinctively Made

Finally, *distinctively made's* properties are recipes and ingredients. Recipe speaks to the various processes used to create products that cater to the needs of Black hair while also considering the safety of what goes on the Black body. The dimensions for these recipes include the processes (crafted, formulated, secret, special) and the care taken to make these products (gentle, care). Ingredients refer to what consumers should hear when looking at a product's contents and where items come from when considering their purchase. The dimensions for ingredients relate to what the products are made with (natural, pure, organic) and what they are made without (sulfate free, paraben free, silicone free).

RESULTS

Shampoo product descriptions promote a commitment to beauty and its achievement through engagement with embodiment practices. By centering beauty as a performative aspect of femininity, products position the female body as both a subject aware of its inability to achieve beauty by its own merits and an object that is both vulnerable and desirable (Mason, 2018). However, as the results show, when shampoo products aim to market their use for Black hair textures, their commitment to beauty as an embodiment of femininity becomes racialized. When selling to consumers with Black hair textures, product descriptions use oppositional language to encourage Black women to engage in beauty practices that manipulate their hair's texture to adhere to more Eurocentric hair rules and norms as their only means of obtaining favorable esthetic evaluations. Using narrative language to describe markers of Blackness in opposition to beauty, product descriptions use their discourse to control how Black beauty is defined. Although products offer shampoos customized for Black hair textures, they use the five senses to communicate that Black women may only embody Black beauty through hair by separating hair from its racialized features of Blackness.

Esthetic Hair Formation: Words You See

Esthetic hair formation uses words to direct attention to and focus on specific hair features consumers see. It encourages consumers to regulate themselves against beauty standards created by these products to determine if they have accomplished the look deemed beautiful. The narrative produced by Black hair care products around the embodiment of beauty develops the standards for evaluating Black beauty. As descriptions construct visual boundaries to judge whether to criticize hair looks as undesirable or celebrate it as desirable, they also provide consumers with a hierarchy they should use to administer their esthetic hair judgment.

Undesirable

By painting a picture of specific qualities related to Black hair textures as undesirable, marketing strategies create a narrative that degrades the consumers' current hair state while offering a solution to get hair to a more desirable state. Products promise to be a "treatment for dry, hair, damaged hair and natural curls" and to hydrate "tight curls." They also call to attention that this hair type has unmanageable qualities and needs control to secure the look required by the external white gaze and male gaze to deem Black hair beautiful.

> Improve hair's overall appearance with this shampoo and moisturizing hair treatment for dry hair, damaged hair and natural curls.
>
> Our luxurious, hydrating shampoo for tight curls cleanses and nourishes dry, thirsty hair.

> This deeply hydrating shampoo blends together fair trade shea butter, argan oil and sea kelp to replenish and seal in moisture to dehydrated strands. Great for 3A to 4C hair types
>
> Dull and frizzy hair in need of smoothness, frizz control, and deep repair. Replenishes moisture while cleaning the hair controlling excessive frizz.
>
> Cupuaçu butter and Flaxseed Milk are combined to restore and repair brittle, dull, unmanageable hair back to its beautiful luster.

These shampoo products connect the look associated with Black hair textures (natural, textured, coiled, or curly) with terms like tangled, damaged, thirsty, full, dehydrated, and frizz to attach Black hair textures to these denigrated hair states. Features are framed as unwanted in these descriptions and urge consumers who see these hair qualities to want a solution to help them rescue their hair from these conditions. Although the images of Black hair textures are deemed incredulous for acceptable visual consumption, these descriptions also achieve the idea of the look hair should aspire to be.

Desirable

When consumers purchase these products, they are a source of the control they need to access their desired look and relieve them from the remorse they are encouraged to attach to their hair's current undesirable state. Products promise that their users can obtain hair that looks "soft, without frizz and with a luminous shine," and hair with enhanced "softness and body" by adding "bounce and shine" to dehydrated hair. The use of these products gives results that you can see, such as "velvety finish and elongated" hair that has "luminous shine and increased hair volume" and hair that is "softer, and with a long-lasting Radiant Glow."

> Curly manes require particular attention in order to stay nourished, shiny and controlled.
>
> ... helps deliver you with Luminous Shine and Increased Hair Volume that also leaves your hair Moisturized, Cleansed, Softer, and with a long-lasting Radiant Glow.
>
> The hydrating formula of this anti-frizz shampoo helps smooth and defrizz curls while enhancing softness and body.
>
> Treat your follicles to a silky, soft transformation that adds bounce and shine with an all-natural recipe.
>
> Orange Blossom extracts accentuate hair with an aromatic fragrance while softly conditioning tresses for a velvety finish and elongate.

The vision these descriptions associate with Black hair textures is that of hair that has not yet arrived but can transform into the beauty it seeks to become. These descriptions set the qualities of beautiful hair and create the criteria used to form a hierarchy for beauty evaluations. Descriptions give consumers visuals that they may use to evaluate the current look of their hair and judge if they have met "acceptable" hair beauty standards. The promise made to consumers is that although Black hair in its current state may not meet acceptable beauty standards, Black hair textures can access beautiful hair. Adding these products to Black hair will give the consumer access to beautiful hair evaluations. Still, Black hair textures can only achieve this by removing the undesirable look and replacing it with the look promoted as desirable.

Shampoo product descriptions use words to create a spectrum from which consumers may make evident beauty and anti-beauty judgments. Marketing strategies provide various qualities to look for in one's hair so that through product descriptions, the consumer can determine where the current state of their hair lies on the undesirable to desirable spectrum. As hegemonic criteria within these data describe desirable and undesirable hair qualities, products use these descriptions to develop an ideal image to form an esthetic judgment. Once established, esthetic hair formation privileges those who closely align with this dominant standard image of beauty based on the body's ability to embody these standards. By using Eurocentric features as the prevailing standard of beauty, these product descriptions frame the qualities of Black women's bodies as the anti-thesis of these standards and deem Black hair textures unattractive. Once racialized, products marketed for racially inscribed features, such as Black hair textures, are used to uphold Eurocentric beauty standards.

Because of this, for Black women to embody both Blackness and beauty, according to these products, they must conform, control, and submit the Black body to standards that differ from its natural state. Within the embodiment of Black beauty, in contrast to the anti-racist esthetic practice that celebrates hair more aligned with Afro-centric features, these products encourage anti-Blackness practices which reinforce social hierarchies of beauty, race, and gender within the Black beauty ideal – setting elongated, looser, and manageable coils as the ideal type to be achieved by the consumer to obtain Black hair beauty. Framing the Black body as the anti-thesis of these characteristics that reflect beauty, these products deny Black hair texture's ability to be read and evaluated as beautiful or feminine if it does not adhere to the previously set beauty regime. Controlling the image of an ideal beauty sustains a hierarchy for beauty and body judgments that maintain the subordination of the Black female body (Collins, [2000] 2009; Thompson, 2009b). These product descriptions' esthetic hair formation determines what attributes must be added to the Black body to sustain the set standards while removing those attributes that contradict said standards – neutralizing any threats to the established standards along the way.

Making Hair Well: Words You Feel

Getting consumers to feel is the goal of the *making hair well* category, which utilizes words to convince consumers that their hair is unhealthy and then prescribes the criteria for healthy hair. These shampoo products frame the Black female body as an object that Black women must continuously work on and treat. By providing references to healing and the means to address what products identify as hair ailments, *making hair well* offers consumers specific hair characteristics, they may use to assess their achievement of hair health through how they feel. Shampoo products connect to consumer emotions and conjure up feelings that create the need for hair protection and restoration to reach optimal health. Products use a combination of emotional protection and tactile feelings to deploy words you feel as a strategy to convince consumers that their hair is ill and needs protection. At the same time, these words tell consumers that the feeling of healthy, restored hair in their everyday lives is only one shampoo wash away.

Emotional Protection
Marketing strategies to conjure specific emotions in the consumer are used to convince consumers that they need to use these products for their hair. Descriptions use stressed, weak, delicate, and fragile to persuade women with Black hair textures that their hair is in danger and needs protection. These products rise to the occasion by recommending consumers use their shampoo to obtain the protection hair needs to be safe from harm. Products aim to make the consumer feel safe by promising to be the "barrier" or "shield" that will safeguard hair from future damage, giving hair the "building block[s]" it needs to get well.

> Antioxidant-rich Fig helps boost hydration while protecting distressed hair from environmental influences
>
> Carrot Root Oil strengthens weak hair, protects against breakage, and promotes growth as well.
>
> This rich super moisturizing ingredient is the building block for healthy, protected hair.
>
> The special charcoal composition penetrates through the cuticle of the hair, strengthening it from the inside out, at the same time creating a protective shield.
>
> Treats the hair while renewing its appearance, recovering from dryness and helping form a protective barrier against pollution.

The healing properties provided by these products address the harm that they say the hair has endured. By offering unseen but felt protection, these products continue to use emotions to connect the consumer to the sensation of safety. The idea of using a product to "boost hydration" that penetrates "through the cuticle of the hair" and strengthens hair "from the inside out" helps demonstrate the way these products are giving protection that hair needs.

Tactile Restoration
Products connect the sense of touch to levels of hair evaluation, allowing consumers to feel whether they have successfully achieved the restorative properties promised by their shampoo. Descriptions provide the hair characteristics that the consumer must obtain to reach the ultimate goal of having healthy hair. As products restore hair to its "healthy" state, the words imply a tactile experience alluding that consumers can feel their hair physically restored.

> This lather-rich formula contains includes olive oil and shea butter to help soften hair, reduce shrinkage, control frizz, eliminate knotting, and restore a healthy moisture balance.
>
> However dry, dull, or brittle your hair is, you can help regain your natural balance of moisture, manageability, shine and softness with Black Vanilla.

> Infused with aloe, this hydrating shampoo gently washes away product build-up to restore shine and body, for clean, healthy-feeling hair.
>
> Gently cleansing and detangling, it seals in vital nourishment, restores dry, damaged textures and stops the cycle of hair dehydration leaving hair moisturized, smooth and soft.
>
> This powerful formula in a bottle with leave your hair and scalp feeling strong and protected.

Restored hair is detangled and knot free, clean, without frizz, soft, and has a healthy balance of moisture. Therefore, hair that feels tangled and dirty with product buildup, dry, damaged, and brittle needs restoration to feel moisturized, strong, smooth, and healthy. These descriptions encourage consumers to assess their need to participate in beauty embodiment practices by engaging the sense of touch. Employing a word cadence, we do this so that you can feel that these products connect the feeling of hair to the attainment of hair health. Products also use elements of shame to promote the use of their products to restore hair while reprimanding hair that does not meet the level of established health standards.

Products use marketing tactics to promote themselves as the source for obtaining the feeling of hair health emotionally and physically. Descriptions articulate Black beauty to Black women as a status only achieved by externally disciplining hair to assimilate to Eurocentric beauty standards. These product descriptions devalue Black hair textures by objectifying its difference as inferior and unhealthy in its natural state (Collins, [2000] 2009). They offer the treatment needed to "fix" hair by changing its properties to those these descriptions define as signals of health. The story presented is that the wellness these hair textures need to obtain beauty requires a cure that others must deliver. These products encourage texturism within the Black community when evaluating the health of Black hair, which maintains social hierarchies that place one's proximity to Whiteness as the standard to assess the embodiment of Black beauty (Davis, 2022). Through conjuring up emotions connected to the need for protection, these products appeal to Black women, offering themselves as the way to fight against hair texture that feels dull, brittle, and damaged through engaging in embodiment practices. At the same time, these descriptions defend hair that feels soft, smooth, and hydrated as characteristics included in definitions of beautiful, healthy hair. Making hair well places beauty within the confines of femininity as it frames the female body as fragile and communicates health as an aspired status achieved through engaging in beauty practices. At the same time, descriptions also covertly push the message that the only solution for Black women to achieve hair health is through tactile restoration, transforming how the hair feels and its texture.

Distinctively Made: Words You Hear, Smell, and Taste

By using the "difference" of Black hair textures to classify the need for separate products, products employ the racialization practice of othering by marketing that products used for Black bodies must differ from those used for non-Black bodies. *Distinctively made* draws attention to this by emphasizing an exclusive blend of unique ingredients in creating these products. Exploring the words consumers hear, smell, and taste while reading these descriptions provides an understanding of how these senses are utilized as a marketing tool to entice consumers to enhance differences for a price. Products aid in users familiarizing themselves with particular words and phrases they should listen out for when selecting a shampoo for their hair type. The methods and ingredients used to make these products help to enhance Black hair textures without inflicting violence or harm to the Black body. The product's ability to be safe and non-toxic is essential and proven by tying the source of ingredients back to smells that are natural, found in nature, and edible enough to taste. Together, the recipe (how products are made) and the ingredients (what products are made of) cater to the words you should hear, smell, and taste as consumers participate in the hair shampoo buying experience.

Recipe

Formulas, framed as recipes, are used to connect how these particular products are made to the sense of taste. The use of recipes being crafted, formulated, secret, and special infers that manufacturers strategically created these products for Black hair. Since these products were created for Black hair, they tout their ability to provide something for hair through a unique blend of ingredients that makes hair well without weighing it down or removing the flavor that makes it distinct. Care is taken to create these products, beginning with using edible ingredients. Using words that connect to taste, products desire to ensure consumers that since they are made with things that are safe enough to put *in* Black bodies, they are also safe enough to put *on* Black bodies.

> Feed your hair with Hair Food Coconut Milk & Chai Spice Sulfate Free Nourishing Shampoo. Infused with the comforting essences of creamy coconut milk and aromatic chai spice, our sulfate free coconut recipe works to give your hair a pick-me-up, liven and volumize your hair and leave your hair looking, feeling and smelling totally luxurious and lovely.
>
> Our deliciously rich and thick Neroli Blossom Cleansing Milk is whipped to perfection! In our beauty kitchen, we churn natural cashew nuts with fruit nectars for a buttery mixture that penetrates the hair shaft to cleanse and smooth follicles.
>
> Inspired by clean, simple ingredients like the ones you'd find in your own kitchen, our recipe for healthy, touchable hair is sulfate free, silicone free, paraben free and mineral oil free. Because what goes on your body is just as important as what you put in it.
>
> Gentle cleansing formula removes dirt and buildup from hair without stripping hair of its natural oils; Uses a blend of Honey & Coconut Oil to deeply penetrate and hydrate natural coils and curls, leaving the hair soft, nourished and with natural shine.
>
> Suave is proud to bring you these formulations so curls can look their best daily.

These products promise to deliver a "recipe" of "simple ingredients like the ones you'd find in your own kitchen" that they have "whipped to perfection" and are safe enough to "feed your hair." Suggesting that blending of items in the kitchen used for cooking healthy meals can also provide hair with nutrients it needs to be well. Inviting consumers to the comfort of the beauty kitchen table, the makers of these products promise to serve excellent hair food prepared to leave hair "soft, nourished and with natural shine."

Ingredients
The ingredients included in product descriptions point consumers toward listening for words as clues to whether these products were made for consumers with Black hair textures in mind. The ingredients used within shampoo products are just as important as what they are made without, and it tells the customer if using this product will bring their hair health or harm. Acknowledging that sulfates, parabens, silicone, paraffin, or other chemicals and ingredients are harmful to Black hair and bodies, descriptions highlight to consumers that these items are not in their shampoos. Information related to what shampoos are free of is included to secure trust in the consumer that these products are gentle and safe for use, unlike the items explicitly marketed for Black women in the past that were proven to be harmful and toxic.

> The rich blend contains 100% aloe vera as the first ingredient along with coconut oil, plumeria extract and papaya extract. Plus, the divine coconut water, white orange and tonka bean scent leaves locks smelling irresistibly good. This sulfate-free surfactant haircare system is vegan, free from silicones, parabens and mineral oil and contains no synthetic dyes.

> Thoughtfully crafted to cleanse and protect coiled, curly or wavy hair, this Dove shampoo is sulfate free, paraben free, dye-free and safe to use on dyed hair. It leaves hair feeling healthy, clean and smelling great while amplifying your natural texture.

> This ultra-soothing, mild formulation thoroughly cleanses with a rich lather that gently eliminates frizz, oil, dirt and other impurities without damaging fragile cuticles. Safe for color treated locks, this vegan, gluten-free and paraben-free product is specially formulated to blend the calming benefits of sulfate free shampoos with the protective, replenishing and intensely hydrating relief of natural extracts and jojoba oil.

> The Vegetable Root Oil Collection by Rucker Roots contain a natural blend of roots that come from the earth's soil.

> Formulated with phytic acid, this shampoo is free of alcohol, sodium-lauryl-sulfate and parabens to make it gentle enough to use every day. Infused with mandarin orange extract and sea kelp, your hair will be smelling fresh and looking good.

Phrases such as "infused with" and "free from" cue the reader to listen to what comes next so that they hear what these ingredients have to say prior to purchasing. Consumers are signaled to listen for ingredients familiar to them as naturally derived from the earth and scents that users are accustomed to smelling in their homes as signs that these products promote wellness. Various flowers and plants in nature, along with herbs, spices, and oils found in the kitchen, are introduced to lure consumers into imagining the many pleasant aromatic possibilities available by using these shampoos for their hair. These descriptions hope to entice the consumer into purchasing not only a shampoo but an enjoyable hair washing experience at the same time.

The distinctively made category essentializes the body as racial by communicating Blackness and Black beauty as a unique type of beauty that needs special attention outside of that provided for the norm. There are risks with essentializing

Blackness in this way. Still, the risks may be worth taking as it moves toward valuing Black hair textures, appreciating uniqueness through their distinguishing features, and creating products that differ from the mass-produced items that are not inclusive of their unique texture. Making recipes different from what already exists problematizes the beauty care industry's exclusion of Black hair textures when creating these products. Descriptions also gender these products by focusing on the fragrance of ingredients and framing the experience as sensual.

By reinforcing the female body as an object maintained for pleasure, these products concurrently promote pleasure as an indulgent experience for women while sustaining pleasure's sexual connotations. Descriptions encourage consumers to embody Black beauty by emphasizing and engaging in beauty practices that enhance the look and feel of Black hair textures in their original state without working toward making it look more Eurocentric. By separating Black bodies from non-Black bodies through othering, the distinctively made category reinforces the social hierarchy of race (Collins, [2000] 2009). At the same time, this category works to deconstruct the beauty hierarchy by challenging the social and political exclusion of the Black female body by making it the subject of their call to engage in beauty practices (Fair et al., 2018; McMillan, 2015). Rather than placing Black beauty in opposition to beauty ideals, it works to position beauty within the norms found in Black hair textures and maintain its properties and characteristics as its focus. The ingredients and recipes created by these shampoos affirm beauty in features of Blackness that are more African than Eurocentric and encourage the embodiment of Black beauty representations bringing more inclusivity in how to interpret beauty on racially inscribed bodies.

DISCUSSION

The present chapter aimed to answer the following research questions: (1) What message does the discourse of shampoo product descriptions marketed to Black hair textures communicate about beauty and Blackness? (2) What message does the discourse of shampoo product descriptions marketed to Black hair textures communicate about Blackness? and (3) How does this discourse define the embodiment of Black beauty through hair?

The discourse of shampoo product descriptions zooms in on hair's mutability to suppress Black hair's unique qualities to pursue qualities that imitate Eurocentric images of beauty, while, at the same time, capitalizing on Black hair texture's uniqueness for profit. Products urge Black women consumers to engage in beauty practices that remove characteristics of Black hair textures they deem undesirable (dry, dull, dehydrated) and add properties counter to the hair's natural state (nourish, shine, and hydrated). By doing so, the discourse communicates the erasure of Blackness from the body as the singular route for securing favorable beauty evaluations. While products value the Black body in consumer culture (Featherstone, 1982) as an untapped specialized market, they use their descriptions to reinforce the current beauty regime rather than expanding beauty standards to include Blackness by considering the beauty in Black hair textures.

By focusing on Black hair textures difference and exclusion, companies use marketing tactics within product descriptions to commodify how beauty is displayed and evaluated on Black bodies through hair. Mass-produced products use gender and racial frames to claim their ability to enhance beauty and Blackness by purchasing products made specifically for Black hair textures. However, since these product descriptions construct the images used to inscribe beauty and Blackness on the body, they use the descriptions to create an image of an ideal beauty type that sustains Blackness as a subordinate representation of beauty by objectifying the look and feel of Black hair textures through defining it in oppositional terms (Collins, [2000] 2009; Thompson, 2009b).

By constructing visual interpretations of racial signifiers through text, marketing strategies encourage the consumption of otherness, creating a racialized space for Blackness consumption. While doing so, these shampoo products marketed for Black hair textures communicate mixed messages about Blackness. Products distinctively made for Black hair textures celebrate Black hair in ways that mimic the anti-racist esthetic tradition that valorizes Afro-centric features on the racialized body and upholds them as the primary representation of Black as beautiful. There are risks associated with racially essentializing the body for marketing purposes in this way as it creates a monolithic view of how Black beauty may be embodied. Although the nuances of the multiplicity and diversity of Blackness across the African Diaspora are beyond the scope of this study, it is essential to note that when there is only one representation of Blackness included within Black beauty; it excludes either Black bodies with features that more closely align with the dominant beauty culture or those misaligned from it. However, as shown through this study, when the definition of Blackness depends on profitable trends of Black culture, companies believe they can use othering in their descriptions to sell their ability to inscribe Blackness onto the body, further separating one from their self-definition of Blackness. By maintaining Blackness as a classification ascribed and achieved, beauty products promote "doing race" through hair stylization (Sims et al., 2020; Tate, 2009) and consuming products as an embodiment identity beauty practice.

Combining the five senses with the descriptions of shampoo products marketed for Black hair textures helps us see how beauty embodiment practices reinforce racialized and gendered practices to subjugate the Black body. These products use gendered discourse to uphold beliefs that all women want to be known and seen as beautiful, supporting femininity as a desired and achievable status. Product descriptions position the body as an object that can obtain and maintain its established beauty standards through participating in beauty practices. By constructing beauty as a status to be protected and restored by the consumer, these products place the burden and rewards of beauty on the consumer's body. The boundaries drawn by shampoo descriptions distort the view of one's current look while reinforcing the need to evaluate and judge one's look. In other words, while descriptors encourage Black women to celebrate the uniqueness of their hair by purchasing products that recognize their hair's specific need, these purchases also confirm the othering of hair as another way to inscribe race onto the body. The discourse used to signal the Black body as its own type of beauty separates the definition of Black beauty's embodiment from the dominant look and feel of beauty, placing it into a category of its own. By refusing to broaden beauty definitions to make Black beauty recognizable, these products discursively construct Black beauty outside the ideal beauty norms (Tate, 2009). By integrating the familiar with the illusion of beauty, shampoo products conjure up an image of hair beauty that Black women should strive for while also telling Black women that the level of beauty they seek is not and does not come naturally (Rooks, 1996). Therefore, products encourage Black women to engage in beauty embodiment practices to sustain the beauty hierarchy, positioning Black beauty as an ever-fleeting status that women must continually work on to maintain.

CONCLUSION

Results from this study contribute to our understanding of how beauty products use marketing strategies to set beauty standards and, specifically, proper Black beauty standards. Shampoo products marketed for Black hair textures regulate how to signify and consume Blackness and beauty. Through shampoo product descriptions, companies create a tension between the embodiment of Black beauty to liberate Black hair texture while simultaneously upholding representations of Black beauty that mirror Eurocentric beauty standards. By moving the focus away from the consumer to the product consumed, this analysis provides new insight into how product labels are discursive and communicate the interpretation of beauty through racialized and gendered embodiment practices. The evidence shows how shampoo products reinforce established racial and gender beauty regimes that reproduce and sustain social hierarchy structures.

This work used shampoo labels from two major US distributors. Future research on the impact of racialized gendered embodiment practices through beauty product consumption should extend the analysis to additional beauty and body products and products marketed to other racial and ethnic groups outside the African diaspora both within and outside US consumer markets. Expanding studies to include different racial and ethnic groups will improve our understanding of how the process of racialization is infused into the discourse of marketing practices. Interviews with manufacturers would help provide a more profound sense of the intentions of those who create and write the texts used in product descriptions for products marketed for specific cultural markers, like hair. Focus groups and individual interviews with product consumers can help us further understand how consumers interpret these messages and their influence on beauty perception. Finally, expanding this study beyond hair to other parts of the body, like skin, to include additional products (e.g., conditioners, lotion, body wash, and cosmetics) will provide a holistic view of the discourse of the beauty industry and consumer culture, their influence in the racialized embodiment experience, and specifically the embodiment of race and Blackness.

NOTE

1. Sarkaesthetics practices is the name of somatic esthetic "practices relating to the body, as it were, as flesh, regarded solely 'from the outside'" (Taylor, 2016, p. 108) given by Paul C. Taylor in his book *Black is Beautiful: A Philosophy of Black Aesthetics*. Taylor identifies three dimensions in sarkaesthetic practices: descriptive which are the norms and principles that govern esthetic evaluations of the body and the practices used to conform them, normative the dimension that prescribes the rules and principles for judgment and pursuit of bodily beauty, and meta-theoretical which is the nature of bodily perceptions and practices.

REFERENCES

Alcoff, L. M. (1999). Towards a phenomenology of racial embodiment. *Radical Philosophy*, 95, 15–26.

Banks, P. A. (2021). *Race, ethnicity, and consumption: A sociological view*. Routledge.

Black, P., & Sharma, U. (2001). Men are real, women are 'Made up': Beauty therapy and the construction of femininity. *The Sociological Review*, 49(1), 100–116. https://doi.org/10.1111/1467-954x.00246

Bordo, S. (2003). *Unbearable weight feminism, western culture, and the body* (10th anniversary ed.). University of California Press.

Brown, S. (2018). "Don't touch my hair": Problematizing representations of black women in Canada. *Journal of Pan African Studies*, 12(8), 64–86.

Butler, J. (2006). *Gender trouble: Feminism and the subversion of identity*. Routledge.

Byrd, A. D., & Tharps, L. ([2001] 2014). *Hair story: Untangling the roots of Black hair in America* (Revised ed.). St. Martin's Press.

Caldwell, P. M. (1991). A hair piece: Perspectives on the intersection of race and gender. *Duke Law Journal*, 1991(2), 365–396. https://doi.org/10.2307/1372731

Charmaz, K. (2014). *Constructing grounded theory*. SAGE Publications.

Collins, P. H. ([2000] 2009). *Black feminist thought: Knowledge, consciousness, and the politics of empowerment*. Routledge.

Craig, M. L. (2006). Race, beauty, and the tangled knot of a guilty pleasure. *Feminist Theory*, 7(2), 159–177. https://doi.org/10.1177/1464700106064414

Davis, K. W. (2022). *Your (afro-textured) hair is beautiful: The trauma of texturism*. WebMD Health News. https://www.webmd.com/mental-health/news/20221201/the-trauma-of-texturism

Fair, F., McMillan, U., Irvin, S., & Jha, M. R. (2018). Subject/object/body: Recent perspectives on beauty and aesthetics in gender studies [*Review of embodied avatars: Genealogies of black feminist art and performance; body aesthetics; the global beauty industry: Colorism, racism, and the national body*]. *Women's Studies Quarterly*, 46(1/2), 215–220. https://ww.jstor.org/stable/26421172

Featherstone, M. (1982). The body in consumer culture. *Theory, Culture & Society*, 1(2), 18–33. https://doi.org/10.1177/026327648200100203

Giddings, P. (2006). *When and where I enter: The impact of Black women on race and sex in America*. Amistad.

Glapka, E. (2018). Postfeminism – For whom or by whom?: Applying discourse analysis in research on the body and beauty (the case of black hair). *Gender and Language*, 12(2), 242–268. https://doi.org/10.1558/genl.30898

Glaser, B. G., & Strauss, A. L. (1967). *The discovery of grounded theory: Strategies for qualitative research*. Aldine de Gruyter.

Havlin, N., & Báez, J. M. (2018). Introduction: Revisiting beauty. *Women's Studies Quarterly*, 46(1), 13–24. https://doi.org/10.1353/wsq.2018.0013

Holmes, T. E. (2020, December 6). *The industry that Black women built*. Essence. https://www.essence.com/news/money-career/business-black-beauty/

Kwan, S., & Trautner, M. N. (2009). Teaching and learning guide for 'Beauty Work: Individual and Institutional Rewards, the Reproduction of Gender, and Questions of Agency'. *Sociology Compass*, 3(6), 1017–1021. https://doi.org/10.1111/j.1751-9020.2009.00243.x

Mason, K. (2018). Gendered embodiment. In B. J. Risman, C. M. Froyum & W. J. Scarborough (Eds.), *Handbook of the Sociology of Gender* (pp. 95–107). Springer.

McMillan, U. (2015). *Embodied avatars: Genealogies of black feminist art and performance*. New York University Press.

Mercer, K. (1994). *Welcome to the jungle: New positions in Black cultural studies*. Routledge. https://doi.org/10.4324/9780203700594

Ndichu, E. G., & Upadhyaya, S. (2019). "Going natural": Black women's identity project shifts in hair care practices. *Consumption, Markets and Culture, 22*(1), 44–67. https://doi.org/10.1080/10253866.2018.1456427

Patton, T. O. (2006). Hey girl, am I more than my hair? African American women and their struggles with beauty, body image, and hair. *NWSA Journal, 18*(2), 24–51. https://doi.org/10.2979/NWS.2006.18.2.24

Rocha, A. R., Schott, C., & Casotti, L. (2016). Socialization of the Black female consumer: Power and discourses in hair-related consumption. *Advances in Consumer Research, 44*, 333.

Rooks, N. M. (1996). *Hair raising beauty, culture, and African American women*. Rutgers University Press.

Sims, J. P., Pirtle, W. L., & Johnson-Arnold, I. (2020). Doing hair, doing race: The influence of hairstyle on racial perception across the US. *Ethnic and Racial Studies, 43*(12), 2099–2119. https://doi.org/10.1080/01419870.2019.1700296

Strauss, A. L., & Corbin, J. M. (1998). Axial coding. In *Basics of qualitative research: Techniques and procedures for developing grounded theory* (2nd ed., pp. 123–142). Sage Publications.

Tafari-Ama, I. M. (2016). Historical sociology of beauty practices: Internalized racism, skin bleaching and hair straightening. *Ideaz, 14*, 1.

Tate, S. (2007). Black beauty: Shade, hair and anti-racist aesthetics. *Ethnic and Racial Studies, 30*(2), 300–319. https://doi.org/10.1080/01419870601143992

Tate, S. A. (2009). *Black beauty: Aesthetics, stylization, politics* (1st ed.). Taylor & Francis. https://doi.org/10.4324/9781315569444

Taylor, P. C. (1999). Malcolm's Conk and Danto's colors; or, four logical petitions concerning race, beauty, and aesthetics. *The Journal of Aesthetics and Art Criticism, 57*(1), 16. https://doi.org/10.2307/432060

Taylor, P. C. (2016). *Black is beautiful: A philosophy of black aesthetics*. Wiley.

Thompson, C. (2009a). Black women and identity: What's hair got to do with it? *Michigan Feminist Studies, 22*(1), 78. http://hdl.handle.net/2027/spo.ark5583.0022.105

Thompson, C. (2009b). Black women, beauty, and hair as a matter of being. *Women's Studies, 38*(8), 831–856. https://doi.org/10.1080/00497870903238463

Vandenberg, A. (2018). Toward a phenomenological analysis of historicized beauty practices. *Women's Studies Quarterly, 46*(1/2), 167–180. https://doi.org/10.1353/wsq.2018.0026

Weitz, R. (2001). Women and their hair: Seeking power through resistance and accommodation. *Gender & Society, 15*(5), 667–686. https://doi.org/10.1177/089124301015005003

CHAPTER 10

MULATA IN REPOSE

Jennifer Báez

School of Art, Art History and Design, University of Washington, USA

ABSTRACT

This chapter provides a close reading and critical analysis of work by two New York City-based Afro-Dominican artists, Joiri Minaya (1990) and Josefina Báez (1960). The author argues that Báez' "Carmen FotonovelARTE" (2020) and Minaya's "Containers" series (2015-2020) play with the trope of repose and mixed-race beauty to chart pathways of Afro-Latina representation that are shaped by yet that radically challenge the colonial script of the mulata. The artists create a space of refusal that transforms repose into a powerful site from which to articulate, problematize, and dismantle oppressive, reductive systems of representation.

Keywords: Multiracial; art history; art; race; gender; intersectional

The undoing of the plot begins because she won't do shit. (Saidiya Hartman, "The Plot of Her Undoing," in *Notes on Feminisms*, p. 6)

A framed and faded giclée print of Francisco Goya's *The Clothed Maja* (1800–05) hung for many years on the living room wall of my great aunt's rent-control Central Park West apartment in Spanish Harlem (Fig. 10.1). As part of a home run by a first-generation AfroLatina, the living room, which doubled as a hair salon on weekends, resembled a museum of the Dominican diaspora, complete with a lineup of Flamboyan tree paintings, faceless clay dolls, and almanacs of the Virgin of Altagracia. The recumbent lady is allegedly a portrait of the artist's lover, the Duchess of Alba, posing provocatively as a *maja* – a 19th-century Spanish nationalist symbol that paradoxically evokes the country's entangled

Fig. 10.1. Author Next to a Print of Francisco Goya's *The Clothed Maja*, 1800–05, New York City, 1993.

Romani and Moorish legacies. In my *tía*'s living room, however, the reclining woman conjured up the terrifying allure of a plantation mistress, the unaffected demeanor of a European heiress on the cover of *¡Hola!* magazine, and the aspirational pursuit that day-lounging stirred on the hearts of New York City-working-class Black diasporic female heads-of-household.

In what follows, I engage the Western iconography of the recumbent pose to invoke an AfroLatina body politic that has stood outside the history of this tradition. How has she, as spectator at times and muse at others, appropriated "repose" as resistance, and how might we think through "repose" to gender Afro-Atlantic esthetics in general? My reflections consider the register of languid abandon of tropicalized women in the media and popular culture against the paradox of the arduous work that is required of them to play such a script in real life. I borrow the phrase "in repose" from the visual arts to capture the gendered and racialized nuances in Western art history that separate the "exotic" and passive reclining nude from the athletic-like Greek (white and male) *contrapposto* standing pose. These nuances are embedded in the phrase's Dominican Spanish translation, *arrecostada(o)*, that is, to lay against or on top of something. Witness its usage in an old rural proverb which equates a woman's romantic disposition to a recumbent and, literally, consumable pose: "como un tajo de aguacate arreco'tá de la'o en una cama de arroz" (like a slice of avocado laying sideways on a bed of rice). I call upon a performance repertoire that, as Diana Taylor (2003) contends, can help us make sense of gross gaps in the imperial archives and retrace lost histories of meaning-making through gesture and posture. In sum, I focus on testimonial artforms that, like family photographs, can flesh out the ghostly dynamics of Afro-Atlantic histories.

The essay examines the work of artists who use their embodied presence as testimonial flesh to intervene, complicate, and, as Saidiya Hartman's declaration in the phrase in the epilogue, "undo" the timeworn plots that conspire to keep women to the script. I propose that Joiri Minaya (1990) and Josefina Báez (1960), two NYC-based Afro-Dominican artists who arrived in the United States on different migration waves, enact an esthetics of "not doing sh*t," a space of refusal that transforms repose into a powerful site from which to articulate, problematize, and dismantle oppressive, reductive systems of representation. I explore how the artists engage the coloniality of repose within what Danielle Child (2019) calls a "working aesthetics" in two pieces: Minaya's *Containers* (2015–2020), a series of photographs of women in floral bodysuits which, I argue, critiques the commodification of repose for the tropical gaze, and Báez' *Carmen FotonovelARTE*, a photobook adapted from George Bizet's legendary operetta and which suggests real repose as a means to escape the infamous plot of the tragic mulatto. I propose these works attempt to undo the representational regimes that construct an archetype for the AfroLatina and that prevent her from breaking off script. But first, what visual genealogies shaped her political formation and why might she be clamoring for real rest?

WHO ARE YOU CALLING *MULATA*?

The AfroLatina, a Black diasporic identity that transgresses the simply Black or Latinx/Hispanic categories, is a liminal creature (Lao-Montes, 2007; Zamora, 2022). She is epistemically tied to indeterminacy because her archetype stands as a haunting embodiment of the *mulata* – a plantation-era nomenclature for a woman of mixed European and African ancestry. The mulata performs the permeability of racial, gender, and class-based boundaries, pulling codes from other female stereotypes that emerged from colonial contexts, such as the orientalized odalisque and, to some degree, the Spanish "gypsy." Just as these characters, the mulata developed around the trope of liminality where borders are considered dangerous because they can, potentially, destabilize the integrity of contained social bodies. Paradoxically, in the United States, the "mixed look" that supposedly verifies mixed ancestry, what Rachel Afi Quinn (2019) calls the "brown aesthetic," is not perceived as threatening to the status quo precisely because the racialized person is not entirely legible as entirely Black. In 19th-century orientalist iconography, we find a similar appeal to the viewer's safe entanglement with Blackness. Women depicted in this iconographic genre are light skinned. What points to their "Africanness" or perceived deviousness are the Moorish accoutrements of the harem, as in Ingres' *Grand Odalisque* (1814), or the presence of a dark-skinned Black servant as in Manet's *Olympia* (1869). These markers of Blackness are not intrinsic to the sitter's own body but located outside of it.

The dueling binary between nature/nation/female and culture/empire/male underpins the script of the mulata that is epitomized in Enrique Grau Araujo's *La mulata cartagenera* (1940) (Fig. 10.2). The painting features a reclining woman of color surrounded by tropicalia. Styled with cornrows and a sheer peasant dress, she glances seductively off frame, her left hand gently pressing down on wildflowers that lay suggestively over her pubic area. Defined in the title as a mulata hailing from Cartagena (a city in the Caribbean coast of Colombia), this woman caters both to the extractivist needs of neoliberal capital from the global north and to the 19th-century national imaginaries of the global south. Centuries of representation, shaped within and against the Spanish colonial experience, naturalized her mystique; her body, at rest, that is, in repose, ostensibly inviting the commodifying gaze. Framed by fruits and flowers, she embodies a hybridity that blends with nature. Additionally, in posing with produce, she does not carry out crude agricultural labor but stands midway in the development chain, between harvest and consumption.

The picture itself has logged quite some overtime. Mobilized as a material presence, Grau Araujo's painting is now part of a clan of classic Latin American artworks that respond to the rising global awareness of inequity compelling institutions in the art world to diversify collections and audiences. She was recruited as early as 2012 for the exhibition Caribbean Crossroads of the World organized by El Museo del Barrio in collaboration with the Queens Museum and the Studio Museum. There, she formed part of a family of canonical pieces charged with fashioning a visual history for the African diaspora in the greater Caribbean. It is precisely the paradox of the picture's active agenda that frames my interpretation of the mulata cartagenera's restful pose. Perhaps she is no longer surrendering to the gaze but waking up to the use-value of her representational labor (Baez, 2022).

The mulata, part of the genealogy of the AfroLatina body, was the most represented mixed-race type in the early modern period (Brienen, 2016). She expressed the threats and potentialities of racial reproduction after the triangular trade configured a negative global discourse around the Black, African body. That historical–cultural construct, as should be expected, flattens reality. There is a difference

Fig. 10.2. Enrique Grau Araujo, *Mulata Cartagenera*, 1940, Oil on Canvas, National Museum of Colombia. *Source*: Enrique Grau Araujo Foundation (courtesy of the Enrique Grau Araujo Foundation).

between the cis female "mulata" hailing from a Spanish Caribbean or Latin American plantation context and the cis female "mulatto woman or mulatta" who issues from the English-speaking antebellum South. *Mulata*/Mulatta, as mentioned, defines liminal figures that straddle the border between whiteness and Blackness and, as such, that produce anxiety in the white supremacist heteropatriarchy. That said, in Ibero-American colonies, race was a fluid concept. One could, in fact, albeit precariously, acquire whiteness through a combination of money, dressing well, and speaking a Hispanicized, urban Castilian (Twinam, 2015). In contrast, in the United States, a drop of Black blood locked the racialized person in a lower status despite brown esthetics privilege. Racial fluidity in colonial Latin America allowed for a dynamic range of mulata stereotypes, which inflects the scripts of AfroLatinidad that carry over to the United States through diasporic immigration.

Mulata/mulatta developed as a term that designated an unbridled sexuality and a sense of self-importance in women with a mixed African bloodline. As a racializing term, it described a skin color that was mid-range relative to a "pure" white and a "pure" black, or what Nina Simone called "yellow" to refer to Saffronia's complexion in *Four Women* (1966). The mulata/mulatta category defined a woman's character based on the privilege that skin color and phenotype afforded her. Historically, whether tied genetically or not to the plantation owner, she was likely to serve in the main house instead of toiling under the harsh sun doing field labor. Racial capitalism, and the social relations it engendered, was the principal author of the script of the vain, lazy, and presumptuous mulata/mulatta who acted upon her privilege. We can find early precedents of this script in Dutch trader Pieter de Marees's *Description of the Gold Coast of Guinea* (1602), which repeatedly mentioned how "ostentatious" "melato" "were kept" in "splendid clothes" (Brienen, 2016). De Marees's book chronicled his experiences in the Gold Coast, and the illustrations circulated worldwide in costume books and maps. The melato shows up in the engraving entitled "How the women comport themselves and how they dress." The trader wrote:

> A. is Portuguese ... and half black, half white and yellowish: such women are called Melato and most keep them as wives, because white women do not thrive much there. They dress very nicely and have many Paternoster and other beads on their bodies. They cut the Hair on their heads very short, like the men, thinking that it becomes them. (Brienen, 2016)

> ... they maintain these Wives in grand style ... and they always dress more ostentatiously and stand out more than any other Indigenous women. (Brienen, 2016)

Skin color was tied definitively to the idea of race in the 18th century. It was then that Enlightenment science, driving an interest in taxonomical knowledge, helped invent race, and the color of skin – despite its instability – became its key index. Casta paintings frequently depicted the mulata dressed in lavish textiles that set her apart from a Black mother to point to a level of cultural, racial, and moral superiority (Katzew, 2005). Casta painting, a genre particular to Spanish America, featured a heterosexual family and their child in 16 different racial combinations resulting from Indigenous, African, and European unions. In these images, skin color indexed a casta's degree of *limpieza de sangre* or "blood purity." This discriminatory regime originated in medieval Spain, where it initially privileged Europeans with no Jewish or Islamic lineages. Casta painting reflected and helped construct a pigmentocracy where white reigned at top and Black stood at bottom, with mixed-races or *castas* signaling racial progress or, conversely, racial regression.

Vanity was a central trait of the mulata/mulatta stereotype. Spanish artist Víctor Patricio Landaluze, working in Cuba, fashioned the mulata as an allegory of the indolent enchantress of the tropics, where her desire for the good life betrayed a sense of narcissism that endangered the social order (Kutzinski, 1994). This portrayal followed a pattern in the transcolonial circum-Caribbean. "Narrativa de una expedición de 5 años contra los negros revueltos de Surinam de 1796" (Narrative of a 5-year expedition against the revolted negroes of Surinam in 1796) was a diary written by John Gabriel Stedman, a Dutch officer in the Scotts Brigade who traveled to Surinam to quell slave rebellions in plantations. The diary includes an engraving of Joanna, his mulatto "wife," which was copied from a watercolor that Stedman made himself in situ (Fig. 10.3). The image portrays her as a sexual object, at once flirtatious and savage, with one breast exposed, while her hat and pearl necklace, far from flattering, highlight her impoverished condition and furnish it as evidence of a conceited personality. Even Haitian vodoun cosmology could not escape the trope of the presumptuous mulata: Erzulie Freda was modeled as a light-skinned and temperamental mulata who sports a fashionable lacy, pink dress and who demands expensive gifts from her devotees. In Latin American countries with a Black demographic majority, the mulata was used to symbolize racial cohesion in the aftermath of chaotic independence movements. However, these nations still deployed the colonial script of the opportunistic mulata (Mitchell, 2020).

Hypersexuality is the most enduring mulata/mulatta trait. As Jasmine Mitchell writes, she is "a sexual invention born from colonial legacies of sexual violence" and she "crystallized a particular kind of Black womanhood in which sexuality is the primary form of labor" (Mitchell, 2020). Whereas the mestiza body was widely represented in the early modern and modern worlds for her potential to whiten the Indigenous bloodline, the term "mulata(o)/mulatta(o)" inflected negatively on reproduction. It derived from the Spanish and Portuguese word for "mule" – the sterile offspring of a horse and donkey. The word is evidence of white anxiety over people of color biologically reproducing with whites and dwindling the "enslavable" dark-skinned labor pool. In addition, the mulata/mulatta's hybridity connected her to a specific brand of sexuality: an African bloodline that endowed her with an apparent heightened appetite for sex, and a European one that, as discussed earlier, reassured whites a safe recreational passage to Blackness.[1]

Tying together the abovementioned tropes is the script that has enjoyed the most currency: the myth of the tragic mulatto. It describes the tragic fate of the mulatto who is unable to adjust to a society that does not accept them as full members of either group (Attiah, 2022). In the Spanish Americas, examples range from Joselito Rodríguez' Mexican drama *Angelitos Negros* (1948) to composer Bobby Capó's song *Capullo y Sorullo*, famously interpreted by merengue legend Johnny Ventura. The myth applied to both men and women although more stories abound for the tragic mulatto woman. Mulata(o)/mulatta(o) is, thus,

Fig. 10.3. A Black Female Slave Holding a Hat, in John Gabriel Stedman, *Narrative of a Five Years' Expedition*, Etching, 1818. *Source*: Courtesy of the John Carter Brown Library (CC BY 4.0).

the product of the violence of miscegenation which resulted from the European expansionist project in the 15th century and the ensuing realities of plantation life in the Americas. The taboo and often violent interracial sexual relations that produced the mulatto determine their identity more so than language, nation, class, or even skin tone. This, much in the same way that creole identity, as Darcy Grimaldo Gribsby (2022) argues, is determined by place of birth over any other attribute. The label packs in a wide range of ideas about sexuality, arrogance, indolence, psychological volatility, and duplicity attached to racial reproduction, in which the body of the mulatto female, especially, is hailed as marker and engineer of societal advancement or degeneracy (Buscaglia-Salgado, 2003; Weinbaum, 2004). An *AfroLatina reading practice,* as Omaris Z. Zamora (2022) argues, acknowledges the AfroLatina's "experience and identity as a fluid body that transgresses various spaces at a time." I argue the practice also acknowledges that the mulata has historically carried the burden of holding a mirror to society's essentialist structures of thought by embodying a liminal, border-marking space.

I return to the family photograph I began with to open the conversation about AfroLatinas mobilizing repose to disrupt essentializing tropes. In performing *Canela* |ka.'n/e/.la| at Trestle gallery in Brooklyn, New York, artist Joiri Minaya, wearing a bathing suit, stretched her body across a white, plastic *chaise longue* and rubbed a mixture of cinnamon and sugar onto her skin as if it were suntan lotion (Fig. 10.4). Her elongated body is a counterpoint to the recumbent Spanish lady in Francisco Goya's *The Clothed Maja*, a decolonial feminist response to the colonial visuality of repose. Playing on the stereotype of the vain and arrogant mulata, Minaya trespasses the imaginary rope that cordons off private hotel beach areas, lounges on the most coveted chair in service-oriented island economies, and slathers on a lotion made of plantation commodities for the pleasure, and to the dismay, of the viewing public.

In *Canela*, class, race, and gender are mobilized against the tropical gaze through the audacity of the artist's recumbent body. When Minaya lays back (*se arrecuesta*) on the beach chair, she performs Max Bredt's *Leisure of the Odalisque* (1860) on a fantasy tropical beach hotel, a site originally made for whites. Grand tourist hotel chains in the Caribbean are largely built on the plots of former sugar plantations. People of color have traditionally not been allowed to exercise repose therein. Minaya's enactment of "not doing sh*t," which we discuss next, protests the violent legacies of the history of enslavement in the hospitality industry.

Fig. 10.4. Joiri Minaya, |ka.'n/e/.la| (Canela), Performance at Trestle Gallery, Brooklyn, New York City. *Source*: Courtesy of Joiri Minaya.

That said, through *mulataje* she also refuses the essentialist fixity of identity and exposes the invention of the script of race by Enlightenment science in the 18th century. By rubbing on the cinnamon mixture, Minaya critiques the global north's fetishization of "tropical" skin color, declaring that the mutability of skin tone proves how unstable it is as a marker of any kind, let alone of "race" and its attendant traits. By rubbing on the mixture, Minaya activates the wounded history of skin politics. This activation is what Buscaglia-Salgado calls *mulataje*, which denotes both a coming-to-terms-with and a blurring of the categories imposed by racial difference. *Mulataje*, according to Buscaglia-Salgado, does not point to "the marked bodies or racial categories, but rather to a history of subversion of those categories." The mulatto subject, the author goes on, can be seen "as the embodiment of metaphorical subjectivity, [and] can be thought of as the very prankster of the imago, always moving beyond, always escaping reduction and definition" (Buscaglia-Salgado, 2003).

As these reflections show, the mulata represented liminality and embodied traits from border-dwelling character types such as the orientalist odalisque. But while the odalisque is firmly associated with the recumbent pose in a 19th-century French-Algerian colonial context, the visual archive of repose for the AfroLatina is best articulated by the transatlantic and postcolonial hospitality industry. Joiri Minaya rescued one such visual archive. By googling "Dominican women," the artist stumbled upon an online dating site for tourists visiting the Caribbean island. The site contained scores of candid snapshots of local women posing for the camera. The snapshots featured women striking S-shaped poses for the viewing pleasure of a largely Euro-American male clientele. Minaya drew connections between these digital images and the colonial visuality of repose and, through her *Containers* series (2015–2020), deployed an esthetics of "not doing sh*t" to disrupt the tropes.

JOIRI MINAYA AND THE ESTHETICS OF "NOT DOING SH*T": A GENEALOGY

Joiri Minaya (b. 1990) is an interdisciplinary visual artist who was born in the United States and grew up in the Dominican Republic. Her work attends to the gaze, to the performativity of tropical identity, and to the slippages of navigating life between the diaspora and the homeland. Her show at Baxter St. gallery in New York City, "I'm Here to Entertain You, but Only During my Shift" (2020), presented large-scale photographs of herself and of other models striking a pose with head-to-toe bodysuits of floral prints set against natural-looking backdrops (Fig. 10.5). These photographs render visible what Saidiya Hartman (2019) called "not doing sh*t"; an act of refusal that reverses the centuries-old plot of women's undoing to tell a counter-story about women undoing the plot. The pictures from "I'm Here to Entertain You …" undo the plot by refusing the reductive systems of representation that demand total transparency from their objects.

The photographs for "I'm Here to Entertain You …" form part of Minaya's Containers (2015–2020) series, which addresses the visual commodification of

Fig. 10.5. Joiri Minaya, Containers #1, Inkjet Print Mounted on Aluminum, 2015–2020. *Source*: Courtesy of the artist.

tropical women, calling attention to their conflation with nature and, thus, their invisibilization. The photographs speak to the strict demarcation between labor and leisure that came into focus through the vacation postcard in Fordist societies. This duality created the illusion that industrialism could create a leisure economy for all, erasing (and feminizing) the labor of those who worked in service. Whether posing as reclining mermaids or in contrapposto with arms akimbo, the models' stance in the Containers series evokes the notion of repose with an affect similar to that projected in vacation postcards. Interestingly, although active scenes may well be depicted in vacation postcards, it need not be the image but the postcard itself, as object and container, that evokes repose. In a similar fashion, the models in Containers project the idea of repose independently of whether they stand or recline. Drawing further attention to the artificial division between labor and leisure, the title of the exhibition itself (I'm here to entertain you, but only during my shift) reveals an understanding that, despite the relaxing appeal that the models project, they were performing for the camera as part of their work shift. Fully aware of their role as performers, these muses hardly surrendered their agency to the camera's invisibilizing gaze. Instead, they displayed knowledge of the use-value of their representational labor.

The containers series involved a performative, embodied process that pit the power to gaze at the other against the ability to hide in plain sight. This dynamic was set in motion through camouflage and restrained mobility. On the one hand, the models' physical effort of holding a pose was dictated by the limitation of the bodysuit. These were recreated poses that the artist found online through her "#dominicanwomengooglesearch" project. On the other hand, the tension of having to hold the sometimes-constrictive poses staged the labor or burden of representation, that is, the grueling work required from women of color to comply with the script of tropicality. On the other hand, the bodysuits mimetizing against the background invoked camouflage as resistance. The floral print was meant to blend with the natural-looking backgrounds, with the models' corporeality fleshing out the floral print, producing a push-and-pull effect that shattered mimetic illusion. The models, in addition, stared back as defying odalisques, shifting the weight of the gaze and making spectators aware of their own positionality within the visual economy of tropical flesh. Interestingly, the models were literally responding to a script. Holding the stances for up to two hours, they listened to a recording that the artist had prepared. The script included extracts from books with titles such as "How to lose your native accent in 10 days" and "How to speak Spanish to your gardener." The title of the exhibition, "I'm Here to Entertain You ...," was a line extracted from this script.

Coming back to refusal, as mentioned earlier, the posing muses in Containers render visible the practice of "not doing sh*t," which carries its own set of esthetic conventions. In The Plot of Her Undoing, Hartman relays that women began to undo the misogynistic plots to subordinate them through radical acts which, far from grand, were intimate and sometimes barely detectable gestures. Plantation life provided a working model. When the enslaved slowed down the pace of work, it sabotaged plantation productivity. Radical passivity is the element of agitation in this type of resistance, and it enlisted the opposite of a spirited display of energy; it demanded instead the performance of repose. Black diasporic performance artists such as Jasmine Jamillah Mahmoud (2024) carry out the work of radical embodied resistance on this front with pieces such as One Hour Performance (Rest Piece), where she lays down to sleep on stage for one hour.

Radical passivity developed a Black Atlantic visuality that echoes what Robert Farris Thompson coined the *esthetics of the cool*, an exclusively African and Afro-Atlantic cultural expression characterized by *transcendental balance* framed by an unbotheredness best recognized in the free-spirit of blues and jazz but also in the visual arts (Thompson, 1973). Women of color mobilize this Black Atlantic visuality to great effect as resistance. It is important to remember that enslaved men had greater opportunities to run away from the plantation and escape from the enslaver's field of vision since they worked out on the field; the movement of women, however, was more restricted (Camp, 2002). Black women's refusal developed more so in forms that challenged plantocratic authority through staredowns, blunt disregard, and targeted slowness. This refusal called for deceleration and for the tempering of affect, but it also exposed invisibilized and invisibilizing labor. At the 2013 American Music Awards, through her hairdo, Rihanna enacted a brand of radical passivity that pulled from the durag tradition of Black apathy to perform incompliance with Predominantly-White-Institution decorum and beauty standards. She wore a doobi or *tubi*, a wraparound technique to keep blowout hair fresh overnight, refusing to perform the propriety of a finished "do." What is more, her bedhead flew in the face of "I woke up like this" ideologies that hyped (white) beauty as effortless, innate, and irreproducible. Rihanna's sleek beehive allowed viewers to appreciate her expertly flat-ironed hair in a way that played on the stereotype of the non-industrious colored folk, while demonstrating that straight hair was achievable through labor – the art of *mulataje* or transformation at its best.

Making beauty work visible is a big aspect behind the AfroLatina/o/x cultural practice of wearing hair curlers in public – a form of appropriating repose as resistance. Long before a 2021 New York Times article noted the trend among young women in South Korea, this was an established practice in Latin America. The practice challenges an imperial patriarchy which sees beauty as unproductive activity, and it confronts the structures of patriarchy at home that have come to expect the invisibility of beauty work. Wearing curlers outside the hair salon calls out the erasure of the time and financial investment required to follow the Western beauty standards which the national heteropatriarchy expects and demands (Child, 2019).

Beauty-as-labor aligns with the theory of beauty of the ancestral Luba peoples from the Democratic Republic of Congo. The Luba believed that beauty was not innate but actively produced through bodily adornment. This concept of beauty is associated with long-term and consistent labor. To adorn your body is to civilize it through cumulative action, to center it, to bring order to chaos, and as such, an imperative. This type of beauty is available to everyone since it is not predetermined at birth, and it positively reflects a person's commitment to improvement. This notion of beauty is agentival and cumulative. Luba traditional beliefs and myths around the institution of kinship additionally honor gender fluidity, whereby personhood is understood as fractal and relational. Both men and women practice elevated forms of hair artistry, adorn their bodies with elaborate tattoos, and have names that are not gendered (Nooter Roberts, 2013). In the Black Atlantic context, beauty-as-labor calls for exposing the labor and skill involved in the task, but not completing it to its fullest expression. It calls for a courting, a taunting of the gaze only to make it aware of its epic failure to reduce the self.

An esthetics of "not doing sh*t" is present in Minaya's *Satisfecha* (2014) video, where she engages issues of affect, domesticity, and agency (Fig. 10.6). Through

Fig. 10.6. Joiri Minaya, Satisfecha (Satisfied), Still Frame from HD Video, 2012.
Source: Courtesy of the artist.

the ritual of connecting over a cafecito, the artist critiques gendered sociality and the politics of respectability in the so-called private sphere. The performance is jarring on multiple fronts. The artist emerges in her underwear, sets a table with coffeeware, proceeds to dip finger-like packages of cloth into a mug filled with coffee, and then stuffs them, one by one, into her mouth. She repeats this process until her mouth is full. She then gets up, clears the table, and leaves. The uneasiness that this scene provokes in the viewer comes from sensing the discomfort of her overstuffed mouth and exposed body, her forced sense of duty, and her disaffection. Coffee culture calls for a chatty disposition. It invites repose. It invites a pause of everyday reality for a cozy conversation with friends or loved ones. Instead, the artist remains mute, not once making eye contact with the imagined guest, performing as an automaton. Here too, an Afro-Atlantic esthetics calls for visibilizing the labor, to demonstrate one possesses the required skills only to deny expectations by not completing the task. In her most recent works, the *Divergences* series, the artist outright rejects the burden-to-represent by literally slipping off her textile *skin* (Fig. 10.7). This marks her entrance into an off-script world, a space of uninterrupted Glissantian opacity.

Fig. 10.7. Joiri Minaya, Shedding II (Los tres ojos), Archival Pigment Print, 2022. *Source*: Courtesy of the artist.

JOSEFINA BÁEZ AND THE EMBRACE OF REPOSE

Josefina Báez mobilizes "Not Doing Sh*t" as poetics, intent on refusing the burden of representation. Báez (b.1960) is a performance artist, painter, writer, poet, and educator whose work revolves around the crossing of all types of borders. Her migratory experience from The Dominican Republic to the United States shaped her identification as a *dominicana ausente* as well as her exploration of embodied presence. Central to her work is her theorization of *El nié*, a place "neither here nor there"; a place of exile where, as Lorgia Garcia-Peña (2016) writes, contradictions of belonging are embraced and redefined. Báez does not engage "repose" to expose it as a representational ploy in tropicality, as is the case with Minaya's *Containers*. Instead, she engages repose as a path to true liberation, which she articulates in her practice as meditative stillness, heuristic play, or intentional leisure.

Báez' *Carmen FotonovelARTE* (2020) is a photo book adaptation of French composer George Bizet's legendary operetta on the tragedy of unrequited love, which uses repose to gain freedom off script. Báez' *oeuvre* is informed by performance, and the script for the photo book traffics on a performative and self-aware type of presence for the main character. The creative team for the project included Kutty Reyes as illustrator, Carmen Inés Bencosme as photographer, Pilar Espinal as the performer, and Esther Hernández Medina as researcher. The story forefronts the tragedy of femicide, amplifying the vulnerabilities and strengths of women and femmes who experience life through the intersectional lens of gender, race, and class. The story unfolds in black-and-white photographs with simple line brush illustrations.

The original character of the French operetta, Carmen, is a seductive Roma or "Gypsy" cigar worker from 19th-century Seville who dies by the hand of her jealous love interest, Brigadier Don Jose. Báez's version is set instead in contemporary times, in the Caribbean city of Santo Domingo where Carmen the "Gypsy" becomes Carmen the AfroLatina (Fig. 10.8). As such, the project stands as a mulata testimonial that thinks through the continuity of orientalist narratives in the global Caribbean imaginary. Caribbean Carmen likewise works at a tobacco factory, evoking the colonial history of trade entangling Spain and the Atlantic world. However, her character is less defined by the factory work environment than by her desire for liberation. In fact, this Carmen invokes repose from wage work to break the script of the tragic mulatto.

Throughout the narrative, Carmen intervenes in archetypal scenes that shaped the mulata as a discursive figure in modernity. Interjecting new representations of beauty, sensuality, race, and freedom for women of color, the photobook offers pathways of liberation for the embodied mulata. In addition, by enjoining a wide audience to perform the "frivolity" of reading a gendered literary form such as the *fotonovela*, the project invites them to participate in an act of modern-day micromarronage, of marooning-in-place, of claiming repose as resistance (Camp, 2002; Witcher, 2002). Carmen embraces "Not Doing Sh*t," which allows her to narrowly escape death – the doomed fate of the tragic mulatto. As she explores her own city, meeting friends and taking in ocean views, tragedy is avoided, and a different, more hopeful path is forged instead.

Fig. 10.8. "Carmen" (Model Pilar Espinal) Posing on Set. *Source*: Picture by Esther Hernández-Medina. Santo Domingo, 2019.

Leisure, as I mentioned, is not merely depicted in this project – the fotonovela. In fact, it compels readers to engage in it. Reading demands the claiming of time and space away from wage work. What is more, when the reading material belongs to a literary genre gendered as "frivolous" or "mindless," it becomes a serious affront to the capitalist heteropatriarchy. Radical feminism has been revisiting gendered practices that were erstwhile considered antifeminist and self-indulgent, and fotonovelas have long been part of this reappraisal. Fotonovelas are a global phenomenon that originally spread wherever there was a need to buttress capitalist infrastructure; hence, its robust presence in Latin America, northern Africa, France, and Italy during turbulent political periods in the 20th century. Cornelia Butler and Jan L. Flora (1978) identified three major types of fotonovelas in 1970's Latin America. The first type helped break primary social ties of the workers to better integrate them into the urban workforce, the second type provided an escape from problems, and the third encouraged the consumption of luxury goods. These plots were aimed at women as they carried on with all their reproductive roles in society: as mothers, as wage workers, and as teachers of culture and values. In essence, they reinforced capitalist ideologies.

Carmen FotonovelARTE, poignantly, reclaims escapism. As Carmen runs errands around the city and faces the challenge of being the sole caretaker of her ill aunt, she finds time to escape to enjoy the view from the ocean-lined avenue of El Malecón. A Marxist reading of the fotonovela would malign escapism since it allows the worker a short-lived pleasure that mystifies the pain of the daily grind. Marxist theory rejected magic realism on similar grounds that "magic and marvelous realist texts lent themselves to assimilationist, or dehistoricizing projects ..." (Puri, 2004). However, an AfroLatina reading of deliberate escapism would rescript it as a path to freedom. Carmen, in fact, quits her job at the tobacco factory after returning from a suspension that allowed her time to clear her head and end an ill-fitting romantic relationship.

Carmen *FotonovelARTE* builds a community of plurality. As Butler and Flora relay, in north and central America, the most popular fotonovela plots involved the breaking up of social ties. Capitalism depends on a mobile workforce, so these plots stressed individualistic adaptability and presented place settings with no identifiable markers or place names. Language is sanitized, hiding class background and ethnicity. Carmen Fotonovelarte is not only antagonistic to the disintegration-integration model, but it actively strengthens ties to place. Carmen speaks with her own language. Far from a "proper" Castilian, her dialog reveals working-class origins, her life experience as a woman of color in Santo Domingo, and her social affiliations. The book also pictures Santo Domingo landmarks unapologetically. This, far from prompting her alienation from her surroundings and her support base, encourages and grounds her sense of place.

Throughout the plot, Carmen plays on the stereotype of the vain mulata to appropriate the script. In one of the scenes, she tries out dresses, overcome with pride. She chooses evening gowns with rich tulle fabric, brocades, silks, and ruffles. Her eyes light up as she looks in the mirror excitedly. This episode recalls the trope of the presumptuous mulata. Feeling the trims and hems of the dresses, fanning them open, she embraces the mulata's extravagant taste for loud colors, fineries, and the good life. Vanity is reconfigured as a committed search for beauty in life, a Luba principle of beauty. Disregarding the typical ending for the tragic mulatto, Carmen performs repose as leisure. Just as Joiri Minaya sheds her textile *skins* in pursuit of opacity for the Divergences series, Carmen too unpacks the representational load. Eating, flirting, gossiping, walking aimlessly throughout Santo Domingo, gawking at the Caribbean Sea. "Not doing sh*t" and owning it.

CONCLUSION

The models performing in Joiri Minaya's *Containers* series (2015–2020) strike a pose in floral bodysuits against backdrops of tropical nature, staring out at the viewer. Commenting on the tropicalization of women of color, the performance makes viewers aware of how these subjects are conflated with nature and landscape. They are invisibilized and, at the same time, obliged to be hypervisible, always available to the capitalist patriarchy's field of vision. The models, in their stillness, invoke a colonial visuality of repose, a complex set of signs evincing the power dynamics rehearsed in the plantation context between mistresses who could rest, and domestics who could merely watch, and conversely, between a master class or slate of artists with the power to gaze, and an enslaved workforce obliged to comply with that gaze. Similarly, Carmen from Josefina Báez's *Carmen*

FotonovelARTE (2020) engages with the notion of repose to break away from a script that would have her suffer the fate of the tragic mulatto. She engages repose figuratively, as leisure and recreation, to escape in place. In this sense, she quits her job at the tobacco factory as well as a questionable love interest, and sets out to enjoy baseball with friends, indulges in low-stakes romance, stares at the beauty of the Caribbean Ocean, and rides on a city bus to see her beloved Santo Domingo. Whereas the Carmen from Bizet's French operetta dies by the hand of a jealous romantic partner, Báez' Carmen does not meet this tragic end, she lives.

In both instances, the engagement with repose subverts the script that shapes the archetype of the AfroLatina, an archetype based on the figure of the mulata – the allegedly vain, lazy, and presumptuous woman whose mixed African ancestry projected the threat of dissolving the artificial boundaries of race, gender, and class. In this essay, through an examination of two contemporary performance pieces, I outlined ways to read repose through an expansive decolonial feminist lens as AfroLatina resistance. Through *mulataje*, Báez and Minaya reject the weight of representing liminality and orientalist fantasies since colonial times. While orientalist iconography appropriated the reclining pose to gender and racialize subjects, repose writ large forms part of a gendered Afro-Atlantic resistance tactics that was born in the plantation and involved radical passivity and marooning-in-place. Reading repose anew in images of racialized and gendered figures allows us to see reclining figures, in particular, and figures at rest, in general, not as surrendering to the gaze but instead as waking up to the use-value of their representational labor.

NOTE

1. See Matt Rife shouting to Zendaya in MTV's Wild n'Out (2015): "you're mixed, I wanna be Black, let's make a lifestyle movie." https://www.buzzfeednews.com/article/stephaniesoteriou/matt-rife-trash-behavior-zendaya-resurfaced-backlash

REFERENCES

Attiah, K. (2022, September 2). Meghan Markle, colorism and the archetype of the tragic mulatto. *The Washington Post*. www.washingtonpost.com/opinions/2022

Báez, J. (2020). *Carmen FotonovelARTE*. I Om Be Press.

Baez, J. M. (2022). Performing representational labor: Blackness, indigeneity, and legibility in global Latinx media cultures. *Feminist Media Studies*, 23(5), 2455–2470.

Brienen, R. P. (2016). Joanna and her sisters: Mulatto women in print and image, 1602–1796. *Early Modern Women*, 10(2), 65–94.

Buscaglia-Salgado, J. (2003). *Undoing empire: Race and nation in the mulatto Caribbean*. University of Minnesota Press.

Butler, F. C., & Flora, J. L. (1978). The Fotonovela as a tool for class and cultural domination. *Latin American Perspectives*, 5(1, Winter), 134–150 (Culture in the Age of Mass Media).

Child, D. (2019). *Working aesthetics: Labour, art and capitalism*. Bloomsbury Publishing.

Camp, S. M. H. (2002). The pleasures of resistance: Enslaved women and body politics in the plantation south, 1830–1861. *The Journal of Southern History*, 68(3), 533–572.

Carrera, M. (2003). *Imagining identity in New Spain: Race, lineage, and the colonial body in portraiture and casta paintings*. University of Texas Press.

De Marees, P. (1602). Description and Historical Account of the Gold Kingdom of Guinea. In A. Jones & A. Dantzig (Eds.), *Fontes historiae Africanae: Series varia*, Series varia (Vol. 5). British Academy.

Garcia Peña, L. (2016). *The borders of dominicanidad: Race, nation, and archives of contradiction*. Duke University Press.

Grimaldo Gribsby, D. (2022). *Creole: Portraits of France's foreign relations during the long nineteenth century*. Penn State University Press.

Hartmann, S. (2019). *Wayward lives, beautiful experiments: Intimate histories of social upheaval*. W. Norton & Company.

Katzew, I. (2005). *Casta painting: Images of race in eighteenth-century Mexico*. Yale University Press.

Kutzinski, V. (1994). *Sugar's secrets: Race and the erotics of Cuban nationalism*. University Press of Virginia.

Lao-Montes, A. (2007). Decolonial moves: Trans-locating African diaspora spaces, *Cultural Studies*, *21*(2–3), 309–338.

Mahmoud, J. [@jasminemahmoud]. (2024, January 26). *The performer laying down on stage wrapped in a blanket* [Post]. Instagram. https://www.instagram.com/p/C2kq9-0PDDX/?img_index=1

Mitchell, J. (2020). *Imagining the mulatta: Blackness in U.S. and Brazilian media*. University of Illinois Press.

Nooter Roberts, M. (2013). The king is a woman: Shaping power in Luba Royal Arts. *African Arts*, *46*(3), 68–81.

Pedrosa, A., & Toledo, T. (Eds.). (2021). *Afro-Atlantic histories*. DelMonico Books.

Puri, S. (2004). Marvelous realism, feminism, and mulatto aesthetics: Erna Brodber's Myal. *The Caribbean postcolonial: Social equality, post-nationalism, and cultural hybridity* (pp. 139–170), Palgrave MacMillan.

Quinn, R. (2019). Spinning the zoetrope: Visualizing the mixed-race body of Dominican actress Zoe Saldaña. *Latin American and Latinx Visual Culture*, *1*(3), 44–59.

Taylor, D. (2003). *The archive and the repertoire: Performing cultural memory in the Americas*. Duke University Press.

Twinam, A. (2015). *Purchasing whiteness: Pardos, mulattos, and the quest for social mobility in the Spanish Indies*. Stanford University Press.

Thompson, R. F. (1973). An aesthetics of the cool. *African Arts*, *7*(1), 41–91.

Weinbaum, A. (2004). *Wayward reproductions: Genealogies of race and nation in transatlantic modern thought*. Duke University Press.

Zamora, O. (2022). Beyond Bodak Yellow and beyond the post-Soul: Cardi B performs AfroLatina feminisms in the trance. *Journal of Black Studies and Research*, *52*(1), 53–63.

Printed and bound by CPI Group (UK) Ltd, Croydon, CR0 4YY
19/08/2024